Goddesses in Religions and Modern Debate

UNIVERSITY OF MANITOBA
STUDIES IN RELIGION

Executive Editor

Larry W. Hurtado

Editorial Board

Alan K. L. Chan
Terence P. Day
Egil Grislis
H. Gordon Harland
Klaus Klostermaier
Dawne McCance
Neal Rose
John G. Stackhouse
M. S. Stern

Volume 1

Goddesses in Religions and Modern Debate

Edited by
Larry W. Hurtado

GODDESSES IN RELIGIONS AND MODERN DEBATE

Edited by

Larry W. Hurtado

Scholars Press
Atlanta, Georgia
1990

GODDESSES IN RELIGIONS AND MODERN DEBATE

Edited by

Larry W. Hurtado

Library of Congress Cataloging in Publication Data

Goddesses in religions and modern debate / edited by Larry W. Hurtado.
p. cm. -- (University of Manitoba studies in religion ; v. 1)
Contents: Goddesses in Chinese religions / Alan K.L. Chan -- The twenty-one taras / Terence P. Day -- Isis, goddess of the oikoumene / Rory B. Egan -- Sakti / Klaus Klostermaier -- Understandings of "the goddess" in contemporary feminist scholarship / Dawne McCance -- The goddess / Joan B. Townsend -- Healing the divisions / Kathleen Wall.
ISBN 1-55540-549-5. -- ISBN 1-55540-550-9 (pbk.)
1. Goddesses. 2. Feminism--Religious aspects. I. Hurtado, Larry W., 1943- . II. Series.
BL473.5.G63 1990
291.2'114--dc20 90-48125
CIP

Printed in the United States
on acid-free paper

Contents

Preface vii

Introduction 1
Larry W. Hurtado

Part One: Goddess Traditions

Goddesses in Chinese Religions 9
Alan K. L. Chan

The Twenty-One Taras: Features of
a Goddess-Pantheon in Mahayana Buddhism 83
Terence P. Day

Isis: Goddess of the *Oikoumene* 123
Rory B. Egan

Śakti: Hindu Images and Concepts of the Goddess 143
Klaus Klostermaier

Part Two: The Modern Discussion

Understandings of "the Goddess"
in Contemporary Feminist Scholarship 165
Dawne McCance

The Goddess: Fact, Fallacy
and Revitalization Movement 180
Joan B. Townsend

Healing the Divisions: Goddess Figures
in Two Works of Twentieth Century Literature 205
Kathleen Wall

List of Contributors 227

Editor's Preface

In the second term of the 1987-88 academic year, the Department of Religion of the University of Manitoba organized a colloquium series on "Goddesses in World Religions and Modern Scholarship". In light of the quality of the individual presentations, the disciplinary diversity of the contributors, and the contemporary interest in the subject of goddesses, the contributors were invited to re-work their presentations for possible publication. The result is this inaugural volume of this new monograph series. All of the original presentations have been revised for publication, and several have been expanded quite substantially, particularly the essays by Chan and Day. The shape of the volume reflects the shape of the colloquium series. We did not attempt a complete mapping of goddess traditions. Instead, we invited contributors to draw upon their scholarly expertise to address the topic of the colloquium series. The essay by Kathleen Wall was not a part of the colloquium series but was prepared specifically for this volume when plans were laid for publication.

This volume is not, therefore, a comprehensive survey of goddess traditions. Rather, these essays embody substantial discussions of particular goddess traditions and controversial questions in current literature on "the divine feminine". All the essays, even the very extensive and heavily documented ones, have been written to be accessible by serious readers, regardless of their particular academic specialty. This collection will, we hope, be a useful resource for a wide variety of readers, including scholars and students in Religious Studies, and Women's Studies.

Much planning and effort has gone into the production of this volume. The scholarly efforts of the contributors will be obvious to the reader. Not so obvious to those who have not tried to shepherd such a work through the editing and production stages is the considerable time involved in "massaging" material into final print form. In this time-consuming labor, several people have made important contributions and I wish to thank them for their assistance. Shelly Bozyk keyboarded the essays into the computer. Chris Read helped greatly in giving initial instruction in formatting the files for printing, and introduced me to the intricacies of "desktop publishing". Helga Dyck helped in the final stages of formatting the essays for publication. I also wish to express thanks for the grant from the University of Manitoba Academic Development Fund, which made possible the launching of this new series. Harry Gilmer and Dennis Ford of Scholars Press cordially responded to numerous queries and were encouraging at each stage.

The purpose of *University of Manitoba Studies in Religion* is to publish work that reflects the study of religion in a public university. The diversity of religious traditions discussed in the following essays, and the disciplinary diversity of the contributors as well, are, in the judgment of the editorial board, fitting attributes for the initial volume of this series. We welcome inquiries from potential contributors of future volumes.

Winnipeg
August 1990

INTRODUCTION

L. W. Hurtado

The high level of contemporary interest in what has been termed "the divine feminine," shared by scholars and the general public, is of course related to the re-examination of the roles and significance of gender in modern culture. In this matter, as in many others, academic study of religion can be fuelled by, and of relevance to, the wider needs and activities of our society. And it is with and an interest in the contemporary questions of our modern world, as well as a dedication to careful scholarship, that the following essays appear. Some of them address contemporary questions quite directly, and others are offered as resources for understanding the various goddess traditions they deal with and for possible use by those who are engaged in current issues of maleness, femaleness and the divine. The contributors do not represent any one school of thought, and have been left free to handle their subjects as they chose. As editor of the volume, my purposes in this introduction are limited to an explanation of the organization of this volume and a few comments on the particular features of the individual essays.

The first thing to point out is what this collection does not do. The volume is not simply a survey of major goddess traditions in the history of religions. A few other works have already provided that sort of more elementary resource.[1] Instead, the plan was to provide (a) more extended analyses than is readily available of several selected goddesses traditions, and (b) scholarly discussions of some important issues in the modern debate about gender and divinity. In addition, the volume reflects the cross-disciplinary plan of the colloquium series for which the original versions of these essays were prepared, with contributions from specialists in various areas of Religious Studies (Chinese Religion, Buddhism, Hinduism, Religion and Modern Thought), and in Classics, Anthropology and English Literature. This combination of detailed examinations of goddess traditions and critical discussions reflecting the modern debate about deity and gender, together with the variety of disciplines represented by the contributors, make this collection a valuable resource for a wide variety of readers, and sets the volume apart from other books on the "goddess" topic.

Goddess Traditions: "Case Studies"

The particular goddess traditions treated are interesting and important in their own right, and the essays in Part One of this collection are substantive contributions to the study of the various religious traditions. Collected here, these essays serve as "case studies" that investigate the varying ways in which goddesses have been conceived and have functioned in world religions. This variety in goddess imagery and function is at once intriguing and corrective of the less-than-well-informed notion one sometimes encounters that when a deity is understood as female she will have a predictable role, imagery and significance for her devotees. In addition to the diversity of goddess figures they deal with, several of the essays emphasize how the respective goddesses have often undergone changes in roles and in the way they are portrayed by devotees as the goddesses are appropriated by different groups of people and/or as the cultures in which the goddesses are reverenced undergo changes across time. These changes and developments in individual goddess traditions further show that understanding the significance and meaning of gender imagery used to represent deities is much more complex than one might at first think.

The weighty essay by Alan Chan, which leads off this volume, is modestly described by him as a "survey" of Chinese goddess devotion. The coverage in this piece, ranging temporally from pre-imperial times on down through many centuries, and across Taoist and Confucian traditions, is certainly broad enough to justify his term. But "survey" is hardly adequate to describe his careful and extensive analysis. One of the interesting emphases of Chan's essay is his demonstration of the changes in function and imagery Chinese goddesses underwent in connection with developments in Chinese culture. The evidence he considers includes iconographic material, religious texts, and poetic texts. His discussion of these poetic texts shows that male erotic fantasies came to play a role in re-shaping the way Chinese goddesses were perceived and portrayed, at least in some circles. Also valuable is Chan's sensitive discussion of the relation of goddesses and myths of immortal women to Chinese social practices (e.g., marriage). And he explains clearly how the symbolic and mythical significance of Chinese goddesses as embodiments of the *yin* side of the binary view of cosmic reality in Chinese tradition.

In view of the interest in China and its traditions that is particularly strong in recent years in the West, Chan's extensive treatment of Chinese goddess traditions is especially timely and valuable. And Chan's essay, though lengthy and full of detailed references in the notes, is accessible as well to readers with limited knowledge of Chinese tradition. This young scholar's study was conducted in connection with a special post-doctoral research fellowship sponsored by the Social Sciences and Humanities Research Council of Canada, and it gives the promise of a vigorous and very productive research career.

Terence Day provides a study of Tibetan goddess tradition that incorporates attention to iconographic details, thorough interaction with important secondary literature on the subject, and an intriguing proposal of his own about how gender differentiation of deities may have functioned, at least for the groups he discusses. The tradition Day investigates includes the *tantric* texts and rather explicit iconography of sexual embraces shocking to some and titillating to others. But he casts a frank and discerning eye over these and a variety of other material, producing an interesting discussion of devotion to the various Tārā figures and offering some probing thoughts on the religious concepts that lie behind the texts, practices and iconography of devotion to these goddesses. Day draws attention to the close pairing of male and female deities and points to evidence indicating that, in some circles at least, male and female divine consorts may have been representations of the same divinity in transcendent and revealed modes respectively. This provocative argument may be of relevance to students of other religious traditions as well. I wonder, for example, if his suggestion might illumine for us how at least some ancient peoples may have understood the relationships of such consorts as Baal and Ashtart (who can bear the epithet "the name of Baal"), or perhaps even Isis and Acerose.[2] Whether Day's proposal is correct, and how far it can go in illumining other examples of male/female deity pairs, are questions that must be left to future scholarly discussion. I suggest, however, that it is well worth considering by scholars in various religious traditions.

Rory Egan's discussion of Isis focuses on the Greco-Roman appropriation of this goddess of Egyptian origin, thereby dealing with the most influential period and form of Isis devotion in which this goddess became the object of reverence for devotees around the Mediterranean basin. In addition to his clear and very readable discussion of the spread of Isis devotion and the way in which she was portrayed, Egan, a Classics scholar, emphasizes that the history of the Isis cult is a process of significant adaptation as she moves from a secondary deity and consort of Acerose in Egypt to her much more impressive status in the Roman era. This movement, out from under the shadow of her consort Acerose, so to speak, makes for an interesting contrast with the development charted by Chan, in which Chinese goddesses, once perceived as powerful deities, came to be given a less significant role in imperial China and were portrayed as idealizations of (male determined) femininity.

Klaus Klostermaier, a well known scholar of Hinduism whose recent textbook on this complex religious tradition is already becoming a favorite choice for university courses,[3] presents here a study of *Śakti* in her various forms. With this form of goddess tradition, we encounter a female deity sometimes portrayed visually and textually in forms decidedly other than what are regarded as "traditional" feminine. The fierce, even cruel form and actions attributed to this goddess offers a very different type of deity from some of the examples considered in the other essays in this volume, and again shows the danger and difficulty of trying to reduce goddess devotion to some common essence. Indeed, the cumulative result of all these four, rather extensive, case studies of goddesses is that "the divine feminine" can represent quite a variety of values, aspirations, practices, beliefs and devotees.

The Modern Debate

Complementing the studies of particular goddess traditions, Part Two of this volume is comprised of two essays that reflect in varying ways the contemporary discussion about gender and divinity, and a study of goddess symbolism in two works of modern literature. Dawne McCance classifies a variety of modern feminist thinkers who probe the relationship of gender and divinity, and provides an analysis of their thought that is at once sympathetic and critical. This essay will serve students as a helpful map of major feminist writers concerned with the question of female images of the Divine, and will give those familiar with some or all of the works she discusses a very useful study because it puts into one frame a variety of positions in the contemporary feminist literature. But, in addition to her helpful exposition of the writers she considers, McCance also offers creative suggestions about issues that are surfaced by the feminist attempts to re-think traditional images of deity, issues that are often not recognized by the thinkers involved in the enterprise. Out of a familiarity with language analysis and modern literary theory (including French literary and feminist theory), she poses questions that deserve to be taken seriously by all concerned with the contemporary critical discussion of gender.

In what is likely to be the most controversial essay in this collection, Joan Townsend delivers an unflinching critique of the idea that there was an original, ubiquitous religion focused on "the Goddess", a single female deity that supposedly dominated religious life before human religion was corrupted with the rise of dominant male deities. Townsend is an experienced archaeologist/anthropologist, acquainted with traditional societies as well as the modern literature she cites, and her scorching critique of "the Goddess" position draws upon this academic training. She sets out the requirements of sound archaeological method and shows that proponents of "the Goddess" view frequently base their arguments on careless and misleading use of artifactual evidence. She also proposes (persuasively, in my view) that the modern "Goddess" position amounts to what anthropologists characterize as a "revitalization movement" rather than a scientifically-based position. The contemporary advocates of this view will have to take account of her explicit and vigorous refutation.

The final essay in this collection, by Kathleen Wall, is an analysis of two novels by major women writers, Doris Lessing and Margaret Atwood. Wall (who has produced a book-length study of goddess typology in literature) brings together two very different kinds of novels, one tending in the direction of serious fantasy and the other set in the "real life" of the modern world, to show that the central characters in both works seem to be clear examples of appropriation of goddess imagery and motifs.[4] Wall's study will be of interest to literary scholars and to readers of the novels in question. But this is not simply a discussion of these works. Wall suggests provocatively that the more open-ended appropriation of goddess imagery and themes by creative writers may be closer to the way in which myths operated and were used in societies now inaccessible to us, ancient societies in which religion was less a set of dogmas and there may have been a rather dynamic interplay between established myths and the on-going needs and desires of people for myth-making.

Given the richness of the following essays in this volume, there is little more for me to write here. Each of them is a worthy contribution on its own. In this collection of studies, they further enrich one another and provide the reader with an interesting, well-researched, sometimes demanding, but accessible body of resources for scholarship and for our continued reflections on ourselves and human religious life.

Notes

1. For an introductory survey of a wide variety of goddess traditions, see David Kinsley, *The Goddesses' Mirror: Visions of the Divine from East and West* (Albany: State University of New York Press, 1988). See also Carl Olson (ed.), *The Book of the Goddess Past and Present: An Introduction to Her Religion* (New York: Crossroad, 1983). Though not true of all the essays in the latter book, some of them reflect the almost evangelistic tone expressed also by Olson and the tendency to regard all goddesses as manifestations of "the Goddess" (which looks rather suspiciously like an anachronistic attribution of a female monotheism to traditions that were evidently polytheistic.

2. For a recent study of Canaanite goddesses and their relationship to Israelite Yahwism, see Saul M. Olyan, *Asherah and the Cult of Yahweh in Israel* (SBLMS, 34; Atlanta: Scholars Press, 1988), and now Mark S. Smith, *The Early History of God: Yahweh and the Other Deities in Ancient Israel* (San Francisco: Harper & Row, 1990). See Egan's essay in the present collection for a study of Isis.

3. Klaus Klostermaier, *A Survey of Hinduism* (Albany: SUNY Press, 1989).

4. Kathleen Wall, *The Callisto Myth from Ovid to Atwood: Initiation and Rape in Literature* (Montreal: McGill-Queen's University Press, 1988).

PART ONE:
GODDESS TRADITIONS

GODDESSES IN CHINESE RELIGION[1]

Alan K.L. Chan

Among the many goddesses in the Chinese pantheon, Kuan-yin, the *bodhisattva* of mercy and compassion, perhaps stands out as the most important and widely worshipped today. Her story, however, is more or less familiar.[2] In this essay, I propose to focus on non-Buddhist, especially Taoist, female deities. This is a large topic. My main concern is to provide a general map for the non-specialist, by surveying the field and exploring uncharted territories, to bring into view the complex world of goddess worship in Chinese religion.

At the outset, it should be made clear that traditional Chinese sources do not always provide a full picture of goddess worship. It is very difficult to reconstruct the origins of any goddess, and to see how the deities were worshipped in early China. This is due, in part, to the fact that mythological narratives were often historicized and moralized in official accounts, through what some scholars have called a process of "reverse euhemerization."[3] Moreover, the writers who were entrusted with the preservation of tradition were almost invariably men, many of whom may not have had any sympathy for goddess worship. Some Confucian scholars, indeed, may even have been hostile to it. Yet, despite the problem of sources, and despite the generally patriarchal structure of society, there is little doubt that goddesses played, and continue to play, an important role in Chinese religious life. The reason for this is not difficult to fathom. Glimpses of the goddess can already be discerned in the religious and philosophical world of early China. Before the goddesses of Taoism can be brought into view, it is necessary to trace the roots of goddess worship in Chinese religion.

Glimpses of the Goddess in Early China

Gods, Ancestors and Shamans

From the so-called "oracle-bone" inscriptions, we know that the worship of deities can be traced at least as far back as the Shang period (second millennium B.C.E.).[4] It was a time when the high god Ti or Shang-ti (Lord on High) ruled the spiritual world. There were nature deities also, such as the god of the Yellow River. There were the astral deities of the sun, the moon, and the stars. Furthermore, divine status must also be accorded to the royal ancestors. They were the ones who bridged the distance between the king and the high god Ti. The question, then, is this: Did goddesses form a part of the divine hierarchy in Shang China?

This is not an easy question to answer, as later sources remember the past from their own perspective. The Shang oracle-bone records themselves, though invaluable, provide only fragments of an immensely rich religious tradition. For our purposes, three such fragments deserve special attention. First, while male ancestors dominated the religious scene, royal ancestresses were by no means neglected. Ancestresses who produced kings were especially well remembered in Shang ritual.[5] Secondly, the names Tung-mu (Mother of the East) and Hsi-mu (Mother of the West) appear in the oracle-bone inscriptions. Their identity is still open to debate; but it is clear that they were divine beings to whom sacrifices were offered.[6] As we shall see, it may be possible to link these figures to goddesses described in later sources. Finally, it must be mentioned that shamanesses (*wu*) played a significant role in Shang religious life. Through divination, music, dance and other rituals, shamanesses were able to mediate between the sacred and the profane. In particular, they were instrumental in seeking rain, ensuring fertility, and performing rites of healing.[7] Indeed, in the words of Edward Schafer, "they were, in fact, lesser goddesses."[8]

Partly because of these considerations, some scholars have suggested that there was a "matriarchal" phase in the Chinese past which survived well into the Shang period.[9] Suggestive as it may be, especially in the context of a study of goddesses, there is little concrete evidence to support this contention. Some women, such as Fu Hao, the famous consort of King Wu Ting, certainly enjoyed high status in the Shang state.[10] But, based on existing evidence, as K.C. Chang plainly states, "there can be no question that both the Shang and the Chou periods were both patrilineal and patriarchal."[11]

When the Chou dynasty (trad. 1122-256 B.C.E.) replaced the Shang, there were both changes and continuity in the religious sphere. The high god, for example, was now known as "heaven" (*t'ien*). The worship of ancestors and nature deities, however, continued. Shamanism remained important, although there are signs of gradual decline as well as indications that male shamans increasingly came to the forefront of religious practice.[12] A late Chou text, the *Kuo yü* (Discourses of the States), describes the origin and function of shamanism in this way:

> Anciently men and spirits did not intermingle. At that time there were certain persons who were so perspicacious, single-minded, and reverential that their understanding enabled them to make meaningful collation of what lies above and below, and their insight to illumine what is distant and profound. [...] Therefore the spirits would descend into them. The possessors of such powers were, if men, called *hsi* (shamans), and, if women, *wu* (shamanesses). It is they who supervised the positions of the spirits at the ceremonies, sacrificed to them, and otherwise handled religious matters [such as the different kinds of offerings, the proper place for sacrifice, ritual vessels and clothings]. As a consequence, the spheres of the divine and the profane were kept distinct. The spirits sent down blessings on the people, and accepted from them their offerings. There were no natural calamities.[13]

The importance of shamanism is not denied; yet, there is a shift in emphasis that renders the magical power of the shamans secondary to their knowledge of the "positions" or status of the deities, and the proper performance of religious ceremonies. Above all, according to this view, the task of the shaman is to maintain religious or cosmic *order*.

More will be said on the question of shamanism later. At this point, what should be underlined is that in Chou and later sources we begin to find clearer glimpses of goddess worship. An exhaustive analysis of these references cannot be entertained here. The following discussion serves to introduce a few of the great goddesses in early Chinese religion.

Nü Wa

In the fourth-century B.C.E. poem *T'ien-wen* (Heavenly Questions), preserved in the famous *Ch'u-tz'u* (Songs of Ch'u) anthology, the poet asks, "By what law was Nü Wa raised up to become high lord? By what means did she fashion the different creatures."[14] The *Ch'u-tz'u* as a whole has preserved a great deal of information concerning various deities and shamanistic practices; it is extremely important to our understanding of early Chinese religion, and we shall have occasions to quote from it again. The *T'ien-wen* itself is made up of a series of questions, over one hundred fifty, in fact, dealing with diverse religious issues. The questions quoted above concern the goddess Nü Wa (or Nü Kua), who is well known in Chinese mythology as the creator of humankind. A later tradition explains that Nü Wa created human beings "by patting yellow earth together."[15] Some scholars have tried to trace Nü Wa to the Shang period, but it must be pointed out that, even in

Chou sources, references to her are rare.[16] It would appear that the cult of Nü Wa did not mature until the Han dynasty (206 B.C.E.-220 C.E.).

In Han sources Nü Wa emerges fully as a major goddess. In addition to her role as creator, she is said to have saved the world by preventing the sky from collapsing. She stopped a flood, and she slew a mythical monster known as "black dragon."[17] She is linked to music, for she had invented the reed pipe (*sheng*), and she is also said to have established the institution of marriage. Iconographically, Nü Wa is often remembered as having a human head and the body of a snake.[18]

The focus of Nü Wa worship is quite clearly on her tremendous power to bring and sustain life. In the *Shuo-wen chieh-tzu*, the earliest Chinese dictionary compiled around 100 C.E., Nü Wa is simply described as an ancient goddess, who gave birth to and transformed the myriad creatures.[19] In this regard, her connection with music and marriage may reflect the practice of ancient fertility rites.[20] It is also noteworthy that since Han times, Nü Wa is often depicted together with Fu Hsi, the deity of the eastern sky and one of the chief originators of culture. A number of accounts report that they formed a brother-sister and/or husband-wife team who gave birth to humanity. In Han stone reliefs, we often see the serpentine coils of Fu Hsi and Nü Wa intertwined to form an inseparable union.[21]

The pairing of Nü Wa with Fu Hsi is best viewed in terms of an attempt to organize the divine hierarchy according to the central values current in the Han period. In the patriarchal setting of the world of high culture, it is difficult to maintain that creation was the work of a goddess alone. With Fu Hsi, however, Nü Wa could play her part in the spiritual world as consort and helper. This fate is by no means limited to Nü Wa. The same may be said for the goddesses of the sun and the moon as well.

Goddesses of the Sun and the Moon

The *T'ien-wen* poem raises another question: "When Yi shot down the suns, why did the ravens shed their feathers?"[22] What the ravens did or did not do, and why, is difficult to tell; but the myth of the archer Yi shooting down the suns is important and well remembered in early Chinese literature. The *Huai-nan tzu* (second cent. B.C.E.), for example, explains: "At the time of [the sage] Yao, the ten suns came out together, burning the crops and killing the trees, and the people had nothing to eat."[23] In addition, various mythical beasts were making havoc. Yao thus ordered the archer Yi to destroy the monsters and to "shoot" the ten suns.

Nine suns were successfully eliminated, or at least subdued; in any case, order was restored.

The myth of the ten suns is recorded also in the *Shan-hai ching* (Classic of Mountains and Seas), another important source for an understanding of early Chinese religion. Here, the focus is not on the sage Yao or the hero Yi, but on the mother of the suns:

> Beyond the south-eastern Sea amidst the Sweet Waters is the Tribe of Hsi-ho. There is a woman named Hsi-ho who regularly bathes the suns in the Sweet Springs. Hsi-ho is the wife of Ti Chün. It is she who gave birth to the ten suns.[24]

The idea that there were ten suns is easily explained. It corresponds to the traditional Chinese ten-day week. The reference to Ti Chün is more difficult, for it involves other complex myths. Suffice it to say that Ti Chün may be identified with the sage-king Shun and with Ti K'u, to whom the origin of the Shang people is traced.[25] Elsewhere in the *Shan-hai ching* it is reported that the suns were carried by ravens, which explains the question raised in the *T'ien-wen*.[26] In later iconography, a raven is usually depicted as residing in the sun (figure 1).

Whether the sun goddess Hsi-ho was originally independent from her "husband," Ti Chün, remains a question. One scholar at least has tried to identify Hsi-ho with Nü Wa.[27] There is also an early tradition which likens Hsi-ho to the charioteer of the sun, without involving sun-birds.[28] Nevertheless, it seems that the myth of the sun goddess is best placed in the larger context of the genesis of the Shang world. The unfavourable picture of the ten suns in the myth of the archer Yi may have originated from a different tradition. Ordinarily, or course, only one sun would appear each day; and even when they appeared together, the result is not necessarily harmful. In the *Chuang-tzu,* we find a dialogue between the sage-kings Yao and Shun. The latter points out that "long ago, the ten suns came out together"; the result, however, is simply that "the ten thousand things were all illuminated."[29]

We may recall that the names Tung-mu and Hsi-mu are mentioned in the oracle-bone records. If the myth of the sun goddess is related to the origin of Shang, could the "Mother of the East" and the "Mother of the West" be the names for the rising and the setting sun? It is also possible that they signify the sun and the moon. According to the *Shan-hai ching,* Ti Chün has another wife by the name of Ch'ang-hsi, who gave birth to twelve moons.[30]

Is the moon goddess Ch'ang-hsi (also known as Ch'ang-yi), then, the same as the "Mother of the West"?[31] Unfortunately, very little is known about Ch'ang-hsi. This is because in later traditions the moon goddess is more commonly identified with another mythological personage named Heng-o (better known as Ch'ang-o), who is none other than the wife of Archer Yi. If Yi's shooting of the suns had anything to do with his association with the moon goddess, there is no mention of it in the literature. The myth of Yi and Heng-o involves new religious themes which became increasingly important in the growing tradition of goddess worship. As the *Huai-nan tzu* remembers it, Yi obtained "the drug of immortality from the Queen Mother of the West. Heng-o stole it and fled to the moon."[32] That is to say, she ingested the drug of immortality, which enabled her to fly to the moon.

The theme of immortality and the goddess known as the Queen Mother of the West will be discussed later. At this point, it is enough to see that in early China, from the Shang to the Han period, goddess worship was evidently well established in Chinese religion. The cult of the moon goddess, in particular, flourished in subsequent centuries, and was celebrated in conjunction with the "Mid-autumn" festival.[33] The once great and powerful Nü Wa and the sun goddess Hsi-ho, however, faded somewhat in later periods. The former's life-giving power came to be shared by other deities, especially by Kuan-yin, beginning with the T'ang dynasty (618-906 C.E.). Hsi-ho suffered a worse fate, for the sun has come to be viewed as a male symbol, and the power of the sun was assigned to the "son of heaven," i.e., the emperor himself. In the *Shu ching* (Book of History), it is said that Yao

> commanded the (brothers) Hsi and Ho, in reverent accordance with the august heavens, to compute and delineate the sun, moon and stars, and the celestial markers, and so to deliver respectfully the seasons to be observed by the people.[34]

Hsi-ho became the brothers Hsi and Ho, and now in charge of the office of astronomy. This may be taken as another expression of the emphasis on "order" to which attention has been drawn earlier.

Transformation of the Goddess in Chinese Literature

One can go on to recount the stories of other ancient goddesses. The goddess of sericulture, for example, has a long and fascinating history.[35] One may mention also the "daughter" of the Yellow Emperor who is revered as the goddess of drought.[36] Equally important is the star goddess known as Chih-nü, the "Weaving Maid," who is still a popular goddess, celebrated especially by women. Her name is already mentioned in such an early work as the *Shih ching* (Book of Poetry), and in the *Shih chi* (Records of the Historian) she is described as "heaven's granddaughter."[37] Corresponding to the star Vega, the "Weaving Maid" is joined by the "Oxherd" (Altair) in later mythology. Their love story, and how they could meet only once a year on the seventh day of the seventh month, proves to have had a lasting hold on the Chinese imagination. That story, however, cannot be treated here.[38]

What is of interest for us here is that romantic love became a part of the world of Chinese goddesses. At the same time, the appearance of the goddess, too, underwent a significant change. Gone is the fierce, dragon-killing Nü Wa; such goddesses as Ch'ang-o (Heng-o) or Chih-nü are commonly depicted as refined and beautiful in later traditions. The star goddess, for example, is pictured in a third-century C.E. poem in this way:

Distant and faint the Herd-Boy Star,
Bright and lustrous the Heavenly River Maid;
Gently plying her slender white hands,
Cha-cha hum her shuttle and loom.
Day after day, her pattern unfinished,
Her tears fall in droplets like rain.
The Heavenly River, shallow and clear,
Divides them now by only a space;
Lovely and tender, with the river between,
Longingly they look but cannot speak.[39]

In this respect, one may indeed speak of a transformation of the goddess in Chinese literature. This development is reflected most clearly in the poetic tradition.

The Goddess of Wu Shan

This discussion may again begin with the *Ch'u-tz'u*, in which we find a poem entitled "Mountain Spirit" (*Shan-kuei*), placed together with other poems in a group known as the "Nine Songs" (*Chiu-ko*). The poem begins with these words:

There seems to be someone in the fold of the mountain
In a coat of fig-leaves with a rabbit-floss girdle,
With eyes that hold laughter and a smile of pearly brightness:
"Lady, your allurements show that you desire me."[40]

There is little disagreement that the "mountain spirit" is a goddess.[41] She may have been a goddess of fertility; but in the eyes of the poet, as the rest of the poem makes clear, she is above all a divine woman of irresistible sensual appeal. She is also not beyond the poet's reach: "She gathers sweet scents to give to one she loves...Dallying with the Fair One, I forget about returning."

The theme of romantic involvement with a mountain goddess is developed most fully in two poems of the *fu* style ("rhapsody" or "rhyme-prose"), attributed to the late Chou poet Sung Yü. At the centre of these poems stands the goddess of Wu shan, or "Shamaness Mountain," generally identified as located in Szechuan province. Since Sung Yü is traditionally regarded as the chief "disciple" of Ch'ü Yüan, the main author of the *Ch'u-tz'u,* we may safely speak of a developing tradition in this instance.

In the first of these poems, entitled *Kao-t'ang fu* (Rhapsody on the Kao-t'ang Shrine), the poet describes how he and his king visited the Yün-meng (literally, "Cloud Dream") marshes in the land of Ch'u. Yün-meng is a sacred site where ancient Ch'u fertility rites were performed. The *Mo-tzu,* for example, describes it together with other key cultic centres as a place where "men and women gather together and observe (religious ceremonies)."[42] This helps to explain the sense of wonder that the visitors felt as they rested on sacred ground. From a terrace the poet and his king looked out towards the shrine of Kao-t'ang, and were amazed by the wonderful play of cloud and mist that seemed to rise from the shrine itself. The poet explains that in the days of old a former king of Ch'u once visited Kao-t'ang, and in a dream saw a woman who identified herself as the woman or daughter of Shamaness Mountain. She went on to say,

> I am a visitor at Kao-t'ang.
> As I hear of my Lord's visit to Kao-t'ang,
> I wish to offer (myself to your) pillow and mat.[43]

The king obliged, and afterwards the goddess left with these words, "On the south side of Shamaness Mountain...in the morning I am the dawn cloud; in the evening I am the moving rain."[44] When the king woke up from his dream, the goddess was gone; he could only look at the "dawn cloud" and the "moving rain," and he built a shrine, named "Dawn Cloud," for her. It is not difficult to see the kind of meanings these expressions would acquire in later works. To mention but one example here, students of Chinese literature will recall that the famous Sung poet Su Shih (1036-1101 C.E.) fell in love with an entertainer-prostitute, named "Dawn Cloud."[45]

The second poem, entitled *Shen-nü fu* (Rhapsody on the Divine Woman), relates how that very night the present king or the poet himself saw the goddess in a dream.[46] Her ethereal beauty and splendour is described in loving detail. She is likened to the rising sun and the bright moon. Could the poet be thinking of the goddesses of the sun and the moon?[47] "Radiant like a flower, lustrous as jade," the goddess is said to be far more beautiful than even Mao-ch'iang and Hsi-shih, both women of legendary beauty. In this poem, the power of the goddess of Shamaness Mountain is clearly not the issue; she is above all a beautiful woman desired by kings and poets.

These two poems established a pattern for later poets. They ensured the goddess of Wu shan a lasting place in Chinese literature. The price for poetic fame, however, is that the original face of the mountain goddess faded into oblivion. Indeed, as the transformation of the goddess deepened, the term "divine woman" (*shen-nü*) itself came to denote a prostitute, and the expression "cloud and rain" became an euphemism for sexual intercourse. These usages still survive today in modern Chinese.

River Goddesses

The divine woman of Shamaness Mountain is not the only goddess favoured by the poets. River goddesses appear frequently in poetry also. The goddess of the Hsiang river, a major tributary of the Yangtze, is especially important in this connection. In the "Nine Songs" section of the *Ch'u-tz'u,* there are two poems entitled *Hsiang-chün* (Goddess of the Hsiang) and *Hsiang fu-jen* (Lady of the Hsiang). Both poems describe an ardent seeker in quest for the river goddess. Because of the language and symbolism employed, there is little doubt that the poet here speaks in the guise of a shaman. It is also possible that the poems are adapted from ritual songs themselves.[48] A more difficult question is whether the two poems are addressed to the same goddess. The majority of traditional commentators have in fact argued that there are two goddesses involved here. They are identified as the two daughters of the sage-king Yao and the two wives of Shun.[49] This, I suspect, represents yet another instance of the kind of ordering of the divine hierarchy that characterizes the development of Chinese religion. In my view, the most likely hypothesis is that the two poems in the *Ch'u-tz'u* address the same goddess, perhaps based on ritual songs performed in spring and autumn festivals.[50]

If the identity of the Hsiang goddess remains in doubt, the poet's understanding of her is consistent with what we have seen in the case of the goddess of Shamaness Mountain. The first poem, "Goddess of the Hsiang," reads,

> The goddess comes not, she holds back shyly.
> Who keeps her delaying within the island,
> Lady of the lovely eyes and the winning smile?
> Skimming the water in my cassia boat,
> I bid the Yüan and Hsiang still their waves

And the Great River make its stream flow softly.
I look for the goddess, but she does not come yet.
Of whom does she think as she plays her reed-pipes?
North I go, drawn by my flying dragon,
Steering my course to the Tung-t'ing lake:
My sail is of fig-leaves, melilotus my rigging,
An iris my flag-pole, my banner of orchids.
Gazing at the distant Ts'en-yang mooring
I waft my magic across the Great River.
I waft my magic, but it does not reach her.
The lady is sad, and sighs for me;
And my tears run down over cheek and chin:
I am choked with longing for my lady.[51]

The poem goes on to describe the shaman's journey on his "flying dragon," most likely a dragon boat, referring to the "cassia boat" mentioned in line four above.[52] The same "quest" theme is repeated in the companion piece, "Lady of the Hsiang." Despite the shaman's effort, the goddess cannot be attained. Since these two poems centre on a failed quest, the goddess herself remains in the background. We can only imagine how desirable and beautiful she is. Later poets, however, have little difficulty in depicting the alluring beauty of the goddess of the Hsiang river.[53]

Like the Hsiang in the south, the Lo river, which flows into the Yellow River in the north, is perceived to have a divine essence. In the *Ch'u-tz'u*, the goddess of Lo river already appears as a target of the poet's love.[54] Her name is Fu-fei, or "Consort Fu," a name which points to her perceived relationship with the god of the Yellow River. Through the brush of the early third-century C.E. prince and poet Ts'ao Chih, the Lo goddess achieves, as it were, a second and transformed immortality. As Ts'ao himself tells us in the preface to his poem *Lo-shen fu* (Rhapsody on the Lo Goddess), his work is inspired by the poems by Sung Yü on the goddess of Wu shan.[55] This should already gi an indication of the nature of Ts'ao's work, and further testifies to a continuing tradition of the goddess' transformation.

In this long poem, the goddess is seen quite simply as the most beautiful woman one can ever hope to find:

From afar, I see her:
She shines like the sun rising above the morning haze;
Moving closer, I observe her:
She dazzles like a lotus coming out of the green water.[56]

The poet proceeds to describe her gentle shoulders, her slender waist, her fine, long neck and nape, and her smooth, white skin. She does not wear makeup. The poet fixes his gaze on her hair, her brows, her lips, her teeth, her eyes; even her dimples do not escape attention. The goddess is of course dressed appropriately in rich and beautiful clothes fit for a divine consort. She is accompanied by other goddesses, including Nü Wa, who appears here as a singer of songs. Seeing the goddess' gleaming eyes, her lustrous jade-like complexion, the way she hesitates and holds back her words, and sensing the fragrance that emanates from her, the poet longs for her and forgets even his meals. After Ts'ao Chih's time, few poets found it necessary to be creative when describing this or any other goddess. The same language is applied to beautiful women, and in some instances to entertainers and prostitutes.[57]

Poets and Shamans

Goddesses of mountains and rivers, as nature deities and associated with fertility cults, commanded serious attention in early China. In one of his journeys to the sacred centres of the land, the first emperor of the Ch'in dynasty (221-207 B.C.E.) reached the shrine of the Hsiang goddess.[58] There, his journey was interrupted by a "great wind." Recognizing the presence of the goddess, the emperor grew angry and ordered some 3,000 convicts to cut down the trees in the area, to punish the goddess. Obviously, unlike the poets, he did not feel any affection for the Hsiang deity.

Nevertheless, it was the poet's vision that shaped the memory of the Hsiang and other goddesses, at least in the world of high culture. In the poems discussed above, it is clear that old religious themes are transformed by the poet's more earthly aspirations. Indeed, in the second century C.E., the *Ch'u-tz'u* commentator Wang Yi has said as much with regard to the "Nine Songs":

> In former times the people living in the area lying between the Yüan and the Hsiang rivers south of Nanying were superstitious and much given to the worship of spirits. In their service of the gods they would sing, play drum, and dance to do them pleasure. It was in this area that Ch'ü Yüan concealed himself after his banishment. Full of grief and bitterness and in a greatly disturbed state of mind, he would go out to watch the sacrificial rites of the local inhabitants and witness the singing and dancing which accompanied them. Finding the words of their songs crude and barbarous, he composed the "Nine Songs" to replace them.[59]

On this point, the great Confucian scholar Chu Hsi (1130-1200 C.E.) adds that Ch'ü Yüan changed the words of the original songs and deleted what was "excessive."[60]

What were these "excessive" elements that offended the poet's sensibilities? One way of approaching this question is to draw attention to the decline of shamanism in Chinese religion. As early as the Chou period, as indicated earlier, there were attempts to explain the origin of shamanism and better define its role within the state cult. At the same time, there were attempts to curb what was considered "excessive" in ritual practices, such as human sacrifice and ritual nudity. The *Li chi* (Book of Rites), for example, relates how a ruler of the state of Lu, concerned about a drought, sought advice regarding the ritual of "exposing" a shamaness in order to seek rain. The advice is not only negative, but compares the shamaness to a "stupid woman."[61]

The *Shih chi* also relates an interesting story which deserves retelling, for it shows the prevalence of human sacrifice and how it was viewed by the ruling elite.[62] The story concerns an official by the name of Hsi-men Pao (fl. 400 B.C.E.). When he first became the governor of the Yeh district, in modern Honan, he learned that the people were taxed to their limit in order to prepare for an annual sacrifice, a sacred marriage, between the god of the Yellow River and a young girl chosen from the villages. The aim is of course to keep the deity satisfied lest he would cause a great flood. The ceremony was very elaborate. For over ten days, the site was lavishly decorated, and the chosen girl was carefully attended to by the shamanesses. On the wedding day, the young bride would be "sent" to the river deity on a "bed"--that is, a boat equipped with all the necessary items of a nuptial bed. This brings to mind Sung Yü's poem *Kao-t'ang fu*, in which the goddess of Shamaness Mountain offered herself to the king's "pillow and mat."

Hsi-men Pao agreed to take part in the ceremony, which was attended by over 2,000 people. When everything was ready, the governor ordered the bride be brought before him. He found her unsatisfactory, and asked the chief shamaness to inform the river god to wait for a few days till he could find a more suitable bride. Immediately he had the shamaness thrown into the river. Then, for good measure, a couple of her disciples were thrown into the river as well, to see why she had not returned. Needless to say, the divine marriage ended right there.

Is it possible that some river goddesses were originally sacrificial victims? The goddesses of the Hsiang and Lo rivers, for example, besides being very beautiful, are also remembered as drowned women who became goddesses.[63] But this may be due to the kind of historicizing tendency that colours much of the Chinese religious tradition. Conceivably some rivers are simply perceived to have a female divine presence, independent of ritual sacrifices. Again, the origins of river goddesses cannot be decided here; probably no one single process can account for *all* water deities. What the *Shih chi* story does show is that early Chinese religious practice is not quite as refined as that portrayed by the poets. It also suggests how a strong official opposition eventually led to the decline of shamanism. In this framework, it is easy to understand why so few accounts of shamanism have survived in official sources. The *Shih chi* story, incidentally, is preserved only because it was thought to be humorous; otherwise, it too may have been deemed "excessive" and not worthy of the historian's attention.[64]

Shamanism itself, despite official opposition, did not disappear. At the beginning of the Han dynasty (ca. 200 B.C.E.), shamans still served the government in the capital Ch'ang-an.[65] But since then they were increasingly relegated to a minor position in the government bureaucracy. Outside the world of officialdom, however, shamanism found new support in popular religion. The *Chin shu* (History of the Chin Dynasty, 265-420 C.E.) tells us how Hsia T'ung (fl. ca. 265 C.E.), a recluse of great learning and moral integrity, condemns his relatives for having employed two shamanesses to perform an ancestral sacrifice. The criticism itself contains nothing new: the shamanesses are accused of "lewd behaviour." What is interesting is a brief description of their appearance: they are very beautiful; they excel in music and dance; and they could make themselves invisible. Their performance begins with the playing of drums and bells, but soon progresses to "swallowing swords and spitting fire." The whole place is enveloped in a dense fog, punctured by flashes of lightning.[66] This type of narrative suggests that a certain ambivalence characterizes the reception of shamanism in traditional China. While it was forced into the background by official criticism, it seems to have retained a powerful hold on the religious imagination of the people. We should keep this in mind when we examine goddess worship in Taoism.

When shamans fell out of favour in the world of elite culture, poets came to replace them as the champions of goddesses. When fertility rites were deemed "excessive," and no longer performed in, for example, the Yün-meng marshes, the poet brought a new meaning to the place and to the goddess of fertility. When "pillows and mats" were no longer used in ritual sacrifices, they acquired a new symbolic significance. In addition, just as it came to be that shamanesses had to be organized into the official hierarchy, goddesses themselves were reinterpreted in such a way that their power and divinity became secondary to their place in the broader cosmic hierarchy. The sun goddess Hsi-ho thus became "officials" in the "government" of Yao. Nature goddesses and fertility goddesses became daughters and wives of sages and heroes of old. The same process that rendered Nü Wa the wife of Fu Hsi, and the Hsiang goddess or goddesses the two daughters of Yao, was applied to other deities. The goddess of the Lo river thus became none other than the daughter of Fu Hsi.[67] Goddesses, too, must be given respectable family backgrounds.

The Taoist Connection

Given these considerations, it may seem surprising that goddess worship survived in China at all. There is, however, another side to the story of the transformation of the goddess which helped to secure her place in Chinese religion. This has to do, first of all, with the philosophical and cosmological worldview that emerged in the Chou period, and secondly, with the rise of religious Taoism.

More specifically, beginning with the second half of the Chou dynasty, the concept of *Tao* or Way gradually became one of the key philosophical categories in Chinese thought. This concept serves to articulate the insight that the multiplicity of phenomena may be traced to a common source. Interpretations of *Tao* are, to be sure, varied; but few in traditional China would reject the claim put forward by the *I ching* (Book of Changes) that *yin* and *yang* constitute the Way.[68]

In its mature form, the concept of *yin-yang* forms the basis of a comprehensive cosmological theory. Materially conceived, *yin* and *yang* refer to the two fundamental forms of *ch'i*, or "breath" of life, which make up the cosmos. *Yin*, identified further with the female, the earth, the moon, the dark, the yielding and submissive, etc., ideally complements the *yang*, the male, heaven, the sun, the bright, the hard and aggressive. Harmony between the two forces, in other words, is deemed vital to the well-being of the physical and spiritual universe.[69] By the turn of the Common Era, the *yin-yang* theory had become a part of the Chinese worldview, a common thread which draws the various schools of thought together. Goddesses, in this framework, are above all characterized by the purity of their *ch'i*, i.e., they represent the essence of *yin*.

This view of the cosmos occupies a central position in Taoism. As an organized religion, Taoism first appeared towards the end of the Han period in the second century C.E. The relationship between religious Taoism and the earlier philosophical writings of Lao-tzu and Chuang-tzu is not easy to define. For our purposes, I would simply suggest that religious Taoism found in the philosophical tradition a source of inspiration and insights. At the same time, the philosophical tradition was reinterpreted in the light of new Taoist concerns. In the *Lao-tzu*, or *Tao-te ching*, the *yin-yang* theory is already mentioned, in the context of an account of the cosmogonic process:

> *Tao* produced the One.
> The One produced the two.
> The two produced the three.
> And the three produced the ten thousand things.
> The ten thousand things carry the *yin* and embrace the *yang*, and through the blending of the material force [*ch'i*] they achieve harmony.[70]

Later commentators often specify that the "One" refers to the "original *ch'i*," and the "two" are the *yin* and *yang* forces. Moreover, in the *Lao-tzu*, the Way is also described as the "mother" of all things. Indeed, the metaphor of the mother and other "*yin* metaphors," such as water, the yielding and submissive, figure prominently in the Taoist classic. Together, they suggest a radically different conception of the *Tao*, when compared with the Confucian and other interpretations. In particular, chapter 6 of the *Tao-te ching* reads:

> The spirit of the valley never dies.
> It is called the subtle and profound female.
> The gate of the subtle and profound female
> Is the root of heaven and earth.

This enigmatic statement, as one can well imagine, has given rise to diverse interpretations. One modern suggestion is that the text here may reflect an ancient myth of a "mother-earth" goddess.[71] Like the more general claim that there is a "matriarchal" period in Chinese history, this view may be heuristically useful, especially in the light of similar myths in other cultures; but little textual or archaeological evidence can be found to support this hypothesis. In early China, it appears that the earth deity was identified as a male god.[72] Furthermore, whether the *Lao-tzu* as a whole espouses a "feminine perspective" remains an open question. Roger Ames, for example, has argued that the *Lao-tzu* envisages an "androgynous" ideal, which seeks to reconcile all opposites.[73] The only point we need to make is simply that certain passages in the *Tao-te ching* provided an impetus for the development of goddess cults in later Taoism.

Immortality and Afterlife

The *Lao-tzu* also points to another theme crucial to religious Taoism: namely, the quest for immortality. "The spirit of the valley never dies," as chapter 6 puts it. Elsewhere in the *Tao-te ching* we find such equally puzzling statements as "He who dies but does not really perish enjoys long life" (chap. 33). In chapter 59, the text speaks of "the way of long life and everlasting vision." Again, scholars may debate the "original" or "intended" meaning of these passages. What is beyond dispute is that, since the Han dynasty, Taoism has been identified as being devoted to the quest for immortality.

Besides the *Lao-tzu*, shamanism may also have contributed to this Taoist preoccupation. As mentioned, shamans were the acknowledged experts in the art of healing. The *Shan-hai ching*, in this regard, refers specifically to a group of shamans who wielded a "drug of no death."[74] It also refers to a "people of no death," and a "kingdom of no death."[75] Although shamanism may have been viewed with suspicion by Confucian officials, the ideal of "deathlessness," a physical or "worldly" immortality, had a profound impact on the development of Taoism.[76] To attain the state of deathlessness, special techniques were developed, including the use of special drugs, breathing and physical exercises, dietary regimens, and sexual practices.[77] The last is of course rooted in the belief that harmony between *yin* and *yang* bears directly on self-cultivation. Alchemy, both in terms of the manufacture of an elixir of life and internally the transformation into a spiritual body, thus became an essential part of Taoism.[78]

The secret to immortality may also be directly conferred by a deity or an "immortal" (*hsien*). Even in non-Taoist sources, there are accounts of a fabulous island off the east coast of China where immortals are said to dwell.[79] In the Han period, a cultic centre in the west, a sacred mountain known as K'un-lun, began to take on increasing importance, assuming the role of the *axis mundi*. The *Shan-hai ching* describes it as the home of the "hundred deities," i.e., the multitude of divine beings.[80] It is in this same context that the shamans in command of the "drug of no death" are introduced. On Mount K'un-lun, as the *Shan-hai ching* and the *Huai-nan tzu* both point out, there is a "tree of no death," which offers longevity to those fortunate enough to taste it.[81] This sacred mountain, as we shall see, is further identified as the abode of the most powerful goddess and bestower of immortality in the Taoist pantheon.

The art of nourishing life is not easily accessible to the common people. Divine guidance in the quest for immortality is a special gift given only to those who truly deserve it. The precise criteria need not concern us at this point. What is more important here is to see how the belief in an afterlife came to complement the ideal of immortality. The two may have originated independently; but roughly by the Han dynasty, they formed a closely related pair which permeated every level of Chinese religion.

Recent archaeological finds at Ma-wang-tui (in Ch'ang-sha, Hunan province) vividly testify to the prevalence of the belief in an afterlife in the Han period. The three Han tombs discovered in Ma-wang-tui, excavated between 1972-1974 and dated to the second century B.C.E., contain a wealth of information concerning early Chinese religion and culture.[82] In Tomb 3, for example, a large number of texts are found, including silk manuscripts of the *Lao-tzu* and the *I ching*, as well as astronomical and astrological treatises. There are also medical texts, which include not only descriptions of diseases and prescriptions, but instructions in the art of nourishing life. In this category, we may include a painting which contains over forty diagrams of physical exercises, involving men and women, old and young.[83]

Tomb 1 is usually dated around 168 B.C.E., and the occupant is believed to be the wife of Li Ts'ang, the Marquis of Tai. Her richly furnished tomb indicates the degree of recognition that women of distinction still enjoyed at that time. For our purposes, the most important find is the priceless silk painting found on top of the innermost coffin of the "Countess". Most likely it was used as a burial shroud.[84] It depicts generally the journey of the deceased woman to the afterworld, but the exact symbolism of the polychrome, "T-shaped" painting is still very much open to debate. The identity of the key figure at the top-centre, with the serpentine tail, has not yet been resolved. She may be a goddess--the depiction calls to mind Nü Wa--or she may be the Countess of Tai herself, "sloughing off her mortal coil," as she reaches her final destination.[85] To her right, below the crescent moon, there is another female figure who could be the moon goddess Ch'ang-o, flying to the moon after having taken the drug of immortality. Some scholars, however, prefer to see her as the Countess.[86] The Countess of Tai may not have attained immortality; but, the effort to preserve her body proves astonishingly successful.[87]

The Ma-wang-tui finds thus illustrate concretely the kind of religious beliefs current since the Han period. They offer us a clear glimpse of the world in which goddess worship developed, despite the official policy to delete "excessive" rituals, and despite the poetic transformation of old religious practices. In Taoism especially, cosmological speculation, beliefs in an afterlife and the hope of immortality combined to yield a rich tradition. Numerous goddesses would find a home in this tradition, as Taoism grew into a fully institutionalized religion in the post-Han era.

The Queen Mother of the West

The Many Faces of Hsi-wang-mu

The most important goddess in the Taoist pantheon is Hsi-wang-mu, the Queen Mother of the West. We have already come across her name, in our discussion of the moon goddess, and some scholars have identified her with the Hsi-mu (Mother of the West) of the oracle bones.[88] The close similarity of the two names certainly speaks well for this hypothesis; but, since the earliest extant references to the Queen Mother date to late Chou times, a strong oral tradition would have to be assumed to account for the continuity. Furthermore, when references to the Queen Mother do appear in the early literature, we are confronted with very different accounts which, unless new archaeological evidence comes to light, render the reconstruction of the goddess' origin largely a matter of conjecture.

Because of her name, the Queen Mother is generally regarded as having been a female deity from the very beginning. There is a second view which argues that the name of the goddess refers originally to a place or state. The *Erh-ya*, in particular, describes "Hsi-wang-mu" as one of the "four wildernesses."[89] The *Hsün-tzu* at one point speaks of a "royal state of the West" (Hsi-wang-kuo), a name which closely resembles that of the Queen Mother.[90] Traditionally, this view is especially popular among Confucian scholars who wish to discount the importance of the Queen Mother.[91] To students of Chinese religion, however, it should present little difficulty, as Hsi-wang-mu or Hsi-wang-kuo may refer both to the place and to its divine and/or earthly ruler. The name Hsi-ho, as we have seen, is also applied both to the sun goddess and to a state or tribe.

A third view regarding the origin of the goddess is more important. It suggests that the Queen Mother may be better understood as originally an androgynous deity, in whom the *yin* and *yang* cosmic forces join in perfect union.[92] Androgyny, to be sure, is not an uncommon motif in world mythology. And, as mentioned earlier, the *Lao-tzu* has also been viewed from this perspective. Some support for this view may be gathered from iconographic sources. The Queen Mother, for example, is sometimes depicted in stone reliefs together with symbols of the sun and the moon, suggesting perhaps her command of both the *yin* and *yang* forces.[93] My only concern is that such iconographic material is of relatively late provenance; it does not necessarily reflect the image of the Queen Mother in the pre-Han and early Han periods.

The Queen Mother, it is true, was described in such an early work as the *Huai-nan tzu* as a great deity on whom cosmic order depends. In a time when the Way no longer prevailed, the *Huai-nan tzu* states, "the Old Mother of the West broke her *sheng* (headdress) in two, and the Yellow Deity sighed and moaned. Flying birds suffered damaged wings, and running animals suffered injured feet"--the consequence, in short, was disastrous.[94] The *sheng* is the characteristic headdress of the Queen Mother, and as Kominami Ichiro has shown, it is also related to the loom, symbolizing the central role of the deity as the "weaver" of cosmic order.[95] But, the affirmation of the goddess' power does not necessarily entail her original androgynous nature. Presumably the *Huai-nan tzu* here regards the "Yellow Deity"--that is, the Yellow Emperor (Huang-ti)--as equally instrumental in the maintenance of cosmic order. Indeed, it may be no accident that the Queen Mother and the Yellow Emperor are mentioned together in the same sentence.

Goddess of K'un-lun

The *Chuang-tzu* also refers to the Yellow Emperor and the Queen Mother. They are seen, together with a number of mythological beings, as deities who have attained the Way.

> Hsi-wei got it and held up heaven and earth. [Fu Hsi, the Big Dipper, the sun and the moon also obtained the Way.] K'an-p'i got it and entered K'un-lun. P'ing-i got it and wandered in the great river. Chien Wu got it and lived in the great mountain. The Yellow Emperor got it and ascended to the cloudy heavens... The Queen Mother of the West got it and took her seat on Shao-kuang--nobody knows her beginning, nobody knows her end.[96]

Shao-kuang is usually glossed as either the name of a cave or a mountain in the far west. The other figures listed include cultural heroes, celestial luminaries, river deities, and the two mountain deities known as K'an-p'i and Chien Wu. The former is a deity on Mount K'un-lun, and is said to have the face of a human being and the shape of a beast.[97] The latter, as we shall see, although assigned to Mount T'ai in the east in later traditions, may be traced to K'un-lun as well. I suspect that the Queen Mother may also have been a mountain deity at one stage of her illustrious career.

The Queen Mother appears several times in the *Shan-hai ching* in a much more concrete way. She is always linked to a mountain, identified differently in the different passages, but situated generally in the western or north-western part of the Chinese religious world. Thus we find the Queen Mother being linked to a "Jade Mountain," a "Mountain of the Snake Shamaness" (also known as "Turtle Mountain"), the "Mountain of the Queen Mother," and Mount K'un-lun.[98] Her power is great, for she has control over evil influences or, according to another interpretation, over certain stars.[99] In two passages, the Queen Mother is portrayed as a deity with a human body, a tail of a leopard, and teeth of a tiger. One of the texts reads,

> South of the western sea, by the shores of the flowing sands, behind the Red River and before the Black River there is a great mountain called the "heights of K'un-lun." A deity resides there, with the face of a human being and the body of a tiger; it has stripes and a tail, both of which are white... There is a person who wears a *sheng* (headdress), with the teeth of a tiger and the tail of a leopard; she dwells in a cave and is named "Queen Mother of the West."[100]

The "cave" in question is usually identified with the "Shao-Kuang" mentioned in the *Chuang-tzu*. Who is the other deity accompanying the Queen Mother on or near the "heights of K'un-lun"?

Mount K'un-lun figures elsewhere in the *Shan-hai ching*. At one point it is said to be the abode of Ti (Sovereign), whence the "Red River" and the "Black River" flow.[101] The divine sovereign Ti is served by a deity known as Lu Wu, who has the face of a human being, the body and claws of a tiger, and nine tails. This figure should be the same as the nameless deity found together with the Queen Mother on the K'un-lun heights. And according to Kuo P'u (276-324 C.E.), Lu Wu is none other than the mountain deity Chien Wu mentioned in the *Chuang-tzu* passage translated above.[102]

In yet another passage, Mount K'un-lun is likewise described as the place of Ti, characterized again by the "Red River" and the "Black River."[103] According to this account, K'un-lun is the home of the "hundred deities," who live in caves; but, instead of Lu Wu or Chien Wu, the guardian of the sacred mountain is now identified as a mythical beast called K'ai-ming, with a large tiger-like body and nine human-faced heads. Could this K'ai-ming beast be the same as Lu Wu? Could the difference between the "nine heads" of the former and the "nine tails" of the latter be due to a scribal error? According to Kuo P'u, the K'ai-ming deity represents the essence of *yang* and commands the "hundred spirits" (*pai-ling*). Does this imply that there may be a *yin* counterpart which assists in ruling the multitude of spirits? These issues cannot be resolved here; my only suggestion is that mountain deities abound on K'un-lun, the cosmic centre, among whom perhaps ranks the Queen Mother also. Together they serve a high god known as Ti. According to some scholars, Ti may be identified with Huang-ti, the Yellow Emperor.[104]

This last assertion is admittedly difficult to prove. Yet, in the *Chuang-tzu*, the Yellow Emperor is also linked to Mount K'un-lun.[105] The *Mu*

T'ien-tzu chuan (Story of Mu, Son of Heaven), an early text of uncertain provenance which focuses on the legendary travels of King Mu of Chou (tenth cent. B.C.E.), including a meeting with the Queen Mother, also speaks of a "shrine of the Yellow Emperor" on Mount K'un-lun.[106] On this basis, one may ask whether the Queen Mother in the *Shan-hai ching* was not one of the Yellow Emperor's chief assistants. According to the *Huai-nan tzu*, "The Yellow Emperor gave birth to *yin* and *yang*."[107] Perhaps the Queen Mother and the K'ai-ming/Lu Wu/Chien Wu deity are seen to embody respectively the *yin* and *yang* forces.[108]

Taking this line of inquiry one step further, it seems that the Queen Mother cult may be traced to shamanistic roots. The hybrid form of the goddess itself brings to mind the pervasive "man-beast" motif in early Chinese art. And shamanism, as a number of scholars have pointed out, has much to do with the shaping of this artistic tradition.[109] Furthermore, in the *Shan-hai ching* the Queen Mother is specifically linked to a "Mountain of the Snake Shamaness"; and the "Mountain of the Queen Mother" itself is placed next to a "Spirit Mountain" (Ling shan) where a number of shamans are said to "ascend and descend."[110] Like Mount K'un-lun, this mountain too assumes the position of a cosmic pillar through which shamans "ascend" to the spiritual realm and "descend" with divine knowledge or communication. Since the *Shuo-wen* dictionary equates the word *ling* (spirit) with *wu* (shamaness), the sacred mountain here may even be the prototype of the "Shamaness Mountain" so dear to the poets.[111] If the words *ling* and *wu* are interchangeable, then the mountain deity who commands the "hundred spirits" is also the lord of the "hundred shamans."

At a time when the divine hierarchy was not yet well organized, when the sacred geography was still not clearly defined, the Queen Mother appears to be a powerful mountain goddess and a patron of the shamans. She is regarded as the essence of *yin*, but subordinate to a high god, perhaps the Yellow Emperor. Later in our discussion, we shall see how this relationship is reversed, as changes to both figures call forth a new interpretation. Here, we note that the Queen Mother is perceived as having power over evil influences, especially natural calamities and diseases; after all, as indicated earlier, shamans have access to the "drug of no death." The goddess is also seen as a key to cosmic order and harmony--this would follow from her pivotal position on Mount k'un-lun. In the "great wilderness," the *Shan-hai ching* adds, one finds not only the "Spirit Mountain" and the "Mountain of the Queen Mother," but also a mountain to which the sun and the moon return.[112] K'un-lun, as cosmic centre and pillar, would encompass all these aspects and more. There is, in other words, no need to see the Queen Mother as having "evolved" from a mountain deity into a cosmic goddess. The picture that emerges from this analysis is simply that of a powerful goddess of a *cosmic* mountain.

In the World of Men

The process to define better the religious world was, however, under way, when the Queen Mother appeared in the various sources. The *Chuang-tzu, Shan hai ching* and other sources picture the goddess from the perspective of their own understanding of the cosmos. Thus, focusing on *Tao,* the *Chuang-tzu* is not interested in the appearance of the Queen Mother. Although the image of a cave-dwelling deity is preserved, the important point is that she has attained the Way. The picture of the Queen Mother in the *Shan-hai ching,* on the other hand, is largely shaped by early religious, shamanistic traditions. What is decisive here is the power of the goddess, reflected both by her appearance and function. The *Huai-nan tzu,* with its own preoccupations, remembers the Queen Mother as a cosmic goddess and a bestower of immortality. It is interesting that the archer Yi, who obtained the drug of immortality from the Queen Mother, is also mentioned in the *Shan-hai ching,* again in the context of Mount K'un-lun.[113]

Just as Yi had sought the favour of the Queen Mother, emperors too aspired to reach the goddess. The meeting between the Queen Mother and an emperor in fact forms a central theme in the mature story of the goddess. The *Mu T'ien-tzu chuan,* as mentioned, includes an episode in which King Mu of Chou visited the Queen Mother. The king presented himself in a formal way, bearing gifts, and was received warmly by the Queen Mother. The two exchanged poems or songs, which include an allusion to the theme of immortality.[114] In this account, though brief and plagued with textual difficulties, the Queen Mother is above all presented as a divine sovereign.[115] She seems to have lost her "mountain" qualities and to have found a new home in the world of elite culture. Still, some of the "wilder" images are preserved, in the Queen's second poem:

> Come to this western land,
> And live in the wild.
> Find your company among tigers and leopards,
> And dwell among ravens and magpies.
> Blessed fate: I shall always be here,
> For I am the daughter of [the high god] Ti.
> Why do you turn to the world of your people,

And rob me of you?[116]

The king did not stay, although the *Shih chi*, which also refers to this meeting, tells us that he enjoyed his visit so much that he forgot about returning.[117]

This story reminds us of the poetic transformation of goddess worship discussed earlier. Did the Queen Mother suffer the same fate as Nü Wa and other goddesses, and become simply a beautiful, refined, but essentially powerless divine woman? Did she become a mere object of desire for poets and kings? In the mature version, as we shall see more clearly, the goddess is certainly portrayed as very desirable. But, the transformation of the Queen Mother is more complex. On the one hand, like other goddesses, she could not escape the visions of beauty and order imposed by the literary elite. On the other hand, the Queen Mother did not lose her power and status as the most important goddess in the Taoist pantheon.

During the Han period, the Queen Mother began to assume a more distinct identity. The various images, such as immortality, cosmic order, and meeting with an emperor, began to coalesce and to yield a fuller picture of the goddess. The initial result, interestingly, appears to be a goddess of immortality in the form of an older woman. Ssu-ma Hsiang-ju (179-117 B.C.E.) writes in his *Ta-jen fu* (Rhapsody on the Great Man):

Now, with my own eyes I see the Queen Mother of the West!
With a head of silvery white hair, she wears her *sheng*
(headdress) and lives in a cave.
Fortunately she has a three-legged raven to serve her.
Even if one were to live forever like this and not die,
Though it be for ten thousand generations, there is little
to rejoice.[118]

The unsympathetic tone of these verses need not concern us. What is of interest is that a number of images are now tied together in the shape of a white-haired deity. Conceivably, the colour white may refer to the goddess' connection with the west, as the two belong to the same category in the Han cosmological system. Nevertheless, in this instance I believe the poet has something more concrete in mind.

The picture of an elderly goddess can also be gleaned from a report of the Han "soteriological" movement devoted to the Queen Mother.[119] In 3 B.C.E., the Hsi-wang-mu cult burst onto the popular religious scene in a major way. The *Han shu* (History of the Former Dynasty) says,

In the first month of the fourth year of Chien-p'ing, the population were running around in a state of alarm, each person carrying a stalk of straw or hemp. People exchanged these emblems with one another, saying that they were carrying out the

> advent procession. Large numbers of persons, amounting to thousands, met in this way on the roadsides, some with dishevelled hair or going barefoot... Some harnessed teams of horses...setting up relay stations so as to convey the tokens. They passed through 26 commanderies and kingdoms until they reached the capital city. That summer the people came together in meetings in the capital city and in the commanderies and kingdoms...and they sang and danced in worship of the Queen Mother of the West. They also passed round a written message, saying, "The Mother tells the people that those who wear this talisman will not die; and let those who do not believe Her words look below the pivots on their gates, and there will be *white hairs* there to show that this is true."[120]

Following this report, the *Han shu* offers an "official" reading of this movement. It includes the observation that "Hsi-wang-mu is the name applied to a (mature, older) woman [*fu-jen*]," and that the "white hairs are the sign of declining years."[121] To the believers, of course, the "white hairs" symbolize something very different: they signal the presence of the goddess and her gift of everlasting life.

This insight, moreover, is perhaps also behind the reference to the Queen Mother in the *T'ai-p'ing ching* (Classic of Great Peace), the earliest in a specifically Taoist scripture. The text is very difficult, but the general sense seems to be this: "To make/let the people live as long as Hsi-wang-mu." The text then explains the words individually. "'Hsi' means everyone preserves the true Way in his chest and heart. 'Wang' refers to the king who succeeds in carrying out the Way of heaven... 'Mu' (mother) is the proof of longevity, and the leader of the spirits."[122]

A similar picture seems to be implied in Yang Hsiung's (53 B.C.E.-18 C.E.) *Kan-ch'üan fu* (Sweet Springs Palace Rhapsody), the subject of which is an imperial sacrifice performed by Emperor Ch'eng (32-7 B.C.E.):

> He recalls Queen Mother of the West, and joyfully salutes her
> longevity.
> He rejects Jade Maiden, expels Consort Fu.
> Jade Maiden has no place to gaze her limpid orbs;
> Consort Fu can no longer flaunt her pretty eyebrows.
> Now He grasps the essential firmness of the Way and Virtue,
> And equal to the gods, consults with them.[123]

In this instance, there is a contrast between the Queen Mother and the other goddesses who are characterized by their alluring beauty. This may be compared with Chang Heng's (78-139 C.E.) *Ssu-hsüan fu* (On Contemplating the Profound Mystery), where the charm and sensual appeal of "Jade Maiden" and "Consort Fu" are described in greater detail.[124] This does not mean that they are, as it were, "bad" goddesses; the implication is simply that they are different from, and inferior to, the

Queen Mother. Yet, in Chang Heng's poem perhaps the poetic transformation of the goddess has touched the Queen Mother as well:

> I visited the Queen Mother at her Silver Terrace;
> And satisfied my hunger with jade-white (magical) mushrooms.
> Wearing her *sheng* headdress, she entertained me
> with a smiling face;
> Gently she chided me for dallying.[125]

The Queen Mother may not yet be a goddess with "pretty eyebrows," "slender waist," and "laughing eyes"; but her silvery white hair is no longer an identifying feature. Given her tremendous power, it should not be surprising that she could maintain a youthful appearance. This seems to be what T'ao Ch'ien (365-427 C.E.) has in view when he writes,

> The Jade Terrace rises above the handsome mist;
> The Queen Mother relaxes her wondrous features.
> Born together with heaven and earth,
> No one knows how old she is.
> Her spiritual transformations never cease.[126]

These lines are taken from one of T'ao's thirteen poems on "Reading the *Shan-hai ching*." Obviously, he did not regard the picture of a mountain deity with teeth of a tiger and tail of a leopard to be of interest or importance. Since T'ao indicated that besides the *Shan-hai ching* he was reading the *Mu T'ien-tzu chuan* also, we may surmise that the image of a divine sovereign was more to his liking.

Queen of the Immortals

In the most celebrated episode of her multi-faceted story, the Queen Mother appears in her full splendour to a second emperor: namely, Emperor Wu of Han (141-87 B.C.E.). Han Wu-ti's well-known interest in the quest for immortality certainly makes him an ideal candidate for the goddess' favour. As Chang Hua (232-300 C.E.) explains, "Han Wu-ti was fond of the Way of the immortals. He made sacrifices to famous mountains and great marshes so as to seek the Way of the divine immortals. Then, the Queen Mother of the West sent her messenger...to tell the emperor that she was coming [to visit him]."[127] Though Chang's work as a whole may have suffered later changes, I see no reason to doubt that this particular story was known from the third century C.E.[128]

To view her appearance first, the Queen Mother is described generally as a majestic divine personage. According to Chang Hua, she arrived in a "carriage of purple clouds," and "three green birds, as large as crows, waited in attendance at her side."[129] Her divinity is also indicated by the clouds of *ch'i* vapour that emanated from her. A later work, the *Han Wu ku-shih* (Old Stories of Emperor of Wu of Han), provides a slightly more detailed description of the goddess. In addition to the royal carriage and mythical birds, the Queen Mother is seen wearing her *sheng* headdress and magnificent shoes. "Jade maidens" accompanied her on this occasion.[130]

When we turn to the *Han Wu-ti nei-chuan* (Inside Account of the Life of Emperor Wu), which contains the fullest account of this famous meeting, a more specific picture emerges. Having completed the proper preparation, the emperor awaited the arrival of the goddess. Her divine entourage was large, and vividly described, but most importantly as the Queen Mother descended from her "carriage of purple clouds," this is what the emperor saw:

> The Queen Mother entered the palace hall, supported by only two servant girls [i.e., the others stayed away]. They could be about sixteen or seventeen, both wearing a dress of fine green silk...they were indeed true beauties. The Queen Mother entered the palace hall and sat facing east. She wore a dress of rich yellow silk....She looked to be about thirty, of just the right (medium) height; her heavenly form was radiant and full, and her beautiful face was without equal in the world. She was indeed a truly transcendent being.[131]

This passage requires little comment. By the T'ang dynasty (618-906 C.E.), this was the common picture of the goddess. Later Taoist accounts of the Queen Mother need only to fit this story into their own narrative. Three noticeable departures, however, should be mentioned. First, the Queen Mother grew a little younger. In Taoist hagiographic accounts, she is said to be about twenty years old.[132] Secondly, since the earlier account in the *Shan-hai ching* cannot be ignored, Taoist sources explain that the fiercely powerful deity with teeth of a tiger is not the Queen Mother herself, but rather the god of the "white tiger" of the west, a servant of the supreme goddess.[133] Finally, just as Nü Wa was coupled with Fu Hsi, a male deity also came to accompany the Queen Mother. This deity, known as the "King Father of the East" (Tung-wang-kung), served as the *yang* complement to the goddess' ideal *yin* essence.[134] However, the arrival of the King Father did not undermine the importance of the Queen Mother. We shall come back to this point shortly.

In this way, the transformation of the goddess is accomplished. Needless to say, her abode on Mount K'un-lun is also treated in a parallel fashion, transformed into a grand celestial palace. The important point, however, is that the Queen Mother retained her religious significance despite attempts to redefine her role in elite culture. While Taoist writers could not transcend the prevalent aesthetic ideals and literary conventions, they certainly did not allow the saving power of the goddess to be eclipsed by the images of feminine beauty. The *Chuang-tzu*, *Huai-nan tzu*, and the popular movement of 3 B.C.E., to name but a few, have already pointed to a goddess of great soteriological significance. In the third century C.E., Chang Hua reported that according to no less an authority than Lao-tzu, "all the people offered sacrifice to the Queen Mother," and that she had command of all ranks of deities in the Taoist pantheon.[135] Although at first the Queen Mother was not specifically a Taoist deity, once she was assimilated into Taoism she became the queen of all immortals. Her dazzling beauty and even her marriage with the King Father did not distract her followers, but in fact enhanced her position in the world of faith.

In the story of the Queen Mother's visit to Emperor Wu, two main themes can be discerned that help us understand better her role in the religious world. First, as a number of scholars have recognized, the date of the meeting is revealing. Placed either on the seventh day of the first month, or the seventh day of the seventh month, this meeting falls within the larger mythological category of a seasonal meeting of the *yin* and *yang* forces. Just as the Queen Mother and the King Father symbolize the harmony of *yin* and *yang* on a cosmic level, the meeting between the goddess and the emperor ensures that the same harmony is maintained in the realm of human experience.[136]

What is even more important is the relationship between the goddess and the emperor which finds concrete expression in the Han Wu-ti story. The Queen Mother is above all the *teacher* of the emperor.[137] It is the Queen Mother who can teach the emperor, and by extension other dedicated and exemplary individuals, the secret to immortality.

This theme is carefully spelled out in the *Han Wu-ti nei chuan*, and reworked in later hagiographic accounts of the Queen Mother. Step by step, the goddess leads the emperor into the teachings of Taoism. She begins by admonishing the emperor for having indulged in worldly pursuits, and emphasizes the importance of curbing one's desires in the quest for immortality. Next, she explains to him the various types of magical drugs, which are placed in a hierarchical order corresponding to the different ranks of Taoist deities and immortal beings. Techniques of self-cultivation, or "internal alchemy," form the next topic of the goddess' discourse. Finally, the teaching is sealed by the transmission of sacred writings to the emperor.[138] Throughout this exchange, the emperor remained humble and attentive; several times he knelt and begged the goddess for knowledge. At one point, the text describes how the Queen Mother gently patted the emperor's back, encouraging and comforting her prized student. This is not at all the same as the kind of romantic encounter that we have seen, for example, between the king of Ch'u and the goddess of Shamaness Mountain.

The point is not that the emperor would become an immortal. He failed, in fact, as the text makes clear. The object of the encounter is best summed up by the Queen Mother herself:

> The reason of my bestowing the writings of the True Form to him now is not that he would necessarily attain the Way. It is because I wanted to show how his sincerity will bear fruits, and how the quest for transcendence is not mistaken, so as to guide those how seek transformation. Moreover, I wanted to let all and sundry know that such spiritual realities do exist in the world, which should repel those misguided individuals who do not believe.[139]

The Queen Mother is here addressing another goddess, whom she has invited to join her at Emperor Wu's palace. The latter, the Lady of the High Origins (Shang-yüan fu-jen), occupies an exalted place in the pantheon second only to the Queen Mother herself. This goddess also possesses sacred texts and talismans, which contain the key to immortality. But, at first, she is reluctant to give them to the emperor, not only because he is unworthy, but because of the rules of propriety regulating the transmission of sacred writings. More precisely, Shang-yüan fu-jen points out that the proper way is for a man to receive them from a male deity, and a woman from a goddess. The Queen Mother has to intercede forcefully on Emperor Wu's behalf, before the Lady of the High Origins agrees to teach him.[140] Although in later traditions the Queen Mother is specifically said to be the mistress of all female Taoist adepts, it is important to recognize that she certainly could and would teach men as well. Sincerity of faith and commitment to self-cultivation promise to move the most exalted of all goddesses. In this way, the narrative conveys unequivocally the centrality of Taoist teaching, now available in the form of revealed scriptures, in the quest for immortality. The Queen Mother is shown to be the divine teacher through whom the goal of everlasting life is made accessible to Taoist emperors, spiritual leaders and adepts, and all believers.

In Taoist hagiographic works, this and other aspects of the Queen Mother are subsumed under the more general category of the essence of *yin*. In particular, this is how the noted Taoist writer Tu Kuang-t'ing (850-933 C.E.) has reworked the earlier material to arrive at a full view of the goddess.[141] According to Tu, "at the beginning," the Way first gave birth to the *yang* essence, which is manifested in the divine being of the King

Father of the East. Then, the Queen Mother followed. Together, they nurture and sustain the well-being of the cosmos and the myriad creatures. As the *yin* essence, the Queen Mother has special power over all "women who have become immortals and attained the Way." Tu Kuang-t'ing next describes her celestial home on Mount K'un-lun, including her attendant "white tiger" deity. The Queen Mother, we are told, received her training from the head of the Taoist pantheon, the Heavenly King of the Original Beginning (Yüan-shih t'ien-wang), who gave her authority over all spiritual beings. She is also entrusted with the responsibility to oversee the transmission of all sacred writings.

On the "historical" level, the Queen Mother has made her mark as well. When the Yellow Emperor was engaged in battle against the forces of disorder, the Queen Mother sent a goddess known as the Woman of Profound Mystery of the Nine Heavens (Ch'iu-t'ien hsüan-nü) to help him (again, by transmitting to him sacred texts and talismans) and thereby saved the world. In this regard, there is a reversal of roles which renders the Yellow Emperor subordinate to the goddess. As the Yellow Emperor became an "historical" figure, he was perceived by Taoist writers as a model student of the Way. In his later years, according to this account by Tu Kuang-t'ing, the Yellow Emperor received from the Queen Mother the teaching of "quietude and non-action," a famous phrase from the *Lao-tzu* which in this context is identified with the Way of the divine immortals.

The meeting with King Mu of Chou comes next, followed by the story of Emperor Wu. The narrative concludes finally with the Queen Mother's visits to the main leaders of the Mao shan sect of Taoism, which was the dominant school of Taoism in medieval China and with which Tu Kuang-t'ing was associated. Specifically, Tu describes how the Queen Mother bestowed her favour on the founding figures of Mao shan Taoism: Mao Ying (fl. 100 B.C.E.) and his two younger brothers, as well as Wei Hua-ts'un (fl. 300 C.E.), the "Lady of the Southern Peak" and key matriarch of this tradition.[142] On both occasions, divine sanction is indicated by the transmission of sacred writings.

Tu Kuang-t'ing's account of the Queen Mother may be taken as the "orthodox" Taoist version. It is, however, not concerned with the worship of the goddess on the social level. Although a detailed discussion of this topic cannot be undertaken here, I should point out that the Queen Mother cult enjoyed widespread support in medieval China. Her high status in the pantheon, her relationship with such eminent figures as Han Wu-ti and Mao Ying, and her role as divine teacher and bestower of immortality all contributed to the popularity of her cult. But this list is far from exhaustive, for believers appealed to her for other reasons as well. For example, towards the end of the Sui dynasty (589-618 C.E.), an official by the name of Chang Hsiang found himself in a desperate situation while suppressing a rebellion. As the rebels laid siege to the city where he made his stand, and proceeded to attack with fire,

> (Chang) Hsiang saw that the people were terrified. On one side of the city there was a Hsi-wang-mu temple. Hsiang climbed to the top of the city (walls), looked towards the temple, and paid obeisance. Crying aloud, he said: "What crime did the people commit, that they should be burnt to death? If the spirit is with you, please send rain to save us."[143]

The rain did come, and Chang Hsiang was able to hold out until reinforcement arrived to defeat the rebels. As the essence of *yin*, the Queen Mother certainly has power over rainfall; but, in principle her power extends to all areas of religious concern. So long as the faith is strong and sincere, she may be counted on to come to the aid of her followers, regardless of the nature of the difficulty.

During the T'ang dynasty, according to Suzanne Cahill, the Queen Mother was worshipped by both men and women. She was especially important to women outside the main social currents. As Cahill puts it,

> Hsi Wang Mu acted as patron deity for all women in Taoism, but she was the special guardian of singing girls, dead women, novices, nuns, adepts, and priestesses. These people stand outside the roles prescribed for women in the traditional Chinese family--the dutiful daughter, obedient wife, and self-sacrificing mother.[144]

The promise of transcendence, the prospect of a free and happy existence as a Taoist immortal, provided a main motivation for worship. In this regard, as Cahill also points out, even the "jade maidens" or servants of the Queen Mother had an important role to play. They provided a more "realistic" model for women, because it would be difficult, if not impossible, to imitate the divine being of the Queen Mother herself.[145]

It should be clear by now that Taoist writers did not share the same view as the poets in their understanding of the goddess. While the appearance of the Queen Mother is described in conventional terms, her power extends beyond traditional limits and can help women to transcend social constraints. In Taoist hagiography, the status and authority of the Queen Mother are emphasized; her beauty and splendour are but "natural" expressions of her majesty. To be sure, all Taoist accounts specify that the King Father of the East came first in the initial cosmic transformation; but once the formal question of priority is settled, the authors could then recount the greatness of the Queen Mother without reservation. The King Father is hardly mentioned again.[146]

Towards a Typology of Taoist Goddesses

Sheng-mu and T'ien-fei

If the Queen Mother of the West did not conform to the image of an ideal woman in the eyes of traditional Chinese men, other goddesses in the Taoist pantheon came to fill that role and to rival the Queen Mother's popularity.[147] The most exalted goddess in this category is the Holy Mother Primordial Goddess (Sheng-mu yüan-chün), the mother of the Most High Lord Lao, i.e., Lao-tzu himself.[148] According to Tu Kuang-t'ing, before the goddess gave birth to Lao-tzu, she was known as the Jade Maiden of Profound Wonder (Hsüan-miao yü-nü). Like the Queen Mother of the West, this goddess too embodies the essence of *yin*. After she had given birth to Lao-tzu, she became the Holy Mother as well as the teacher of her son. Finally, when her task was completed, she returned to heaven and took her rightful place as a queen of the Taoist cosmos. From young girl to mother and divine queen, the life of the goddess reflects the ideal of a traditional Chinese woman. Her role as queen, as Livia Kohn has suggested, may be compared with the family matriarch and ancestress.[149] Her role as teacher, on the other hand, distinguishes her as a high Taoist deity.[150]

The goddess known as T'ien-fei (Celestial Consort), to take but one more example, also reflects the same dynamics of cultural values and religious identity. This goddess, still very popular today, was originally a local deity of the southeast China coast.[151] Tradition has it that she was born into the Lin family in the tenth century C.E. As a young girl, she already showed signs of being gifted with the power of a shamaness, by means of which she saved her brothers from being drowned at sea. She became the patron deity of all seafarers, and was given the official title of T'ien-fei in 1281.

As Judith Boltz has pointed out, a fifteenth-century text adds that the goddess showed both "an awesome goodness born of her innate spirituality and an extraordinary filial devotion."[152] Although she did not marry while on earth, as would be expected of any ordinary filial daughter, she became a divine consort, which would more than qualify her as a model for traditional women. Besides her main function as the protector of seafarers, she is also appealed to by women for the precious gift of children. One story has it that a certain woman, who remained barren for ten years after marriage and who tried every other religious avenue, gave birth to a son after she had prayed to T'ien-fei.[153] A later title, granted in 1683, identifies the goddess as the Celestial Queen or

Empress (T'ien-hou). Among the faithful, she is more intimately known as Ma-tsu, the short form of a name meaning grandmother.

The examples of Sheng-mu and T'ien-fei demonstrate that Taoist goddesses generally do not stand opposed to the traditional feminine virtues. A number of themes in their stories, as will be shown below, also characterize the lives of other goddesses. What should be emphasized at this point is that their religious significance is not diminished because of it. They remain at the same time transcendent beings. It would be less than just, in other words, to reduce all Taoist goddesses to a kind of glorified traditional Chinese woman. The real question is to see how transcendence and tradition both find expression in the goddess story. Though it is not possible to examine individual goddesses in any detail, I would like to draw attention to the rich body of "goddess literature," and to a number of recurring motifs in the lives to Taoist goddesses. Three hagiographic works, in particular, form the basis of this analysis: namely, Tu Kuang-t'ing's collected hagiographies of female immortals, the tenth-century encyclopedia *T'ai-p'ing kuang-chi,* and a later collection attributed to the Taoist master Chao Tao-i (fl. 1294-1307).[154]

Development of Hagiographic Literature

These collections are fairly late documents and reflect the mature tradition of Chinese religious biography. A more detailed study would have to take into account earlier hagiographic works, such as the *Lieh-hsien chuan* (Lives of the Various Immortals) attributed to Liu Hsiang (79-8 B.C.E.) and the *Shen-hsien chuan* (Lives of the Divine Immortals) by Ko Hung (284-364 C.E.).[155] In addition, there is a whole genre of traditional literature which bears on this topic, including the *chih-kuai* (records of the strange) stories that flourished in the Six Dynasties period (third to sixth centuries C.E.), and the later *ch'uan-ch'i* (transmissions of the marvellous) tradition.[156] These stories often preserve elements of popular belief, and some contain "biographies" of female immortals as well. Among the other relevant sources, special mention should also be made of the biographies of "exemplary women" (*lieh-nü*) found in independent works and in the dynastic or standard histories.[157] They may provide parallels and contrasts, which help to distinguish the goddesses of Taoism.

If the authenticity of the *Lieh-hsien chuan* may be accepted, then religious biographies of goddesses have been a part of Chinese literature since the Former Han dynasty. The current version of this text contains some seventy biographies, five of which are devoted to female immortals.[158] References to other divine women are also found in about twelve entries. Since Ko Hung refers to this work in his writings, it would appear that the *Lieh-hsien chuan* was in existence before the fourth century C.E. The difficulty, however, is that the current version may be corrupt and no longer reflects the original.

Ko Hung's *Shen-hsien chuan* is likewise beset with textual uncertainties. In the current ten-*chüan* (part or chapter) version of this work, *chüan* 7 contains the biographies of six goddesses. In *chüan* 10 there is an entry on one Pan Meng, who is said to be of unknown origins, and "some say that she is a woman."[159] There are, as in the *Lieh-hsien chuan*, references to various female immortals embedded in other entries also. In the case of Shen Hsi, for example, his wife attained immortality as well. When Shen Hsi first reached the celestial realm, he saw the divine Lao-tzu. There were several hundred attendants, as he recalled later, the majority of whom were women.[160]

The six main female figures included in Ko Hung's work differ from those found in the *Lieh-hsien chuan*. Ko does refer to one of the latter in the preface to his compilation, and in general criticizes Liu Hsiang for not having done a more thorough search. However, since the current versions of both works are suspect, the possibility that Ko Hung deliberately refrained from repeating Liu Hsiang's selections cannot be determined further. All of the main figures, in any case, found their way into later hagiographic collections.

By the time of T'ao Hung-ching (456-536 C.E.), a key figure in the Mao shan sect of Taoism, goddess literature was evidently quite common. In T'ao's *Chen-ling wei-yeh t'u* (Chart of the Ranks and Functions of the True Spirits), which stands as one of the earliest attempts to present an organized account of the Taoist pantheon, goddesses occupy a prominent position.[161] There is, first of all, a special section devoted to over fifty senior "female realized persons" (*nü-chen*), led by the Queen Mother of the West. Another section outlines fifteen categories of "jade maidens." On a lower level, there is yet another section devoted to about fifteen lesser *nü-chen*. When combined with the female figures found in the various ranks of the divine hierarchy, we have a sizable group of Taoist goddesses. Although T'ao's "chart" does not provide biographic details, it indicates the extent to which goddesses have become an accepted part of religious Taoism. A sixth-century hagiographic work, the *Tao-hsüeh chuan* (Lives of Taoist Masters) by Ma Shu (ca. 522-581 C.E.), thus includes an entire *chüan* devoted to female immortals.[162] By the second half of the ninth century C.E. when Tu Kuang-t'ing arrived on the scene, the time was indeed ripe for a special work on the goddesses of Taoism.

Two versions of Tu Kuang-t'ing's *Yung-ch'eng chi-hsien lu* (Records of the Immortals Assembled in the High-Walled City), in fact, are found in the *Tao-tsang* (Taoist Canon).[163] Except for the Queen Mother of the West and the Woman of Profound Mystery of the Nine Heavens (Chiu-t'ien hsüan-nü), the two versions contain hagiographic accounts of different goddesses.[164] According to Tu's preface, he sets out to record the story of "women who have attained the Way and risen into (the ranks of) transcendent beings from antiquity to the present."[165] It also makes clear that since the Queen Mother of the West heads all female transcendent beings, her biography is to be given first, followed by that of the Primordial Goddess--that is, the Holy Mother of the divine Lao-tzu.[166] The title "High-Walled City" (Yung-ch'eng) similarly reflects the priority of the Queen Mother, for it refers to her seat of power on Mount K'un-lun.[167]

It is difficult to ascertain the relationship between the two current versions of Tu's work. Here, I shall assume that they together make up the bulk of the original, primarily because the *T'ai-p'ing kuang-chi* quotes from both versions.[168] The majority of Tu Kuang-t'ing's selections are included in the *Li-shih chen-hsien t'i-tao t'ung-chien hou chi* (Comprehensive Mirror on the Successive Generations of True Immortals Who Embody the Way, Later Anthology) attributed to Chao Tao-i.[169] This work is the most extensive hagiographic collection devoted to female immortals in the Taoist Canon, containing 120 entries.

Cosmic Goddesses

Goddesses are generally referred to as *nü-chen* or *nü-hsien* in Taoist works. These terms have been variously translated as female "immortals," "transcendents," "realized" or "perfected" beings, or a combination of them. In this essay, these words are simply used interchangeably. A Taoist goddess is always characterized by her spiritual perfection and transcendence, which in turn is characterized by her immortality. For heuristic purposes, two main types of Taoist goddesses, and a number of variations and recurrent themes may be distinguished.

There are, first of all, what may be called cosmic goddesses, such as Hsi-wang-mu, Shang-yüan fu-jen and the Holy Mother, who occupy a high position in the divine hierarchy. What distinguishes them from other female deities is their original divine nature, their superior and inborn *yin* essence. They did not, in other words, become transcendent beings, but are divine "from the beginning." In addition to the high goddesses, we may include in this category the many daughters of the Queen Mother.

Many of these are connected with the revelation of the *Shang-ch'ing* (Supreme Clarity) scriptures to the visionary Yang Hsi (fl. 350 C.E.), which laid the foundation of Mao shan Taoism.[170] Cosmic goddesses in general hold the key to the transmission of sacred writings and talismans.

Because of their divine origins, however, they are often known only by their lineage and titles. The only "personal" details that emerge from their biographies are usually limited to their age and general appearance. As a rule, they are young and very beautiful. A good example would be the fourth daughter of the Queen Mother, the Primordial Goddess of the Southern Ultimate (Nan-chi yüan-chün), who appeared once during the Han dynasty to teach a noted immortal, and later to Yang Hsi.[171] She looked about sixteen or seventeen, and her "heavenly form is radiant and full"--the exact same phrase used in the description of the Queen Mother herself (see earlier discussion). Another cosmic goddess who merits special attention is the twenty-third daughter of the Queen Mother, the Lady of the Flowers of the Clouds (Yün-hua fu-jen).[172] On Shamaness Mountain, she helped the sage Yü to overcome the great flood of Chinese mythology. Her biography is instructive in a number of ways. It brings out clearly the central role of divine teacher played by Taoist goddesses. It includes a long discourse on basic Taoist teachings. Last but not least, Yün-hua fu-jen is identified with the divine Woman of Shamaness Mountain, and Tu Kuang-t'ing strongly criticizes the poet Sung Yü for having profaned the great goddess.[173] This testifies concretely to the difference between Taoist writers and secular poets to which references have already been made. Tu is equally critical of Ts'ao Chih's poem on Fu-fei, the goddess of the Lo river. He describes it as "the diabolic, superficially polished words of literary men."[174]

As distinguished from the cosmic goddesses, most Taoist immortals have a human origin and occupy a lesser place in the pantheon. There are, however, exceptions to both counts. First, a separate category should be reserved for those goddesses who have been banished from heaven to a life on earth for some minor offenses. The biography of Tu Lan-hsiang, for example, describes how she was found as a three-year-old girl by an old fisherman on the shore of Lake Tung-t'ing. She grew up into an extraordinary beauty--a sign of her divine origin--and was eventually recalled to her celestial station.[175] Invariably these goddesses return to heaven, and usually the person or family with whom they were associated while on earth benefit from their presence. The old fisherman who found and raised Tu Lan-hsiang was both physically and spiritually rejuvenated. In the end, he too became a student of the Way.[176]

With respect to rank, there are a few women who, despite their human beginnings, managed to achieve a high divine status. The most distinguished member of this group is undoubtedly the matriarch of Mao shan Taoism, Wei Hua-ts'un, the Lady of the Southern Peak.[177] After years of training and practice, she achieved the rank of "primordial goddess" (yüan-chün), which is the highest for a female immortal, and was welcomed into the celestial realm personally by the Queen Mother and other high deities.

In one respect the case of Lady Wei is rather unique, because she has made it to the top on her own merits. The other goddesses in this category are usually related, by birth or marriage, to some important male figures. Lady Li of the Fang-chang Terrace, for example, is identified as a high goddess; but we do not even known her personal name.[178] She is known only as the daughter of Li Ch'ing-pin and the sister of Li Ling-fei, both high-ranking deities in the divine hierarchy. In the early Shang period, she "attained the Way and rose into the heavens in broad daylight." Next, we are told of her presence at the revelation to Yang Hsi, where she appeared as a beautiful girl of thirteen or fourteen. The remainder of the narrative is devoted to a number of her poems.

Lesser Immortals

When we turn to the less exalted goddesses with a human origin, individual details are more forthcoming. Again, one group is simply connected with famous male immortals. Thus, the wife and daughters of Chang Tao-ling, the "founder" of religious Taoism, have all become immortals.[179] The wife and daughter of Chang Heng, the son of Chang Tao-ling, have likewise come to enjoy the delights of a celestial existence.[180] More generally, the moral and religious merits of one's ancestors may be sufficient for spiritual realization. The short biography of Tou Ch'iung-ying, for example, informs us that she had reaped the benefit of the good deeds performed by her ancestor seven generations ago.[181] Similarly, Liu Ch'un-lung succeeded in becoming an immortal because her ancestors had "*yin* virtues," or "hidden" virtues pertaining especially to the caring and saving of lives.[182] In the case of Pao-ku, the daughter of the Taoist master Pao Ching, the wife of the more famous Ko Hung, and whose ancestors had accumulated stores of merit, it would be surprising indeed if she could not join them in the world of perfected immortals.[183]

Taoist religious biographies should certainly be viewed with reference to traditional social values. In the "Comprehensive Mirror" collection, we even find two cases where an independent goddess has been turned into the sister of a male immortal.[184] But, this does not mean that Taoist goddesses cannot achieve greatness independent of their relations. The case of Wei Hua-ts'un again proves to the contrary. An equally telling example is the goddess Li Chen-to, the sister of the rather mysterious figure Li Pa-pai, whose name reflects the legend that he was "eight hundred" (*pa-pai*) years old.[185] Although she is said to have followed her brother's lead in search of the Way, her biography specifies that she attained perfect transcendence ahead of him.

This may be compared with two other accounts that focus on a goddess and her husband. In both cases, the woman is explicitly described as being spiritually superior to her spouse. The wife of Ch'eng Wei, despite the fact that she is remembered only by her husband's name, became an immortal while her husband failed.[186] The second account is devoted to Lady Fan, whose husband Liu Kang is a major immortal and teacher of other goddesses.[187] Yet, as they engaged in friendly games to determine who had the stronger magical power, Lady Fan proved to be the winner every time. The last "test" came when they were about to leave the world and rise into the heavens. Liu Kang needed a tree for a springboard--that is, his *ch'i* essence was not quite pure and light enough for unassisted levitation. Lady Fan, on the other hand, simply sat down and effortlessly rose into the sky like a floating cloud.

The lives of Taoist goddesses thus do not always conform with the dominant social values. Lesser goddesses in the Taoist pantheon are mostly independent women who because of their own effort and dedication have come to realize spiritual transcendence. They come from all walks of life: princesses and court ladies, daughters of high officials, poor widows, nuns, wine sellers, peasant girls, prostitutes, and others. One interesting minority group consists of old women, who could be several hundred years old, but are always distinguished by their youthful appearance. A typical case may be Ch'ang Jung, who is identified as the daughter of a Shang king. She pursued Taoist cultivation in a mountain, and lived on a certain type of roots. She was over two hundred years old but looked about twenty, and was known for her compassion and power to heal. Eventually, she soared into the sky and disappeared.[188] The connection with a mountain, a plant diet, and the power to heal are common themes, and reflect the continuing influence of shamanism.

Two variations should also be mentioned. Due to their special diet, some have developed distinctive physical features: long bodily hairs (usually green, suggesting closeness to nature) and a complexion as fine and bright as a flower.[189] Secondly, since prior to her final liberation the adept often dwells alone in a mountain, there is real concern for her safety. In one case, an adept was even raped, even though she seems to have been quite advanced in her quest, as indicated by her green hair and her face which resembled a white flower.[190] After the assault, she regressed to the form of an old and sick woman, and died shortly after. Usually, however, the woman would either be protected by guardian spirits or she possessed magical power to defend herself against demons, wild animals, and wicked men. In at least two cases, Buddhist monks are portrayed as the evildoers who received severe but deserved punishment from the goddess. The polemical dimension of Taoist hagiography should not be overlooked in a more detailed discussion.[191]

Another issue which cannot be addressed here concerns the relationship between "nature" (*hsing*) and "training" (*hsüeh*) in the quest for transcendence. Although religious discipline and self-cultivation are clearly important, in some cases the narrative emphasizes the inborn nature and preordained destiny of an individual. I mention one example. Wang Feng-hsien was a poor peasant girl, who at fourteen met and played with a group of young divine companions. She was transformed; she refused to eat or drink, and her skin became so transparently clear that it seemed hardly human. By means of a bamboo pole she was able to travel to the celestial realm. There she was told that she had "the bones of an immortal," although her destiny required her to live on earth for fifty years. The prophecy was later fulfilled.[192] The strict dietary control described here does involve discipline and effort, but it is not the decisive factor in this particular instance. This case is also instructive because of its anti-Buddhist polemic. In heaven, as Wang Feng-hsien reports, there are no images of buddhas and *bodhisattvas*.[193]

For our purposes, we may consider the case of Wang Feng-hsien as a variant of the main group of lesser immortals. A representative of the latter is typically drawn towards the Way from a very young age. The reason is not always given, but not infrequently a life-transforming event is involved. Most commonly it is a meeting with a divine teacher. A more dramatic experience is reported in the story of Chang Lien-ch'iao, who at the age of eight or nine was lured into a well by a lotus flower. She miraculously returned and developed a "laughing sickness"; Chang explained that "someone" was tickling her from behind.[194] She recovered and joined a Taoist monastery soon afterwards.

Regardless of the circumstances, once awakened to the Way the future immortal shows signs of being different from ordinary human beings. It may be her unusual beauty, her reverent devotion to Taoist worship, her love of quietude, or her ability to recite long Taoist scriptures that sets her apart. Sickness too may be a distinguishing feature, because it signals the passing away of the "old" self and the beginning of a spiritual transformation. Invariably, the adept ceases to partake of ordinary food. At a minimum she stops eating meat and any kind of strong-smelling vegetable. The more advanced avoid cereals, and the most gifted do not eat at all. The avoidance of grain helps to purify one's *ch'i* essence, which is itself life-sustaining and a prerequisite for transcendence.[195] Then, it is only a matter of time before the person reaches liberation.

One group of narratives emphasizes the ethical dimension of Taoist cultivation. It is the moral goodness of the adept which enables her to join the ranks of divine immortals. More commonly, however, the ethical component is simply assumed and a long process of training defines the life of a future goddess. From the study of scriptures, dietary practices and meditation, to the use of special immortality-inducing drugs, the adept journeys through her earthly tenure as an apprentice of *Tao*. Finally, when her training is completed, she assumes her new station in the divine hierarchy. The basic procedure involves what is known as the "deliverance from the corpse" (*shih-chieh*), which takes the form of a magical death--the adept is buried but later the coffin is found empty with only a token, usually her shoes or clothing, left behind.[196] The more advanced rise into the sky in broad daylight, open to view by all, and the most successful are honoured on that occasion by the presence of immortals and celestial animals, who ride on multi-coloured clouds and perform music to welcome their latest companion. This type of narrative not only shows how an individual becomes an immortal, but, more importantly, also marks her as belonging to a community, to a long tradition of Taoist seekers. In this way, the experience of a fortunate few may serve to enrich the lives of all Taoist believers.

Marriage and Celibacy

During the training phase of her career, the adept might perform acts of wonder, which include healing, the foretelling of future events, and communication with divine beings. One theme, in particular, deserves special mention. It relates how a future goddess becomes "pregnant" through divine intervention. This causes suspicion and invites danger, as the integrity of the adept comes to be questioned. The brother of Li Chen-to, for example, although himself a Taoist master, did not understand the significance of the event and was about to kill her. Li Chen-to rose high into the sky and gave birth to a Taoist scripture.[197] On the level of worship, this explains why the goddess was appealed to by women for safe childbirth. From the perspective of hagiographic narrative, this brings out further the extraordinary nature of the main character, and reaffirms the centrality of Taoist scriptures. But, what interests me most is the apparent tension between traditional "womanly" duties and the demands of spiritual commitment that emerges from this type of story.

To conclude our preliminary survey, I would suggest that this tension between tradition and transcendence offers a strong hermeneutical vantage point to understand the complex world of Taoist goddesses. On the one hand, the quest for spiritual purity calls for a chaste and virtuous life. On the other hand, being "virtuous" in the traditional setting means the fulfillment of one's duty as a daughter and obedient wife. How far does "chastity" extend in this context? To some Taoists, it is true, sexual practice is actually a valued form of self-cultivation. It remains, however, an esoteric teaching not easily accessible to the majority of Taoist followers. The question, rather, is whether total dedication to the Way necessarily involves a celibate life. In other words, the ideal of personal salvation and the obligations of traditional life, especially marriage and procreation, often come into conflict, which demands a response on the part of Taoist writers.

The example of Li Chen-to cited above provides one solution to this problem. She was pure, but she also became a "mother" by giving birth to a sacred scripture. In more general terms, intercourse with divine beings, the possibility of a divinely-induced pregnancy, and giving birth to a scripture or any sacred object, may be viewed as elements of a Taoist response to charges of violations of traditional mores.

Satisfying as this may be, miraculous occurrences of this nature, nevertheless, are rare. An equally solid response must be found within the common parameters of traditional life. Taoist religious biographies, in this regard, are sensitive to the complexity of life-situations. There is no attempt to reduce the variety of human experience into one ideal set of circumstances. Indeed, Taoism proves to be flexible and accommodating on this score, as it allows for both main options. Celibacy and marriage are both legitimate avenues to spiritual perfection. Buddhist influence may be discerned in the emphasis on celibacy; but, for our purposes, it is enough to note that this openness and flexibility contribute to the wide appeal of religious Taoism in Chinese society. The more important question is how the two paths are reconciled in Taoist hagiographies.

Celibacy is obviously not a requirement for transcendence, as numerous married women, mothers and grandmothers have become divine immortals. According to one account, a mother rose into the heavens in broad daylight, carrying her five children.[198] Marriage is also not a necessary condition, as indicated by the many women who prefer a life of solitude in the mountains. While neither necessary nor sufficient, celibacy does play a significant role in the lives of some individuals. It adds to the sense of determination and "extraordinariness" which characterizes the adept. The niece of Wang Hui, for example, was attracted to the Way while young, did not consume ordinary food, and in general conforms nicely to the model of a "basic" Taoist immortal. Her biography adds that when she grew up, she "vowed never to marry."[199]

In this and other similar cases, parental consent is given. The parents may be Taoist followers themselves, or at least they recognize the significance of their daughter's aspiration. Some may even try to help, for example, by building a separate room to facilitate her devotion and quiet self-cultivation. But, in the world of traditional China, parents are not always so understanding and supportive. Some fear that demons may be at work, or the parents may be opposed to Taoism. The father of Hsieh Tzu-jan, for example, was incensed by her Taoist practice, which went contrary to the long-standing commitment of the family to the Confucian tradition. He locked her in a room for over forty days, and it was not until he saw that she actually blossomed without food that he became convinced of her extraordinary being.[200] Hsieh Tzu-jan went on to become a major Taoist figure, and was recognized as having been taught personally by the Queen Mother of the West herself.

To pursue her goal, the future immortal may have to argue, persuade, or even rebel against her family. The parents of Ts'ai Hsün-chen and Li T'eng-k'ung were against their wishes to leave the family and seek Taoist training; but, as the text puts it, "the parents could not rob them of their will."[201] They succeeded in becoming immortals, and served as a source of inspiration for later adepts.[202]

A different situation confronted Pien Tung-hsüan, whose ethical and spiritual development already reached a high level by the age of fifteen. She, too, vowed not to marry and wished to join a Taoist establishment. Her parents, however, could not bear to see her go. Pien Tung-hsüan served them until they passed away before she took leave of the world.[203] Like Hsieh Tzu-jan, Pien was a major figure who received special favour from the Queen Mother. A much stronger reaction is reported in the biography of Liu Yen, an entertainer who met an old woman and was awakened to the Way. She begged her mother to let her leave, but was refused. She then cut her hair, put on a simple garment, and left for the mountains.[204]

What if the young woman were unable to oppose the demands of her parents? How would parents persuade their daughter not to abandon the claims of tradition? The story of Wei Hua-ts'un is again of paradigmatic significance. At the age of twenty-four she was forced to marry, despite her readiness to sever all worldly connections. She raised two sons, and then retired to a quite room to resume Taoist practice. After three months or so, she received her first revelation. Still, we are told, Lady Wei continued to look after her family and did not ascend to the Taoist heavens until she was past eighty years old.[205] Her example thus illustrates concretely how a "virtuous" woman may come to fulfill her religious aspirations without sacrificing her worldly duties. The biography of P'ei Hsüan-ching relates how she took to Taoist practice at a young age. Since her parents were Taoist followers also, they did not interfere with her devotion. Nonetheless, they did make a marriage arrangement for her. When P'ei told them of her desire to live a celibate life, they replied, "Even Lady Wei of the Southern Peak once followed her husband before she became a high goddess."[206] This silenced her objections.

This type of argument must have been very popular. In one biography, for example, we find the following verses attributed to a goddess: "Nung-yü had a husband and they both attained the Way; Liu Kang and his wife ascended together to be immortals."[207] We have already come across the story of Liu Kang and his wife, Lady Fan. Nung-yü and her husband both excelled in music and disappeared together into the sky on the back of a mythical bird.[208] The implication here is that not all adepts are destined to live a celibate life. Other divine couples may be found to support this view as well. Another poem, also attributed to a goddess, expresses a similar sentiment: "Even Ko Hung had a wife/ Even the Queen Mother had a husband."[209] In this way, marriage is thus shown to be at least not an obstacle, if not a positive step itself, in the quest for transcendence.

One final question must be addressed. What difficulties confront a married woman who wishes to become an adept? How would her husband and/or in-laws react to her religious pursuits? In the case of Lady Wei, her husband never found out that she was a great goddess. One may assume that he was not unsympathetic, for he did not object to her secluded devotion. The husband of Yang Ching-chen was more supportive. He agreed, at her request, to move to a separate room with their four children.[210]

A less favourable reaction is depicted in the biography of Hsüeh Hsüan-t'ung. After twenty years of marriage, she decided to devote herself to spiritual cultivation. Initially claiming illness as an excuse, Hsüeh retired to a separate room, where she prayed and read scriptures. There she stayed for thirteen years, and her sincerity and effort eventually moved no less a goddess than Lady Wei herself to grant her a pill of immortality. Her husband remained unaware; he mocked and laughed at her, and generally thought her very foolish. The narrative comments that Hsüeh thus often "netted the suspicion of 'Tung-ling'."[211] In the biography of Tung-ling Sheng-mu (The Holy Mother of Tung-ling), we read that she was a student of Liu Kang. Her husband was so against her Taoist work that he falsely accused her of demonic practice, and had her imprisoned. She flew out of a window and disappeared.[212]

Just as their husbands and family may react differently, the adepts themselves also respond to their situations in diverse ways. Lady Wei waited until her sons were well advanced in their official careers before she took her place in the celestial hierarchy. The case of P'ei Hsüan-ching is equally instructive. As we have seen, citing the precedent of Lady Wei, her parents made her marry one Li Yen. Soon after the marriage, she told Li of her calling and that she could not fulfill her conjugal duties. Since Li was himself a believer, he gave his consent and in fact saw two goddesses visiting his wife. To "compensate" for his loss, the narrative continues, one night "a celestial maiden descended into Li Yen's room. A year or so later she returned and presented him with a boy, saying that he was Li's son... Three days later...a white *feng* [mythical bird] carried Hsüan-ching soaring into the northwestern sky."[213] In this way also, the conflicting demands of tradition and Taoist transcendence are satisfactorily reconciled.

Some adepts, indeed, are especially remembered for their love of family. Ch'i Hsüan-fu died of an illness when she was three, but was revived by a Taoist deity. Her destiny was thus manifest from the start. She married, and was badly mistreated by her cruel in-laws. Still, she insisted that it was her duty to serve them with love and respect.[214] Yang Ching-chen, to take but one more example, while in heaven, actually asked to be returned to earth so that she could serve her husband's family.[215] A balanced analysis, however, must take into account a rather different scenario as well. Yang Cheng-chien, for example, was asked to prepare a feast for her husband's family; but she could not bring herself to kill a fish. She ran away from home, met a Taoist teacher, and never returned.[216]

A reading of the story of Ch'i Hsiao-yao should suffice to bring this discussion to a close.[217] From the start, she seemed to have been a "problem" child. When her father taught her the "rules for women," Ch'i said that they were merely for "ordinary" people, and chose to study the *Lao-tzu* instead. Because of her unconventional behaviour, her parents had difficulty arranging a match for her. When, finally, she was married into a peasant family, she could not get along with her husband and in-laws. They all accused her of neglecting the duties of a wife, as Ch'i would devote all her time to prayer and meditation. When confronted, she boldly asked to be sent back to her own parents, who in turn forced Ch'i to return to her husband. Even neighbours were convinced that she was possessed by evil spirits, or was perhaps a demon herself. In short, there was no room for compromise; Ch'i had to choose between the life of a Taoist adept and that dictated by the norms of traditional society. Her choice was clear. She was vindicated in the end by a spectacular ascension.

Concluding Remarks

The range of experience reflected in Taoist hagiographies is truly impressive. What underlies the careful preservation of details can only be a sincere devotion to the goddesses themselves. If constructing a typology of Taoist goddesses is to be entertained, individual circumstances and nuances must be taken into account, so as to avoid the danger of a procrustean treatment. There is overlap between cosmic goddesses and lesser immortals. Within these broad categories, there is a web of similarities and differences which renders a typological study extremely complex. This, however, also makes a study of Taoist goddesses richly rewarding.

Goddess worship in Chinese religion has a long history. Although the origins of the ancient goddesses, such as Nü Wa, can hardly be reconstructed, and despite the fact that our knowledge of early Chinese religion, especially shamanism, remains fragmentary, their influence can be discerned in Taoist religious biographies. The power to heal, and to ensure fertility, for example, characterizes both goddesses and shamans. The obvious but nonetheless important point is that religious Taoism did not develop out of an historical vacuum. The decline of Nü Wa and the sun goddess, and the changing conceptions of the Queen Mother of the

West, to name but two, are concrete indications of the historical rootedness of the goddess story.

The poetic tradition, besides its intrinsic value as literature, is important for this reason also. It shows how Taoism interacted with the dominant culture, was influenced by it, and yet maintained its own distinctive and independent stance. Despite the tendency to downplay the importance of goddess worship in elite circles, the voice of the *yin* essence is not to be denied. On a doctrinal level, Taoist "theologians" realize the significance of the *yin* principle, as the basis of growth, as the quiet which precedes movement, as the soothing darkness which gives way to light and which returns to protect all living beings from the blinding intensity of *yang* forces.

On this level, to be sure, there is room for different interpretations within Taoism itself. While some celebrate the life-giving power of *yin*, others may view it with fear. On the level of worship, however, there is little disagreement. The consensus is that goddesses can offer deliverance, dispense reward and punishment, and ultimately bring salvation to both women and men. Goddesses do serve as a model for many women; but it would be a mistake to reduce their power and function to that of a role model alone. A more comprehensive study would no doubt require further investigation of the performance of rituals, sectarian and regional differences, and other factors that accompany goddess worship. In this essay, I am content simply to map the general contours, and to suggest avenues for future research.

The story of Taoist goddesses, I believe, is best viewed in relation to traditional social and moral values. As Taoism grew into a pillar of Chinese culture, its self-understanding could no longer be restricted to certain classical texts such as the *Lao-tzu*. Its pantheon could no longer be inhabited only by hybrid deities of raw and awesome power. Its universe was informed by the same hierarchical structure which underlies traditional politics and society. As Taoism increasingly came into contact with the lives of the people, it could not avoid being shaped, motivated and directed by the same set of values which governed society at large.

What is decisive is that Taoism, at the same time, sought to go beyond the kind of limitations that it diagnosed as diseases of culture. It offered the riches of transcendence, which is not "anti-culture," but a perfect reality devoid of suffering and the constraints of finitude. The hierarchical structure of the world remains operative in the celestial realm. But it ceases to be oppressive; it depicts an ideal order, characterized by harmony and freedom. When articulated, this vision in turn helps to shape the lives of the people. In the final analysis, it is in this meeting of traditional cultural values and transcendence that Taoist goddesses find their true home.

Notes

Abbreviations

ch.	*chüan*
HWTNC	*Han Wu-ti nei-chuan*
HY	Harvard-Yenching Index to Taoist Literature
SPPY	*Ssu-pu pei-yao*
TT	*Tao-tsang*
TCHC	*Li-shih chen-hsien t'i-tao t'ung-chien hou-chi*
TPKC	*T'ai-p'ing kuang-chi*
YCCC	*Yün-chi ch'i-ch'ien*
YCCHL	*Yung-ch'eng chi-hsien lu*

1. I wish to acknowledge gratefully the financial support of the Social Sciences and Humanities Research Council of Canada towards the research embodied in this essay.

2. See, for example, Diana Paul's essay on Kuan-yin (1983, 161-175); see also Kinsley 1988, chap. 2, and Maspero 1981, 166-171. A fine, concise discussion of Kuan-yin is presented in Jan Yün-hua 1981, 138-144.

3. This is a complex issue, and the reverse, i.e., "euhemerization," is also a factor in the development of Chinese mythology. See the early studies by Maspero 1924, Karlgren 1946, and Bodde 1961; a more recent and sophisticated example is William Boltz 1981. A number of scholars have challenged the methodological validity of this approach to Chinese myths. See, e.g., the critical discussion in Teiser 1985-86. Interestingly, both Boltz and Teiser see the theme of order as an underlying focus of Chinese mythology. They also agree that the distinction between myth and history (Boltz) or between "supernatural and humanistic mentalities" (Teiser) confuses the issue in this context, despite their different estimation of the usefulness of the concept of "euhemerization." Cf. Boltz 1981, 151-152 with Teiser 1985-86, 16-17, 41-43. It is most encouraging that more scholars are now turning their attention to this important and underdeveloped field of Chinese studies. For a general discussion of the methodological issues; see esp. Girardot 1976, and Girardot and Major 1985-86. In general, I have no objection to using the concept of "reverse euhemerization," so long as the mythological core is recognized, and provided that one does not reduce Chinese mythology to any one particular formula. What is at issue is the meaning and significance of history,

which called forth more than one interpretation in traditional China. Even after the triumph of Confucianism, the conflict of interpretations remained a constant reality. In Chinese, the following studies are still among the best: Ch'en Meng-chia 1936a, and Chang Kwang-chih 1959; 1962. An English summary of Chang's second article is reprinted in Chang 1978, chap. 8. There is also a large body of Japanese literature on this topic; see Wang Hsiao-lien 1972 for a general introduction.

4. On Shang religion, see Akatsuka 1977; Ch'eng Te-k'un 1960, chap. 13; and Maspero 1978, book 2. Other, more specific studies will be cited in subsequent notes. On the oracle-bone records, see Keightley 1985.

5. Keightley 1978, 217. Indeed, according to Ch'en Meng-chia (1936, 149), ancestors and ancestresses were treated equally in Shang rituals.

6. On these figures and the kind of sacrifices offered to them, see esp. Ch'en Meng-chia 1936, 131-132, and Fracasso 1988, 19-30.

7. The second half of Ch'en Meng-chia 1936a, 532-576, is devoted to this topic; see also Chang Kwang-chih 1983, chap. 3; Chow Tse-tsung 1979 and 1981; and Schafer 1951.

8. Schafer 1980, 15.

9. On this question, see Eberhard 1968, 108-117; Chang Kwang-chih 1983, 9, n. 1.; Fracasso 1988, 24-26; van Gulik 1974, 5-9. Ho Ping-ti 1975, 274-279, examines the evidence for a matrilineal society in early China.

10. Fu Hao, in addition to her duties as royal consort, led military expeditions as well. The famous Fu Hao tomb discovered in 1976, despite the continuing disagreement as to the identity of the occupant, shows that women of the royal family commanded much respect and recognition. See Fong 1980, 177-182; p. 42 provides a list of the tomb contents.

11. Chang Kwang-chih 1978, 185, n. 1; cf. pp. 75-66.

12. Ch'en Meng-chia 1936a, 533; Schafer 1951, 156-158.

13. *Kuo yü*, 18, *Ch'u yü*, part 2; as trans. in Bodde 1961, 391. Some details are left out by Bodde; but the general sense is clear. This excellent study is now available in Bodde 1981 also.

14. *Ch'u-tz'u*, as trans. in Hawkes 1985, 130 (lines 97-98). Literally, the second question asks, "Nü Wa has a body; who could have fashioned it?" That is to say, if the goddess created humanity, then who created her? Hawkes uses the *pin-yin* romanization; for the sake of consistency, all Chinese words are romanized in this essay according to the Wade-Giles system.

15. Bodde 1961, 388.

16. Ch'en Meng-chia 1936a, 536. Besides the *T'ien-wen*, the *Shan-hai ching, ch.* 16, contains another early reference to the goddess, which speaks of ten deities known as "the intestines of Nü Wa." The implication, according to Yüan K'o, is that these divine beings grew out of the "body" of the goddess. See Yüan K'o 1983, 389, and the long note to this entry.

17. *Huai-nan tzu* (SPPY), *ch.* 6.7a; trans. in Bodde 1961, 386-387, and Le Blanc 1985, 158-159. The detailed notes in Le Blanc's work are helpful.

18. A second-century C.E. poem, for example, speaks of Nü Wa's "serpent torso"; as trans. in Knechtges 1987, 273 (line 153). For a general discussion of Nü Wa, see also Maspero 1924, 52-54; Karlgren 1946, 229; Schafer 1980, 37-41. In Chinese, there is the useful source book by Yüan K'o 1982; pp. 16-49 discuss basically all of the main references to Nü Wa in the early literature.

19. *Shuo-wen chieh-tzu, ch.* 12B (Reprinted, Hong Kong: Chung-hua shu-chü, 1979, p. 260).

20. Ch'en Meng-chia 1936a, 536; Schafer 1951, 156. On the use of music and dance in ancient Chinese fertility rites, see esp. Chow Tse-tsung 1979, 17-26.

21. See, e.g., Pirazzoli-t'Serstevens 1982, 174, figure 120, and Loewe 1979, 41, figure 9.

22. Hawkes 1985, 129 (line 56). Instead of ravens, some scholars take the sun-birds in question to be crows. The word may also mean simply a black bird.

23. *Huai-nan tzu* (SPPY), 8.5b-6a; cf. Allan 1981, 302, and Chang Kwang-chih 1978, 165. There is another tradition which remembers Yao himself as the archer; see Yüan K'o 1982, 269. The ten suns figure also in another poem, the *Chao-hun,* in the *Ch'u-tz'u*: "And ten suns...come out together, melting metal, dissolving stone"; Hawkes, 224 (line 20). Hawkes is probably following Wen I-to's emended reading; the current text reads: "The ten suns come out one after the other." Cf. *Shan-hai ching, ch.* 14, Yüan K'o 1983, 218, where the myth of the ten suns is related to shamanistic traditions. All quotations from the *Shan-hai ching* are taken from Yüan's critical edition, and will be identified by their *chüan* and page numbers.

24. *Shan-hai ching,* 15: 381; as trans. in Allan 1981, 298. Yüan K'o argues that on the basis of two other versions the word "south-eastern" should be emended to read "eastern."

25. Yang K'uan 1982, 223-246; Ch'en Meng-chia 1936a; 488; Allan 1981, 299-300.

26. *Shan-hai ching* (n. 23 above), 14: 354. Allan further suggests that Ti Chün may be "the father of the sun-birds" (p. 298).

27. As cited in Eberhard 1968, 85-86; cf. Schafer 1980, 40-41.

28. For example, see the poem *Li-sao,* in the *Ch'u-tz'u*: "I ordered Hsi-ho to stay the sun-steed's gallop" (Hawkes 1985, 73 [line 189]). There is also a reference to Hsi-ho in the *T'ien-wen* (Hawkes, 128 [lines 45-46]), on which the Later Han commentator Wang Yi comments, "Hsi-ho is the charioteer of the sun"; as cited in Akatsuka 1977, 448. See also Maspero 1924, 11, for a similar passage from the *Huai-nan tzu.*

29. *Chuang-tzu* (SPPY), chap. 2, as trans, in Watson 1968, 45; modified.

30. *Shan-hai ching,* 16: 404. Akatsuka, for example, is of the opinion that Tung-mu and Hsi-mu are related to the worship of the rising and setting sun, or more precisely to the shamanesses in charge of sun worship (p. 451).

31. Ch'en Meng-chia 1936, 132, favours this view and equates Tung-mu and Hsi-mu with the deities of the sun and the moon, respectively. See Fracasso 1988, 28-30 for a survey of opinions on this question.

32. *Huai-nan tzu,* 6.10b; as trans. in Le Blanc 1985, 184. On the moon goddess, see also Maspero 1924, 14-16, and Eberhard 1968, 87-92.

33. Eberhard, 87-92, 46-49.

34. *Shu ching, Yao-tien,* as trans. in Needham 1959, 3.188. I am not aware of any cult devoted to the sun goddess in contemporary Chinese religion. Worship of Nü Wa, however, is still very much a part of Chinese religious life. I have recently visited a couple of Nü Wa temples in Hong Kong and Macau, for example.

35. On the identity of the "first sericulturalist," see Kuhn 1984, and Bodde 1975, 263-272.

36. See Ch'en Meng-chia 1936a, 525-526, and Schafer 1951, 162-169.

37. *Shih chi* (SPPY), 27.12a; or simply "daughter of heaven," or "child of the lord of heaven" according to other accounts. The *Shih ching* poem is entitled *Ta tung* (no. 203 in the standard Mao edition); see Loewe's (1979, 112-113) discussion of Waley's and Karlgren's translations.

38. See Kominami 1974, Yüan K'o 1982, 160-168, and Loewe 1979, 112-115.

39. As trans. in W.C. Liu and I.Y. Lo, eds. *Sunflower Splendor: Three Thousand Years of Chinese Poetry* (Bloomington and London: Indiana University Press, 1975), 32, no. 5. Cf. poem #2 in this same section (p. 31), which is not concerned with a goddess but an ordinary woman: "Fair is the woman upstairs,/ Bright as the moon at her window./ Lovely is her rouge-powdered face,/ Slender are her white hands./ At one time she was a singing-girl,/ Now she is a wanderer's wife./ He went away and has not returned,/ An empty bed, hard to keep alone."

40. As trans. in Hawkes 1985, 115 (lines 1-4).

41. See Hawkes' introductory comments (115).

42. *Mo-tzu,* 31, *Ming-kuei;* as cited in Wen I-to 1959, 97. According to Wen (99), the name "Kao-t'ang" is also derived from a term meaning ritual or cultic centre.

43. Sung Yü, *Kao-t'ang fu,* in *Wen hsüan, ch.* 19 (Tokyo, 1974), p. 440; cf. Schafer 1980, 45.

44. *Wen hsüan,* 19: 440; Schafer 1980, 45.

45. See Lin Yutang, *The Gay Genius: The Life and Times of Su Tungpo* (Westport, Connecticut: Greenwood Press, 1971), 359-368.

46. The present text has "king"; but most likely it is a mistake. See *Wen hsüan,* 19: 454, n. 1, and Schafer 1980, 196, n. 108.

47. There is a poem in the *Shih ching* which may bear on this topic. The poem *Tung-fang chih-jih* (no. 99), in Legge's (1970, 153-154) trans., reads: "The sun is in the east,/ And that lovely girl/ Is in my chamber./ She is in my chamber;/ She treads in my footsteps,/ And comes to me. The moon is in the east,/ And that lovely girl/ Is inside my door./ She is inside my door;/ She treads in my footsteps,/ And hastens away." The usage of "sun" and "moon" as symbols of love and beauty can thus be traced to the beginning of Chinese poetry. Furthermore, the word translated here in the sense of "treading on one's footsteps," according to Chow Tse-tsung (1979, 10-11), is related to ancient marriage rites, and by extension to sexual acts. Significantly, the origin myth of the Chou royal clan relates how Hou Chi was conceived after his mother trod on the footprint made by the high god Ti. See the poem *Sheng-min* in the *Shih ching* (no. 245, trans. in Legge 1970, 465). Wen I-to (1959, 73) suggests that the "treading" on footsteps or footprints may refer to a type of shamanistic ritual dance performed in fertility rites. This should suffice to show that the poetic transformation of religious themes has a long and complex history.

48. See Chiang Liang-fu 1984, 290-298; Hawkes 1985, 105-106; cf. Hawkes 1967.

49. This is how Chu Hsi (1130-1200), for example, sees them in his commentary on the *Ch'u-tz'u*; see *Ch'u-tz'u chi-chu* (1987, 33, 35). Another possibility is that "Hsiang Chün" refers to a male deity, perhaps the sage-king Shun, and "Hsiang fu-jen," to his consort(s). Chiang Liang-fu (1984, 305), for example, supports this view. In this case, the voice of the first poem would be that of a female shaman.

50. Hawkes 1985, 100, citing Aoki Masaru. See, however, Chiang Liang-fu's critique of Aoki (298-299).

51. As trans. in Hawkes 1985, 106-107.

52. See Hawkes 1967, 74-76. The present-day "Dragon Boat" festival, celebrated every year on the fifth day of the fifth month, is dedicated to Ch'ü Yüan, the reputed author of the "Nine Songs." See esp. Wen I-to 1959, 221-238.

53. On the treatment of the Hsiang goddess in T'ang poetry, see Schafer 1980, 118-131.

54. Hawkes 1985, 74 (lines 221-32); 129 (lines 68-69); 296 (line 14).

55. *Lo-shen fu*, in *Wen hsüan, ch.* 19 (Tokyo, 1974), p. 467.

56. *Ibid.*, p. 469.

57. Schafer 1980; cf. Cahill 1985.

58. *Shih chi* (SPPY), 6.14b-15a. This passage is translated and discussed in Hawkes 1985, 104.

59. As trans. in Hawkes 1967, 73, n. 5; cf. the slightly different and less literal translation in Hawkes 1985, 96. The *Han shu, ch.* 28B (Peking: Chung-hua shu-chü, 1983), 6.1666, also reports that the people of Ch'u "believe in the power of shamans and spirits and are much addicted to lewd religious rites"; as trans. in Hawkes 1985, 18.

60. Chu Hsi, *Ch'u-tz'u chi-chu* (Hong Kong, 1987), p. 29. Ch'u Yüan's authorship is not the issue here; the songs themselves reflect earlier religious materials.

61. *Li chi, T'an kung*, B. 34b (Shih-san-ching chu-su ed.); see James Legge, trans., *The Sacred Books of China: The Texts of Confucianism*, part 3, The *Li Ki*, I-X, in *Sacred Books of the East*, vol. 27 (Oxford: Oxford University Press, 1885; reprinted Delhi, 1968), p. 201. This negative assessment should be contrasted with the statement reported in the *Lun-yü* (Analects), 13-22, "The Master said, 'The southerners have a saying: If a person is without canstaqncy, he cannot serve as a shaman or healer. How well said!'" (D. C. Lau, trans., *Confucius. The Analects* [Harmondswroth: Penguin Books, 1979], 122, modified). Shamans were obviously much respected before they bacame the object of criticism and ridicule.

62. *Shih chi*, 126.10b-11b. This passage is translated in J.J.M. de Groot 1982, 6.1196-1198. Though outdated, this work (first published in 1910) is still useful for the numerous sources it has collected on shamanism.

63. On this theme, see Eberhard 1968, 37-41.

64. The story of Hsi-men Pao was appended to the chapter on "comic figures" by Ch'u Shao-sun (fl. ca. 35 B.C.E.); it did not come from Ssu-ma Ch'ien himself. Hsi-men Pao is mentioned in *Shih chi*, 29.2b, but only as an official who improved irrigation and thereby the lives of the people.

65. *Shih chi*, 28.13b. See Schafer 1951, 157-159 for other references.

66. *Chin shu, ch.* 94 (Peking: Chung-hua shu-chü, 1982), 8.2428; cf. de Groot 1982, 6.1212. Also, see *Chin shu, ch.* 84, 7.2184, for another reference to shamanism.

67. According to Hawkes (1985, 91), the *Ch'u-tz'u* commentator Wang Yi has already made this identification. I cannot find this in my text, however, which only says that "Fu-fei is a divine woman" (*shen-nü*). The earliest reference to Fu-fei as the daughter of Fu Hsi appears to be the commentary to Ts'ao Chih's *Lo-shen fu* in the *Wen hsüan*.

68. Fung Yu-lan, *A History of Chinese Philosophy*, vol. 1, *The Period of the Philosophers*, trans. D. Bodde (Princeton: Princeton University Press, 1983), 384.

69. There is a vast body of literature on this topic. A good account is Needham 1956, 2.232ff; cf. John Henderson, *The Development and Decline of Chinese Cosmology* (New York: Columbia University Press, 1984).

70. Chap. 42; as trans. in Wing-tsit Chan 1981, 176. Strictly speaking, *ch'i* extends beyond the "material" to include the spiritual dimension as well. See the good discussion in Benjamin Schwartz, *The World of Thought in Ancient China* (Cambridge: Harvard University Press, 1985), 179-184. All subsequent quotations from the *Lao-tzu* are taken from W.T. Chan's translation.

71. See, for example, Ellen Marie Chen 1969 and 1974. This theme is also developed in Barbara Reed's essay on "Taoism," in Arvind Sharma, ed., *Women in World Religions* (1987), 163-165.

72. See Maspero 1978, 98-101; Ch'en Meng-chia 1936, 117. In later periods, however, the earth deity, Hou-t'u, was seen as a female figure. Under the influence of the *yin-yang* cosmology, there was a tendency to equate "earth" with *yin*, because "heaven" was clearly perceived to be a *yang* phenomenon. Thus, the *Cambridge History of China*, vol. 1, *The Ch'in and Han Empires*, ed. D. Twitchett and M. Loewe (Cambridge: Cambridge University Press, 1986) renders Hou-t'u as "Earth Queen." But it seems that the change was not completed perhaps until the T'ang dynasty. According to Tsung Li and Liu Ch'ün (1987, 187-193), citing the *Hou Han shu*, *Chin shu* and other sources, an empress was associated with the worship of a male earth deity from the Han to the Sui dynasty. This too would satisfy the demands of the *yin-yang* cosmology. This question deserves further attention.

73. Ames 1981. Ames is esp. critical of Needham's "'feminine' interpretation of Taoism" (p. 23) and his assumption of a matriarchal society in ancient China.

74. *Shan-hai ching*, 11: 301 (n. 23 above).

75. *Ibid.*, 6: 196-197; 15: 370; cf. 18: 444, where a "mountain of no death" is mentioned.

76. On this whole question, see esp. Yü Ying-shih 1964-65. Professor Yü writes, "The whole development of immortality...from its beginning in the late Warring States period down through Han times may be best characterized by one word: worldliness" (119).

77. The various techniques and practices are discussed in Maspero 1981, books 5, 8-9; Robinet 1979; and esp. Kohn 1989a. On sexual practices, see Harper 1987.

78. On the various aspects of Taoist alchemy, see Needham 1974-1980, vols. 5.2-4, and Kohn 1989a. On the notion of "spiritual body" in Taoism, see Schipper 1982.

79. For example, *Shih chi*, 28.9a. See generally Needham, vol. 5.2, pp. 93-113.

80. *Shan-hai ching*, 11: 294. It should be noted that the various references to K'un-lun in the *Shan-hai ching* do not always agree and may reflect different conceptions of the cosmic centre. For an attempt to link Mt. K'un-lun to the myth of a primordial "chaos" (*hun-tun*), see Girardot 1983.

81. *Shan-hai ching*, 11: 299, and 300, n. 4; *Huai-nan tzu* (SPPY), 4.2b.

82. The literature on Ma-wang-tui is too large to be enumerated here. A basic report is provided in *Wen wu* (1975.1: 47-57, 61). See also Jan 1977, Loewe 1979, 17-30, and Pirazzoli-t'Serstevens 1982, 41-60.

83. Four reports on the medical texts, including the *Tao-yin t'u*, can be found in *Wen wu* (1975, 6: 1-19); drawings of selected figures are provided on pp. 8-9. See also the excellent study by Catherine Despeux, "Gymnastics: The Ancient Tradition," in Kohn 1989a, 225-261.

84. It has also been suggested that the painting was used as a funerary banner, i.e., a banner used in funeral processions. But as Yü Ying-shih (1987, 368-369) has shown, it is much more likely that the painting served as a burial shroud. On this painting, see the major study by Loewe 1979, and Seidel 1982.

85. Loewe 1979, 59. Other suggestions include Fu Hsi and the sun goddes, Hsi Ho. See Chung Ching-wen, "Ma-want-tui Han-mu po-hua ti shen-hua shih Yi-yi," in *Chung-hua Wen-shih lun-ts'ung* 2 (Shanghai, 1979), 75-98; and Chou Shih-ch'i, "Ma-wang-tui Han-mu po-hua jih-yüeh shen-hua ch'i-yüan K'ao, in *ibid.*, 99-103.

86. It is thus generally agreed that one of the two female figures represents the Countess, or more precisely her *hun* soul. If, as Yü Ying-shih has suggested, the painting is related to the ritual of "summoning the soul," then it may be more fitting to see the Countess as being still in a "fluid" state, as opposed to the already "transformed" figure with the serpentine tail. Yü's (1987) study is not limited to the Ma-wang-tui painting, but provides an excellent account of the belief in an afterlife in early China.

87. As Needham puts it, "when the body was finally uncovered it was found to be like that of a person who had died only a week or two before." See Needham, 5.2. 304; see esp. figures 1333 and 1334.

88. Ch'en Meng-chia 1936, 131-132; Chang Kwang-chih 1978, 157; Seidel 1982, 99-100.

89. As trans. in Fracasso 1988, 3.

90. Fracasso (p. 2) trans.: "Yü studied under (the ruler) of Hsi-wang-kuo." The context suggests that the ruler, as opposed to the state, is the subject here. Fracasso discusses other similar references in n. 2.

91. Pi Yüan (1730-1797), e.g., writes: "The common people believe that Hsi-wang-mu is a divine being. This is not so. Hsi-wang-mu is the name of a state." He then cites the above sources and a few others to support his claim; religious accounts of Hsi-wang-mu are regarded as basically nonsense. As cited in Chu T'ien-shun 1982, 248-249. The equally famous scholar Chao I (1727-1814) shares a similar view; as quoted in Tsung Li and Liu Ch'ün 1987, 435-436.

92. Kominami 1974; Seidel 1982.

93. Kominami 1974, 62-69. These symbols, however, are not unique to representations of the Queen Mother. We may recall that the Ma-wang-tui silk painting also employs the

symbolism of the sun and the moon. They may simply be artistic conventions, conveying a general religious sense, as opposed to a specific meaning such as androgyny.

94. *Huai-nan-tzu*, 6.8b; as trans. in Le Blanc 1985, 173, slightly modified.

95. Kominami 1974, 46-48. In his essay, Kominami also demonstrates the relationship between the myth of Hsi-wang-mu and that of the "Weaving Maid" (Chih-nü). In addition, his discussion of Mt. K'un-lun as cosmic centre is also helpful.

96. *Chuang-tzu*, chap. 6; as translated in Watson 1968, 81-82.

97. Kuo Ch'ing-fan, *Chuang-tzu chi-shih* (1985), 249.

98. *Shan-hai ching* (n. 23 above), pp. 50, 305-306, 397, 407.

99. See the discussion in Loewe 1979, 90; Fracasso 1988, 9-10.

100. *Shan-hai ching*, 16: 407; trans., Loewe 1979, 91; modified. The phrase "it has stripes and a tail" (*yu-wen yu-wei*) may be corrupt. This passage is quoted in the Sung dynasty encyclopedia *T'ai-p'ing yü-lan, ch.* 38, but without the word *yu*. *Wen-wei* may mean a "striped tail"; but it may be a mistake also. Other entries speak of mythical beasts with "nine tails," for example. If we emend *wen* to read "nine," the sentence would mean that the nine tails "are all white." Another possibility should also be mentioned. In the section known as *Hsi-shan ching* (*Shan-hai ching*. 2: 51-52), certain mountain beasts are described as having "striped tails," on which Kuo P'u comments that the word *ch'ang*, "long," is a variant for *wen*. Perhaps the deity has a "long tail" rather than a "striped" one.

101. *Shan-hai ching*, 2: 47. Literally, K'un-lun is described as Ti's "lower capital" (*hsia-tu*), perhaps implying Ti's "earthly" domain.

102. *Shan-hai ching*, p. 48, n. 3

103. *Shan-hai ching*, 11: 294. Again, K'un-lun is identified as Ti's *hsia-tu*.

104. Yüan K'o 1983, 285-286, n. 3; 294-295, n. 2. See also Yang K'uan, in *Ku-shih pien* (1982), 7A.196-197, and Seidel 1987, 29.

105. *Chuang-tzu*, chap. 12: "The Yellow Emperor went wandering north of the Red Water [or River], ascended the slopes of K'un-lun, and gazed south" (Watson 1968: 128-129). Chap. 18 describes K'un-lun as "the place where the Yellow Emperor rested" (Watson, 192).

106. *Mu T'ien-tzu chuan, ch.* 2 (1937), p. 7. According to tradition, this text was discovered in a tomb in the third century C.E. See *Chin shu, ch.* 51, 5.1432. Modern scholarly opinions vary as to its date and authenticity. Because the language is archaic, and because such early texts as the *T'ien-wen* and the *Shih chi* already refer to the kings' legendary travels (cf. n. 117, below), I take it as a late Warring States product, roughly third century B.C.E.

107. *Huai-nan tzu*, 17.4a. On the Yellow Emperor, see also Jan 1981, and Le Blanc 1985-86.

108. In later traditions, as we shall see, the Queen Mother is paired with a male deity known as Tung-wang-kung, who represents the *yang* complement to the goddess' *yin* essence. Yet, the connection with the Yellow Emperor was not altogether forgotten. The two, e.g., appear in Taoist alchemical formulae together. See Strickmann 1979, 150. For a general discussion of the Queen Mother, see also Cheng Chih-ming, *Chung-Kuo She-hui Yü Tsung-chiao* (Taipei, 1986), esp. 7-35.

109. See, e.g., Loewe 1978, and Chang Kwang-chih 1983, chap. 4.

110. *Shan-hai ching*, 16: 396.

111. *Ibid.*, n. 1.

112. *Ibid.*, p. 394.

113. *Ibid.*, pp. 198, 294.

114. *Mu T'ien-tzu chuan, ch.* 3, p. 15; cf. Dubs 1942, 227.

115. Since the phrase "the state of Hsi-wang-mu" appears three times in the text (pp. 13 and 24), and since the king presented himself as a gift-bearing guest, some scholars have taken this as "proof" of the original nature of the Queen Mother as an earthly sovereign. See nn. 90-91 above. See also the comments by the editors of the Ch'ing dynasty collection, *Ssu-k'u ch'üan-shu*, appended to the *Mu T'ien-tzu chuan*, "Supplement," p. 3.

116. *Mu T'ien-tzu chuan*, p. 16. Again, textual uncertainties surround these verses. Generally, I take them to be an invitation; but cf. Fracasso 1988, 5, n. 8; Dubs 1942, 227, n. 17.

117. *Shih chi* (SPPY), 43.1b; cf. *Shih chi*, 5.2b.

118. *Shih chi*, 117.31b; cf. Hervouet's French translation cited in Loewe 1979, 94; and D. Knechtges, *The Han Rhapsody* (Cambridge: Cambridge University Press, 1976), 39.

119. The relevant texts are translated and discussed in Loewe 1979, 98-101. Cf. Dubs 1942, which treats it as a "mystery" cult; Overmyer 1976, 139 describes it as a "popular ecstatic cult." We may even include messianic and eschatological expectations in a description of this movement.

120. *Han shu, ch.* 27C, 5.1476; as trans. in Loewe 1979, 99. My emphasis. On the basis of Dubs 1942, 235, I have changed Loewe's "manikin of straw" to "stalk of straw" in the first sentence. Loewe's more specific reading is probably influenced by a later reference, which he cites on p. 119.

121. *Han Shu*, 27C, 5.1476. Cahill 1986, 157 translates the first sentence as "Hsi Wang Mu is for women to praise," which is suggestive but changes the grammatical structure of the original.

122. Wang Ming 1979, 68. Cf. Kaltenmark 1979, 40.

123. As trans. in Knechtges 1987, 2.33, 35 (11. 159-164).

124. In *Hou Han shu, ch.* 59, 7.1930; also collected in *Wen hsüan, ch.* 15. Chang Heng's description of the two goddesses calls to mind Ts'ao Chih's *Lo-shen fu*. Cf. Knechtges 1976, 55-56. Also see T. Pokora, "Huan T'an's Fu on Looking for the Immortals," *Archiv Orientali*, 28 (1960): 353-367, for another poem in this tradition; p. 364, n. 74, discusses the two goddesses. Very little is known about "Jade Maiden." The term has come to signify generally a lesser goddess in the service of the Queen Mother.

125. *Hou Han shu, ch.* 59, 7.1930.

126. A.R. Davies, *T'ao Yüan-ming (AD 365-427): His Works and Their Meaning* (Cambridge: Cambridge University Press, 1983), 1.154-155; modified. The Chinese text is quoted in 2.126.

Cf. James R. Hightower, *The Poetry of T'ao Ch'ien* (Oxford: Oxford University Press, 1970), 231.

127. Chang Hua, *Po-wu chih, ch.* 3 (1939), p. 17; trans. in Loewe 1979, 116; modified.

128. While commenting on the *Han Wu-ti nei-chuan* (to be discussed shortly), the editors of the *Ssu-k'u ch'üan-shu* point out that although Chang Hua's work as a whole may be corrupt, this particular story appears to be genuine, for it is already quoted by Li Shan (fl. 660 C.E.) in his commentary on Ts'ao Chih's *Lo-shen fu*, in the *Wen hsüan*. Reprinted in *Han Wu-ti nei-chuan* (1937), p. 1.

129. As trans. in Loewe 1979, 116.

130. Loewe 1979, 117.

131. *Han Wu-ti nei-chuan* (1937), p. 2; abbreviated HWTNC hereafter. I have translated their clothings generally; the original specifies a type of striped-pattern for the attendants and a multi-coloured robe with a rich yellow background for the Queen Mother. This work is traditionally attributed to the Han historian Pan Ku (32-92 C.E.); but most scholars would agree with Schipper (1965) in placing it towards the end of the Six Dynasties period in the sixth century. Further, as the *Ssu-k'u* editors point out, this work may have suffered later changes as well.

132. Tu Kuang-t'ing, *Yung-ch'eng chi-hsien lu* (TT 560-561, HY 782) *ch.* 1.13b; abbreviated YCCHL. Works in the *Tao-tsang* (Taoist Canon; abbreviated TT) are identified by their fascicle number and by the serial number assigned to them in the Harvard-Yenching Index to Taoist Literature (Sinological Index Series, no 25; abbreviated HY). On this and other Taoist works, see the discussion below. Also see Cahill 1985-86, which focuses on Tu's "biography" of Hsi-wang-mu; this particular passage is translated on p. 134. In this essay, the word "biography" is used in the sense of religious biography.

133. YCCHL, 1.10a-10b.

134. *Ibid.*, 1.9a-9b. This development could be traced to the Later Han period; see Kominami 1974, 58-61. Tu Kuang-t'ing (1.12b-13a) cites a Han folk tune which mentions the two together.

135. *Po-wu chih, ch.* 1, p. 5; taking the word *fu*, "give" or "hand over," in the sense of its cognate, to "offer sacrifice."

136. Kominami 1974, 56-62, 73-74; Loewe 1979, 120-123.

137. Seidel 1983, 340-348, discusses this theme in some detail. Although goddesses are not mentioned in this context, it seems to me that in religious Taoism both female and male deities are distinguished by their role as teacher. Cf. Seidel 1982, 103-104.

138. HWTNC, pp. 4-6; YCCHL, 1.14b-17a. These themes are repeated throughout the entire narrative in both works. Generally, the latter account is indebted to the former. It is shorter, more concerned with conveying the basic information. For example, HWTNC (p. 1) describes how the emperor reacted in surprise when a divine messenger came to announce the Queen Mother's visit; YCCHL (1.13a) is satisfied simply to report the announcement itself. The HWTNC is a work of literature; it is concerned not only to provide information, but to paint both the physical and emotional scene as well. Tu Kuang-t'ing's account, on the other hand, includes other events in the life of the Queen Mother which will be discussed later.

139. HWTNC, p. 11; YCCHL, 2.8b (biography of Shang-yüan fu-jen). The second sentence may also be rendered in the sense that the transmission of scriptures would help the emperor stand firm in his own quest for transcendence, so as to lead him towards spiritual realization.

140. YCCHL, 2.7a-9b. HWTNC, pp. 10-13, is much more detailed and colourful. Here, Shang-yüan fu-jen at first even denied that she had these scriptures. She received some strong words from the Queen Mother; "her face betrayed her sense of shame" (p. 12), as she finally agreed to transmit the scriptures, via a male deity, to the emperor.

141. YCCHL, 1.9a-20b. As we shall see, there are in fact two versions of Tu's work. The biography of the Queen Mother is essentially the same in both versions. On Tu's life and place in the history of Taoism, see Cahill 1985-86.

142. YCCHL, 1.9a-20b. On the Mao shan sect of Taoism, see Strickmann 1977 and Robinet 1984. On Wei Hua-ts'un, see Schafer 1977. Two other female figures, Pien Tung-hsüan and Hsieh Tzu-jan, are mentioned in this account as "students" of the Queen Mother. They will be discussed later.

143. *Sui shu, ch.* 71, 6.1657.

144. Cahill 1986, 155.

145. Cahill argues that Taoist goddesses provide two models for different groups of women: "The jade girls set an example of submission and skillful service for prostitutes and performers, while the Queen Mother sets an example of attainment and power for Taoist priestesses and adepts. Both models stood outside women's normal roles in the household. A woman unwilling or unable to follow either of these examples in her present life might hope to go to the Queen Mother's paradise after her death" (1986, 158). I am not entirely convinced that different types of goddesses can be made to correspond to different groups of women. As I shall argue, Taoist hagiographies take into account a wide range of experience and offer hope of transcendence in one's lifetime to all women. Secondly, I do not see the Queen Mother as primarily a role model. This seems to limit the saving power of the goddess to the sociological level. Nonetheless, Cahill's study is very helpful.

146. Aside from the initial comments, YCCHL only mentions the King Father once more, in 1.13a, to the effect that all adepts who "attained the Way and ascended to heaven" must pay homage to the King Father and the Queen Mother. The biography of the King Father himself, as found in the *T'ai-p'ing kuang-chi, ch.* 1, is very short by comparison and contains little concrete details.

147. Worship of Hsu-wang-mu gradually declined after the T'ang dynasty. Besides her non-conformity and the arrival of other Taoist goddesses, one must also mention the challenge of Buddhism. Overmyer (1976, 139) has shown that the popular Buddhist goddess Lao-mu (Venerable Mother) represents a "later manifestation" of the Queen Mother.

148. See Livia Kohn 1989. Buddhist influence is a significant factor in the shaping of this goddess. Kohn's essay includes a translation of Tu Kuang-t'ing's (YCCHL) biography of the Holy Mother.

149. *Ibid.*, 64.

150. I disagree with Kohn on this point. While she considers the goddess' role as teacher to be essentially defined by "the arts of the bedchamber," i.e., sexual practices in the context of Taoist self-cultivation, I see no reason to limit the goddess' expertise to any one particular area. Indeed, a distorted picture of the goddess may result from a onesided emphasis on

sexual practice. A medieval text, e.g., speaks of the Queen Mother of the West in this way: "[She] had no husband, but she liked to copulate with young boys"; as trans. in van Gulik 1974, 158. This is the kind of misinterpretation that one should carefully avoid. The key here is again the goddess' power and her possession of sacred writings and talismans. In more general terms, Taoist goddesses must be viewed not only in terms of their indebtedness to tradition, but as I shall argue, in terms of a dialectic of tradition and transcendence; cf. n. 176, below.

151. Here, I rely esp. on J. Boltz's (1986) excellent study. In Japanese, there is the standard work by Li Hsien-chang (1979).

152. J. Boltz, 217.

153. *San-chiao yüan-liu sou-shen ta-ch'üan* (Origins of the Three Teachings, a Comprehensive Account in Search of the Sacred), ed., Yeh Te-hui (Shanghai, 1909), 4.16b. Although this passage is not included in her discussion, see J. Boltz 1986, 219, for a description of this work; the translation of the title is also hers. Buddhist influence is evident in the story of T'ien-fei. In fact, she has been referred to as the Taoist version of Kuan-yin.

154. Tu Kuang-t'ing, YCCHL; see n. 163 below. The *T'ai-p'ing kuang-chi* (Peking, 1981) is not a specifically Taoist work. But *ch.* 56-70 are devoted to "female immortals" (*nü-hsien*). It quotes from diverse sources, including Tu's work, and contains a total of 86 entries; cf. n. 168 below. For Chao's work, see below n. 169.

155. Liu Hsiang, *Lieh-hsien chuan* (Tokyo, 1975). There is a French translation of this work by M. Kaltenmark (1953). Ko Hung, *Shen-hsien chuan* (1794). Fukui Kōjun's (Tokyo, 1983) Japanese translation of this work is most helpful because of the long introduction and notes. It contains the Chinese text also; but it is incomplete.

156. Anthony Yu's recent study (1987) contains a list of the major titles in this genre; see esp. pp. 399-400, and the extended bibliographic discussion in pp. 401-402, n. 4. The *Sou-shen chi* (In Search of the Sacred), by the Chin dynasty scholar Kan Pao (fl. ca. 317), is particularly important to a study of Chinese goddesses; see Bodde 1942. Also see the more general study by Lo Chin-t'ang 1979.

157. The *Lieh-nü chuan* (Biographies of Exemplary Women) by Liu Hsiang is most important in this regard. See Marina Sung 1981, and Theresa Kelleher's essay on "Confucianism" in Sharma 1987.

158. Note that Ch'ang Jung (no. 50, p. 703), whose story will be discussed below, is identified as a man in the standard edition; but quotations of this story in other sources indicate otherwise. Ch'ang Jung is certainly understood as a goddess in later Taoist sources.

159. *Shen-hsien chuan* (1794), 10.10a; this entry is omitted in Fukui's edition.

160. *Shen-hsien chuan, ch.* 8, in Fukui 1983, 251-254.

161. T'ao Hung-ching, *Chen-ling wei yeh t'u* (TT 73, HY 167). T'ao's major work, *Chen-kao* (Declarations of the Perfected, TT 637-640, HY 1010), is also important and forms a main source for later hagiographers. See Robinet 1984.

162. This work is now lost; but there is a reconstructed version in Ch'en Kuo-fu 1963, 454-504. The last section or chapter, *chüan* 20, is evidently devoted to female immortals, as all sources which quote from Ma Shu's work agree. The fact that the biographies of goddesses are placed at the end of the work is indicative of the patriarchal prejudice which did not leave Taoism untouched. At least one other work, the *Hsü hsien chuan* (Supplement to the

Lives of Immortals, TT 138, HY 295), by Shen Fen, follows this pattern. It contains the biographies of three major figures, Hsieh Tzu-jan, P'ei Hsüan-ching and Ch'i Hsiao-yao, all of whom will be discussed below, placed at the end of *chüan* A.

163. First, there is the six-*chüan* version of the YCCHL (TT 560-561, HY 782) cited above. The Sung dynasty Taoist anthology *Yün-chi ch'i-ch'ien* (Seven Lots from the Bookbag of the Clouds, HY 1026) by Chang Chün-fang (fl. 1015) contains a shorter version of Tu's work (*ch.* 114-116, TT 701). The latter contains Tu's preface as well; this work will be cited as YCCC hereon. There is a brief discussion of this work in John Lagerway, "Le Yun-ji qi-qian: structure et sources," in K. Schipper, *Index du Yunji Qiqian* (Paris, 1951), 1.63, nn. 123-24.

164. YCCHL has 37 entries, whereas YCCC has 27 (one of which is devoted to two goddesses). With respect to the biography of the Queen Mother, the two accounts are generally the same. Nevertheless, the following differences, besides minor writing or character variants, may be noted. The description of King Mu of Chou, first of all, differs in the two versions. YCCHL is more detailed. One section is found in both accounts, but it is prefaced in YCCHL by the words, "it is also said." Could it be that the YCCHL version represents a later elaboration of the YCCC biography of the Queen Mother? YCCHL has one extra paragraph on the Queen Mother's visit to the Yellow Emperor (1.11a-b), and a brief episode involving Lao-tzu (1.11b). In place of the latter, YCCC (114.6b-7b) inserts an account of the meeting with Mao Ying. This is peculiar because Mao Ying reappears later in the narrative, and in the YCCHL as well. I suspect that the YCCC version was the earlier one. First, as it stands YCCC has two separate accounts of the Mao Ying story, no doubt derived from different sources. This makes the narrative rather awkward and breaks up the chronological sequence which guides the composition. Presumably a later redactor saw the difficulty, reworked the story, and added the new material. Secondly, the biography of the Queen Mother in the *T'ai-p'ing kuang-chi* (abbreviated TPKC), which cites a *Chi-hsien lu* in this instance (see n. 168 below) is much closer to the YCCC version. I should add that the later account in Chao-Tao-i's work (see n. 169) seems to have combined both these versions of the Queen Mother story. With respect to the biography of Chiu-t'ien hsüan-nü, YCCC is slightly longer. It details the various sacred objects that the goddess presented to the Yellow Emperor (114.17b-18a), and has an extra sentence at the end. Chao Tao-i's version is quite clearly based on that of the YCCC.

165. YCCC, 114.1a.

166. YCCC, 114.4b. This may be taken as another indication that the YCCC version was the earlier of the two, for it begins with the biography of the Queen Mother. TPKC also begins with the story of Hsi-wang-mu. YCCHL, on the other hand, begins with that of the Holy Mother. It seems that the Holy Mother has become increasingly important since the Sung period; Chao Tao-i's work also begins with the Holy Mother.

167. YCCC, 114.4a-b.

168. The TPKC cites the *Yung-ch'eng chi-hsien lu* as its source nine times, two of which are not found in the two current versions, three are found in YCCHL, and four in YCCC. It also quotes from a *Chi-hsien lu* 17 times, four of which are found in the two versions (two each). I assume that these two titles refer to the same work. In another Sung dynasty encyclopedia, the *T'ai-p'ing Yü-lan* (*ch.* 661-68), quotations are also made from a *Chi-hsien lu*. In at least six cases, the quotation is taken from YCCHL. In two cases, the quotation is found in YCCC. In one case, the quotation is not found in the two versions, but agrees with TPKC, which also cites the *Chi-hsien lu*. Since Tu Kuang-t'ing's preface (YCCC, 114.4b) indicates an originally ten-*chüan* work, I take it that the total number of biographies preserved in the three sources probably make up most of the original. More precisely, according to the 12th-cent. bibliography *T'ung-chih* (*ch.* 67), by Cheng Ch'iao (1104-62), the original 10-*chüan* work

contained a total of 109 entries. In sum, I would suggest that the YCCC version represents the earliest selected edition of Tu's collected biographies of Taoist goddesses. It generally prefers those biographies which deal with what I shall call "lesser immortals." YCCHL, on the other hand, contains esp. the biographies of "cosmic goddesses." Among the various sources cited by the TPKC, the most significant for our purposes is a lost work entitled *Nü-hsien chuan* (Lives of Female Immortals); but I have not yet been able to determine its provenance.

169. Chao Tao-i, *Li-shih chen-hsien t'i-tao t'ung-chien hou chi* (TT 150, HY 298; hereafter abbreviated TCHC), in six *chüan*. This is the last part of a truly comprehensive hagiographic collection, which is divided into a main collection, a "Supplement" (*Hsü-pien*) and the "Later Anthology." For a discussion of Chao's "masterpiece," see Judith Boltz 1987, 56-59, 246. According to Boltz, the supplemental collections "appear to date to the late fourteenth or early fifteenth century." The evidence, however, seems inconclusive. The fact that a reference to a late fourteenth-century figure is found in the "Supplement" does not render the entire second collection a late product. I see little reason to doubt Chao's authorship, granted that some changes and additions may have found their way into the collection at a later date.

170. See, for example, YCCHL, biographies nos. 1-13; TCHC, nos. 1-8, 31-38, 45 and 52. On Yang Hsi and the Shang-ch'ing revelation, see Strickmann 1977, and Robinet 1984. Most of these goddesses are already mentioned in the T'ao Hung-ching's *Chen-ling wei-yeh t'u*. Often, the poems recited by them at the revelation to Yang Hsi would be recorded. These can usually be traced to the *Chen-kao* (Declarations of the Perfected) by T'ao Hung-ching. In this category, I would include also such ancient deities as the moon goddess Heng-o and the star goddess Chih-nü.

171. YCCHL, no. 6, Nan-chi Wang-fu-jen (2.16a-18a). She first appeared to Wang Pao, who later became the teacher of Lady Wei of the Southern Peak. Cf. TCHC, no. 32 (3.2a-b), which is a much abbreviated version. TCHC notes that one account identifies the goddess as the third, and not the fourth, daughter of the Queen Mother.

172. YCCHL, no 7, Yün-hua fu-jen (3.1a-4b); TPKC, no. 3, 56.347-349, citing *Chi-hsien lu*. Except for minor variants, the two are the same. TCHC, no. 6 (2.4a-7b), is slightly shorter.

173. YCCHL, 3.4b; TCHC omits this reference. As we shall see more clearly (n. 191, below), TCHC generally tries to stay away from polemics.

174. YCCHL, no. 17, Fu-fei, 5.20a.

175. YCCHL, no. 19, Tu Lan-hsiang, 5.21b-22b; essentially the same as TPKC, no. 42, 62.387. TCHC, no. 102, 5.17b-18a, is a summary. A different account, focussing on the romantic encounter between Tu and Chang Shuo, is found in the *Sou-shen Chi* (see n. 156 above), *ch.* 1; cf. TPKC, 272.2144, which cites a "Separate Biography of Tu Lan-hsiang."

176. YCCHL, no. 19, Tu Lan-hsiang, 5.21b-22b. See also Wang Kuan-fu (no. 53) and Ts'ui Shao-hsüan (no. 65), in TPKC, 63.396, and 67.414-416, respectively. The latter is unique to TPKC; although Ts'ui was a major figure and, according to several traditional bibliographic catalogues, had her own biography. A similar account of Wang Kuan-fu is found in YCCC, 116.8b-9b. A variation of this theme is that sometimes a goddess may descend to help specific individuals. This type of story almost always involves romance. Not surprisingly then, it is found mainly in the TPKC, the encyclopedic interest of which is not defined by any particular doctrinal or theological orientation. For Tu Kuang-t'ing and other Taoist masters, this kind of story would represent yet another example of the "superficially polished words of literary men." A good example is the biography of Hsüan-t'ien erh-nü (The Two Women of the Mysterious Heavens), in TPKC, no. 4, 56.349. In this connection,

let me mention another interesting case that indicates the kind of changes Taoist works made to earlier accounts. TPKC, no. 23, 59.368, is devoted to the immortal Nü-chi, citing the *Nü-hsien chuan*. It informs us that Nü-chi attained the Way after having learned "the art of nourishing one's nature and prolonging life." The account of Nü-chi in the *Lieh-hsien chuan* (no. 67, pp. 722-723), however, is more explicit: the Taoist art in question nourishes one's nature by means of "sexual intercourse." The narrative further intimates that Nü-chi set up a separate room where she entertained young men and practised her art for thirty years. As in the TPKC account, the biography of Nü-chi in YCCHL (6.9b-10a) and the shorter version in TCHC (2.13b) have both "censored" these details. For Tu Kuang-t'ing and Chao Tao-i, goddesses are much more than experts in the "arts of the bedchamber"; cf. n. 150, above.

177. TPKC, no. 7, Wei fu-jen, 58.356-361, citing *Chin-hsien lu* and an independent biography. It is not found in the two current versions of Tu Kuang-t'ing's work; but I would be most surprised if the original did not include this major figure. Perhaps because the story of Lady Wei was so widely known and readily available that the editors of the two selected versions of Tu's work did not see any need to repeat it. The TCHC account (no. 44, 3.7a-8a) is much shorter, but adds a poem by the famous poet Tu Fu (712-770) and information on the shrine of Lady Wei.

178. YCCHL, no. 4, Chao-ling Li fu-jen, 2.13b-15a; cf. the much shorter version in TCHC, no. 36, 3.3b-4a. Note that the title Chao-ling is mistakenly reversed to read Ling-chao in the latter. Lady Li is already mentioned in T'ao Hung-ching's *Chen-ling wei-yeh t'u*, p. 6a. See also TCHC, no. 45, the biography of Chiu-hua an-fei (3.8b-9b), which contains similar details.

179. TCHC, 2.13b-14b, is devoted to the wife and four daughters of Chang Tao-ling. YCCHL, 6.4a-5b, provides a much more detailed biography of Chang's wife, Sun fu-jen; cf. TPKC, 60.371-372.

180. This Taoist figure is not to be confused with the Han poet of the same name. The story of Chang Heng's wife and daughter is reported in TCHC, 2.14b-15b. The story of the daughter, Chang Yü-lan (no. 24), is very interesting; cf. the parallel--that is, different wording of the same basic story--account in TPKC, no. 31, 60.375. One of the main themes in this story will be discussed below (cf. n. 197). Where the immortals dwell is not always easy to tell. The expression "celestial existence" is thus intentionally vague. YCCC, 115.8a-9b, the biography of the Wang woman, explains that all immortals become celestial beings and "do not dwell in mountains" (9a). The similar account in TCHC (no. 97, 5.11b-13a), however, changes this to read that they all become immortals and "dwell in sacred mountains [*ling-shan*]" (12b). As a major religion, Taoism obviously cannot be reduced to any one particular set of doctrines.

181. YCCC, 115.3b; same as TCHC, no. 59, 4.4a.

182. YCCC, 115.4a; TCHC, no. 61, 4.4a-4b is slightly more detailed. Cf. the biographies of Chao Su-t'ai (TCHC, 4.1b-2a) and Chou Yüan-chih (TCHC, 4.2b). These accounts are very brief. The figures are assigned a similar position in the divine hierarchy, and all are mentioned in T'ao Hung-ching's *Chen-ling wei-yeh t'u*. In cases where individual details are lacking, I surmise, moral goodness serves as a general explanation for their spiritual perfection. The translation "hidden virtue" is Seidel's (1987).

183. YCCC, no. 4, 115.2a-3a; cf. TCHC, no. 69, 4.8b-10a, which has an extra section on the reappearance of the goddess in a later period. On Ko Hung and his father-in-law, Pao Ching, see Needham, 5.3: 75ff. Ko's "autobiography" is translated in Ware 1981.

184. TCHC, no. 28, Hsü-mu, 2.18b-19a, is turned into the elder sister of Hsü Sun, who was a founder of a major Taoist sect in the third century C.E.; cf. YCCHL, 6.1a-2a, and TPKC, 62.386-387. The second case concerns the high goddess Ma-ku (TCHC, 3.5a-b), who becomes the younger sister of Wang Fang-p'ing; cf. YCCHL, 4.10b-13a, and TPKC, 60.369-370.

185. TCHC, no. 11, 2.10a-11a; TPKC, no. 36, 61.381-382. A number of Taoist figures have come to be known by that name. Here, the TPKC account identifies Li Pa-pai as Li T'o (fl. ca. 325 C.E.). See Seidel 1969-70 for an account of this and other related figures in early Taoist history.

186. TCHC, no. 87, 5.4a-4b; TPKC, 59.367.

187. YCCHL, no. 35, 6.17a-18a; TPKC, no. 28, 60.372-374 adds a long section on a later "sighting" of the goddess in the T'ang period. Lady Fan also appears in the *Shen-hsien chuan*, which is identical to the first part of the TPKC account, up to the goddess' ascension. TCHC, 4.6a-7a, is a summary of the TPKC's longer version. Lady Fan appears in another story also; see TCHC, no. 68, Yün Ying, 4.7b-8b. This story is not included in the *Nü-hsien* section of the TPKC, but is found in 50.313-315, under the name of the male protagonist in the section on male immortals. Similarly, the story of the goddess of Yang-p'ing, in YCCC, 116.9b-11a, is recorded in TPKC, 37.235-236. Wang Fa-chin (YCCC, 115.5b-8a, and TCHC, 4.16b-19a) is mistakenly identified as a man in TPKC, 53.327. Generally, TPKC, *ch.* 1-55, contain useful information to a study of Taoist goddesses. In one story (50.309-310), for example, we read that Liu Kang, Mao Ying, the Queen Mother, Ma-ku, Hsieh Tzu-jan, and other deities gathered together in a fabulous celebration, on the night of the "Mid-autumn" festival. The section on "shamans" (*wu*), *ch.* 283, should also be useful; and at least one goddess included in TCHC (Mei-ku, 2.13a-13b) is found in the section entitled "gods" (*shen, ch.* 291-315).

188. Ch'ang Jung, in YCCHL, no. 27, 6.9a; TPKC, 59.362; TCHC, 2.8b-9a. Cf. n. 158, above.

189. See the biographies of Mao-nü (*Lieh-hsien chuan*, no. 55, p. 708; TPKC, 59.365; TCHC, 2.12b-13a), Ch'in kung-jen (TPKC, 59.365-366; TCHC combines this with the Mao-nü narrative), Yü-nü (TPKC, 63.391-392), and Hsiao-shih ju-mu (TPKC, 65.407).

190. TPKC, 63.391-392.

191. Hsü hsien-ku (YCCC, 115.12a-12b; TPKC, 70.435; TCHC, 4.13a-13b) and K'ou ksien-ku (YCCC, 115.12b-14a; TPKC, 70.435-436; TCHC, 4.19b-20b). What is equally noteworthy is that the TCHC accounts have deleted all negative references to Buddhist monks, identifying the villains as simply unruly men. This suggests that Taoist hagiographic writings do reflect different preoccupations.

192. YCCC, 116.11b-15b; TCHC, no. 50, 3.13a-15a is much shorter. Cf. TPKC, 61.380-381, biography of P'ang-nü; YCCC, 115.5b-8a, biography of Wang Fa-chin. The biography of Yang Ching-chen is the most explicit: it plainly states that her spiritual realization is due to "nature," and not "training" (TPKC, 68.423). One Taoist hagiographer at least is clearly concerned with this issue; see J. Boltz's (1987, 59) discussion of the 12th-century work by Ch'en Pao-kuang.

193. YCCC, 116.14b. In this instance, the TCHC (3.14b) retains the anti-Buddhist reference. This is probably due to the fact that earlier in the narrative Taoism, Buddhism and Confucianism are ranked in that order in a hierarchical structure, each given their place in the work of spiritual transformation.

194. TPKC, no. 56, 64.399; cf. TPKC, 65.406, the biography of Yü-ch'ing nü-tzu.

195. For example, the wife of Wu Ch'ing "stopped eating because she had a headache" (TPKC, 67.418). Also see the biography of Miao-nü, in TPKC, 67.416. For a general discussion see Maspero 1981, Schipper 1982, and Kohn 1989a.

196. See Robinet 1979 and her special study, 1979a, on this subject.

197. TCHC, no. 11, 2.10a-11a; the account of Li Chen-to in TPKC, 61.381-382, provides more information on Li's brother but omits this story. The same theme, however, can be found in the biographies of Chang Yü-lan (TPKC, 60.375; parallel version in TCHC, 2.15a), and Pao-nü (TPKC, 61.381).

198. TCHC, no. 19, biography of Chang Wen-chi, 2.14a.

199. TPKC, no. 81, Wang-shih nü, 70.436; parallel version in TCHC, no. 51, 3.15a-16a, under Wang-shih. The same theme marks the biographies of Ho hsien-ku, one of the famous "eight immortals" (TCHC, no. 95, 5.8a; TPKC, 62.390, under Ho Erh-liang, relates a different legend), and Yü hsien-ku (TCHC, no. 114, 6.9a).

200. TPKC, no. 63, 66.408-413, citing *Chi-hsien lu*; the TPKC version is also important for its anti-Buddhist sentiments. Hsieh Tzu-jan's biography in TCHC, no. 96, 5.8b-11b, is different and focuses on her studies with the T'ang dynasty Taoist master Ssu-ma Ch'eng-chen (647-735); a shorter, but similar account is also found in Shen Fen's *Hsü hsien chuan* (TT 138, HY 295), *ch.* A.16b-19a. According to the *T'ung-chih* (see n. 168 above), *ch.* 67, there was a "Separate Biography of Hsieh Tzu-jan" in three *chüan* as well.

201. TCHC, no. 98, 5.13a.

202. The biography of Yang Pao-tsung (TCHC, no. 105, 5.20a) specifically states that she was inspired by Ts'ai and Li.

203. YCCC, 116.4a-8a; the account in TPKC, 63.392 is a short summary.

204. TCHC, no. 111, 6.8a.

205. TPKC, 58.356-361; TCHC, 3.7a-8a.

206. TCHC, no. 93, under P'ei Yüan-ching, 5.6a. TPKC, 70.434, citing *Hsü hsien chuan*, has "bearing children" instead of "following her husband." Cf. *Hsü hsien chuan*, A.19b-20b.

207. TPKC, no. 70, Feng-chih, 68.425.

208. The story of Nung-yü is already found in the *Lieh-hsien chuan*, no. 35, p. 680, under Hsiao Shih. Cf. YCCHL, 6.8a-8b; TPKC, 4.25-26; TCHC, 2.11a-11b.

209. TCHC, no. 52, Tzu-su yüan-chün, 4.1a.

210. TPKC, 68.422.

211. YCCC, 116.15b-18a; slightly shorter in TPKC, 70.437-38. The pill of immortality was to be taken eight years afterward; thus Hsüeh had to endure her husband in the interim.

212. YCCHL, no. 36, 6.18a; the accounts in the *Shen-hsien chuan*, *ch.* 7, and TPKC, 60.374, are identical. A similar account is also recorded in TCHC, 4.7a-7b. Tung-ling sheng-mu and a few others are served by a "green bird," which calls to mind the story of the Queen Mother of the West.

213. TCHC, 5.5b-6b; TPKC, 70.433-434.

214. TPKC, no. 78, 70.434-435; her filial piety was of course later rewarded.

215. TPKC, no. 69, 68.423.

216. TPKC, no. 54, 64.397. Cf. the biography of Sun hsien-ku, i.e., the matriarch of the Ch'üan-chen sect of Taoism, Sun Pu-erh (1119-1183), in TCHC, 6.17a, where it is said that she "abandoned her three sons."

217. TPKC, 70.438; TCHC, no. 94, 5.6b-8a; *Hsü hsien-chuan*, A.20b-21b.

Main References

Akatsuka Kiyoshi. 1977. *Chūgoku kodai no shūkyō to bunka: In ōchō no saishi.* Tokyo: Kadokawa shoten.

Ames, Roger T. 1981. "Taoism and the Androgynous Ideal." *Historical Reflections,* special issue on "Women in China," ed., R. Guisso and S. Johannesen, 8: 21-45.

Allan, Sarah. 1981. "Sons of Suns: Myth and Totemism in Early China." *Bulletin of the School of Oriental and African Studies,* 44: 290-326.

Bodde, Derk. 1981. *Essays on Chinese Civilization.* Ed., Charles Le Blanc and Dorothy Borei. Princeton: Princeton University Press.

______. 1975. *Festivals in Classical China.* Princeton: Princeton University Press.

______. 1961. "Myths of Ancient China." In *Mythologies of the Ancient World.* Ed., S.N. Kramer. Chicago: Quadrangle Books. Pp. 367-408.

_______. 1942. "Some Chinese Tales of the Supernatural: Kan Pao and His *Sou-shen chi.*" *Harvard Journal of Asiatic Studies,* 6: 338-357. (Reprinted in Bodde 1981, 331-350).

Boltz, Judith M. 1987. *A Survey of Taoist Literature: Tenth to Seventeenth Centuries.* China Research Monograph, 32. Berkeley: Institute of East Asian Studies, University of California.

______. 1986. "In Homage to T'ien-fei." *Journal of the American Oriental Society,* 106: 211-232.

Boltz, William G. 1981. "Kung Kung and the Flood: Reverse Euhemerism in the *Yao Tien.*" *T'oung Pao,* 67: 141-153.

Cahill, Suzanne. 1986. "Performers and Female Taoist Adepts: Hsi Wang Mu as the Patron Deity of Women in Medieval China." *Journal of the American Oriental Society,* 106: 155-168.

______. 1985-86. "Reflections of a Metal Mother: Tu Kuang-t'ing's Biography of Hsi Wang Mu." *Journal of Chinese Religions*, 13-14: 127-142.

______. 1985. "Sex and the Supernatural in Medieval China: Cantos on the Transcendent Who Presides over the River." *Journal of the American Oriental Society*, 105: 197-220.

______. 1984. "Beside the Turquoise Pond: the Shrine of the Queen Mother of the West in Medieval Chinese Poetry and Religious Practice." *Journal of Chinese Religions*, 12: 19-32.

Chan, Wing-tsit, trans. 1981. *The Way of Lao Tzu*. Indianapolis: Bobbs-Merrill Company, Inc., 1963; reprint.

Chang Hua (232-300). *Po-wu chih*. Ts'ung-shu chi-ch'eng ch'u-pien edition. Shanghai, 1939.

Chang Kwang-chih. 1983. *Art, Myth, and Ritual: The Path to Political Authority in Ancient China*. Cambridge, MA: Harvard University Press.

______. 1978. *Early Chinese Civilization: Anthropological Perspectives*. Cambridge, MA: Harvard University Press.

______. 1962. "Shang-Chou shen-hua chih fen-lei." *Bulletin of the Institute of Ethnology, Academia Sinica*, 14: 47-94.

______. 1959. "Chung-kuo ch'uang-shih shen-hua chih fen-hsi yü ku-shih yen-chiu." *Bulletin of the Institute of Ethnology, Academia Sinica*, 8: 47-79.

Chao Tao-i (fl. 1300). *Li-shih chen-hsien t'i-tao t'ung-chien hou-chi*. TT 150.

Chen, Ellen M. 1974. "Tao as the Great Mother and the Influence of Motherly Love in the Shaping of Chinese Philosophy." *History of Religions*, 14: 51-64.

______. 1969. "Nothingness and the Mother Principle in Early Chinese Taoism." *International Philosophical Quarterly*, 9: 391-405.

Ch'en Kuo-fu. 1963. *Tao-tsang yüan-liu k'ao*. Enlarged edition. Peking; reprinted, Taipei, 1975.

Ch'en Meng-chia. 1936. "Ku-wen-tzu chung chih Shang Chou chi-ssu." *Yen-ching hsüeh-pao,* 19: 91-155.

______. 1936a. "Shang-tai ti shen-hua yü wu-shu." *Yen-ching hsüeh-pao,* 20: 485-576.

Cheng Te-k'un. 1960. *Archaeology in China.* Vol. 2. *Shang China.* Toronto: University of Toronto Press.

Chiang Liang-fu. 1984. *Ch'u-tz'u hsüeh lun-wen chi.* Shanghai: Ku-chi ch'u-pan she.

Chin shu. Peking: Chung-hua shu-chü, 1982.

Chow Tse-tsung. 1981. "Ku-wu tui yüeh-wu chi shih-ko fa-chan ti kung-hsien." *Tsing-hua hsüeh-pao,* New series, 13: 1-25.

______. 1979. "Chung-kuo ku-tai ti wu-i yü chi-ssu, li-shih, yüeh-wu chi shih ti kuan-hsi." *Tsing-hua hsüeh-pao,* New Series, 12: 1-59.

Chu Hsi (1130-1200). *Ch'u-tz'u chi-chu.* Reprinted, Hong Kong: Chung-hua shu-chü, 1987.

Chu T'ien-shun. 1982. *Chung-kuo ku-tai tsung-chiao ch'u-t'an.* Shanghai: Jen-min ch'u-pan she.

Chuang-tzu chi-shih. 1985. 4 vols. Ed., Kuo Ch'ing-fan. Peking: Chung-hua shu-chü, 1961; reprint.

Dubs, Homer H. 1942. "An Ancient Chinese Mystery Cult." *Harvard Theological Review,* 35: 221-240.

Eberhard, Wolfram. 1968. *The Local Cultures of South and East China.* Trans., Alide Eberhard. Leiden: E.J. Brill.

Fong Wen, ed. 1980. *The Great Bronze Age of China.* New York: Metropolitan Museum of Art.

Fracasso, Riccardo. 1988. "Holy Mothers of Ancient China: A New Approach to the Hsi-wang-mu Problem." *T'oung Pao,* 74: 1-46.

Fukui Kōjun. 1983. *Shinsenden*. Selected translations of the *Shen-hsien chuan*. Tokyo: Meitoku shuppansha.

Girardot, N.J. and John S. Major. 1985-86. "Introduction." *Journal of Chinese Religions*, "Symposium Issue: Myth and Symbol in Chinese Tradition," 13-14: 1-14.

Girardot, N.J. 1983. *Myth and Meaning in Early Taoism*. Berkeley: University of California Press.

______. 1976. "The Problem of Creation Mythology in the Study of Chinese Religion." *History of Religions*, 15: 289-318.

de Groot, J.J.M. 1982. *The Religious System of China*. 6 vols. Leiden: E.J. Brill, 1910; reprinted, Taipei: Southern Materials Center.

van Gulik, R.H. 1974. *Sexual Life in Ancient China*. Leiden: E.J. Brill, 1961; reprint.

Han shu. Peking: Chung-hua shu-chü, 1983.

Han Wu-ti nei-chuan. Ts'ung-shu chi-ch'eng ch'u-pien edition. Shanghai, 1937.

Harper, Donald. 1987. "The Sexual Arts of Ancient China as Described in a Manuscript of the Second Century B.C." *Harvard Journal of Asiatic Studies*, 47: 539-593.

Hawkes, David, trans. 1985. *The Songs of the South: An Anthology of Ancient Chinese Poems by Qu Yuan and Other Poets*. Harmondsworth: Penguin Books.

______. 1967. "The Quest of the Goddess." *Asia Major*, 13: 71-94.

Ho Ping-ti. 1975. *The Cradle of the East*. Hong Kong: Chinese University Press.

Hou Han shu. Peking: Chung-hua shu-chü, 1982.

Huai-nan tzu. SPPY. Reprinted, Taipei: Chung-hua shu-chü, 1974.

Jan Yün-hua. 1981. "The Bodhisattva Idea in Chinese Literature: Typology and Significance." In *The Bodhisattva Doctrine in Buddhism*. Ed., Leslie Kawamura. Waterloo, Ontario: Wilfrid Laurier University Press. Pp. 125-152.

_____. 1981a. "The Change of Images: The Yellow Emperor in Ancient Chinese Literature." *Journal of Oriental Studies* (Hong Kong), 19: 117-137.

_____. 1977. "The Silk Manuscripts on Taoism." *T'oung Pao*, 63: 65-84.

Kaltenmark, Maxime. 1979. "The Ideology of the T'ai-p'ing ching." In *Facets of Taoism*. Ed., Holmes Welch and Anna Seidel. New Haven: Yale University Press. Pp. 19-52.

_____, trans. 1953. *Le Lie-sien tchouan*. Peking: Université de Paris, Publications de Centre d'études sinologiques de Pékin.

Karlgren, Bernhard. 1946. "Legends and Cults in Ancient China." *Bulletin of the Museum of Far Eastern Antiquities* (Stockholm), 18: 199-365.

Keightley, David. 1985. *Sources of Shang History: The Oracle-Bone Inscriptions of Bronze Age China*. Berkeley: University of California Press, 1978; reprint.

_____. 1978. "The Religious Commitment: Shang Theology and the Genesis of Chinese Political Culture." *History of Religions*, 17: 211-225.

Kinsley, David. 1988. *The Goddesses' Mirror: Visions of the Divine from East and West*. Albany: State University of New York Press.

Knechtges, David, trans. 1982, 1987. *Wen xuan, or Selections of Refined Literature*. Vols. 1-2. Princeton: Princeton University Press.

_____. 1976. *The Han Rhapsody: A Study of the Fu of Yang Hsiung (53 B.C.-A.D. 18)*. Cambridge: Cambridge University Press.

Ko Hung (284-364). *Shen-hsien chuan*. Lung-wei pi-shu ed., 1794.

Kohn, Livia. 1989. "The Mother of the Tao." *Taoist Resources*, 1/2: 37-113.

Kohn, Livia, ed. 1989a. *Taoist Meditation and Longevity Techniques.* Ann Arbor: Center for Chinese Studies, University of Michigan.

Kominami Ichiro. 1974. "Seiōbo to shichi seki denshō." *Tōhō gakuhō*, 46: 33-81.

Kuhn, Dieter. 1984. "Tracing a Chinese Legend: In Search of the Identity of the 'First Sericulturalist'." *T'oung Pao*, 70: 213-245.

Le Blanc, Charles. 1985-86. "A Re-examination of the Myth of Huang-ti." *Journal of Chinese Religions*, 13-14: 45-63.

______. 1985. *Huai-nan tzu: Philosophical Synthesis in Early Han Thought.* Hong Kong: Hong Kong University Press.

Legge, James, trans. 1970. *The Chinese Classics*. Vol. 4. *The She King or Book of Poetry*. Hong Kong: Hong Kong University Press.

Li Hsien-chang. 1979. *Boso shinkō no kenkyū.* Tokyo: Taizan bunbutsusha.

Liu Hsiang (79-8 B.C.E.). *Lieh-hsien chuan.* Tokyo, 1975.

Lo Chin-t'ang. 1979. "Popular Stories of the Wei and Chin Periods." *Journal of Oriental Studies* (Hong Kong), 17: 1-9.

Loewe, Michael. 1979. *Ways to Paradise: The Chinese Quest for Immortality.* London: George Allen and Unwin.

______. 1978. "Man and Beast: The Hybrid in Early Chinese Art and Literature." *Numen*, 25: 97-117.

Maspero, Henri. 1981. *Taoism and Chinese Religion*. Trans., Frank Kierman, Jr. Amherst: University of Massachusetts Press.

______. 1978. *China in Antiquity*. Trans. Frank Kierman, Jr. Amherst: University of Massachusetts Press.

______. 1924. "Légendes mythologiques dan le *Chou King*." *Journal Asiatique*, 204: 1-100.

Mu T'ien-tzu chuan. Ts'ung-shu chi-ch'eng ch'u-pien edition. Shanghai, 1937.

Needham, Joseph, et al. 1956, 1959, 1974-1980. *Science and Civilisation in China*. Vols. 2, 3, 5.2 - 5.4. Cambridge: Cambridge University Press.

Overmyer, Daniel L. 1976. *Folk Buddhist Religion: Dissenting Sects in late Traditional China*. Cambridge, MA: Harvard University Press.

Paul, Diana. 1983. "Kuan-yin: Savior and Savioress in Chinese Pure Land Buddhism." In *The Book of the Goddess, Past and Present*. Ed., Carl Olsen. New York: Crossroad. Pp. 161-175.

Pirazzoli-t'Serstevens, Michèle. 1982. *The Han Dynasty*. Trans., Janet Seligman. New York: Rizzoli.

Robinet, Isabelle. 1984. *La révélation du Shangqing dans l'historie du taoisme*. 2 vols. Paris: l'École française d'Extrême-Orient.

______. 1979. *Méditation taoiste*. Paris: Dervy Livres.

______. 1979a. "Metamorphosis and Deliverance from the Corpse in Taoism." *History of Religions*, 19: 37-70.

Schafer, Edward. 1980. *The Divine Woman: Dragon Ladies and Rain Maidens in T'ang Literature*. Berkeley: University of California Press, 1973. Reprint, San Francisco: North Point Press.

______. 1977. "The Restoration of the Shrine of Wei Hua-ts'un at Lin-ch'uan in the Eighth Century." *Journal of Oriental Studies* (Hong Kong), 15: 124-137.

______. 1951. "Ritual Exposure in Ancient China." *Harvard Journal of Asiatic Studies*, 14: 130-184.

Schipper, Kristofer. 1982. *Le Corps taoiste*. Paris: Librairie Arthème Fayard.

______. 1978. "The Taoist Body." *History of Religions*, 17: 355-386.

______, trans. 1965. *Le Han-wou-ti nei-tchouan, l'empereur Wou des Han dans la légende taoiste*. Paris: l'École française d'Extrême-Orient.

Seidel, Anna. 1987. "Traces of Han Religion in Funeral Texts Found in Tombs." In Akizuki Kan'ei, ed. *Dōkyō to shūkyō bunka*. Tokyo: Hirakawa shuppansha. Pp. 21-57.

______. 1983. "Imperial Treasures and Taoist Sacraments: Taoist Roots in the Apocrypha." In *Tantric and Taoist Studies in Honour of R.A. Stein*. Vol. 2. Ed., M. Strickmann. Bruxelles: Institut Belge des Hautes Etudes Chinoises. Pp. 291-371.

______. 1982. "Tokens of Immortality in Han Graves." Review article, with an appendix by Marc Kalinowski. *Numen*, 29: 79-122.

______. 1969-70. "The Image of the Perfect Ruler in Early Taoist Messianism: Lao-tzu and Li Hung." *History of Religions*, 9: 216-247.

Sharma, Arvind, ed. 1987. *Women in World Religions*. Albany: State University of New York Press.

Shen Fen (10th cent. C.E.). *Hsü hsien chuan*. TT 138.

Shih chi. SPPY. Taipei: Chung-hua shu-chü, 1960.

Strickmann, Michel. 1979. "On the Alchemy of T'ao Hung-ching." In *Facets of Taoism*. Ed. H. Welch and A. Seidel. New Haven: Yale University Press. Pp. 123-192.

______. 1977. "The Mao Shan Revelations: Taoism and the Aristocracy." *T'oung Pao*, 63: 1-64.

Sui shu. Peking: Chung-hua shu-chü, 1982.

Sung, Marina. 1981. "The Chinese *Lieh-nü* Tradition." *Historical Reflections*, 8: 63-74.

T'ai-p'ing kuang-chi, chüan 56-70, *Nü-hsien*. Peking, 1981.

T'ao Hung-ching (456-536). *Chen-ling wei-yeh t'u*. TT 73.

Teiser, S.F. 1985-86. "Engulfing the Bounds of Order: The Myth of the Great Flood in *Mencius*." *Journal of Chinese Religions*, 13-14: 15-43.

Tsung Li, and Liu Ch'ün. 1987. *Chung-kuo min-chien chu-shen*. Hopei: Jen-min ch'u-pan she.

Tu Kuang-t'ing (850-933). *Yung-ch'eng chi-hsien lu*. TT 560-561, 701.

Waley, Arthur. 1973. *The Nine Songs: A Study of Shamanism in Ancient China*. London, 1955; reprint, San Francisco: City Lights Books.

Wang Hsiao-lien. 1972. "Jih-pen hsüeh-che ti Chung-kuo ku-tai shen-hua yen-chiu." *Ta-lu tsa-chih*, 45/1: 31-38.

Wang Ming. 1979. *T'ai-p'ing ching ho-chiao*. Peking: Chung-hua shu-chü, 1960; reprint.

Ware, James R. 1981. *Alchemy, Medicine and Religion in the China of A.D. 320: The Nei P'ien of Ko Hung*. Cambridge: MIT Press, 1966; reprint, New York: Dover.

Watson, Burton, trans. 1968. *The Complete Works of Chuang Tzu*. New York: Columbia University Press.

Wen-hsüan. Zenshaku Kanbun taikei edition. Tokyo, 1974.

Wen I-to. 1959. *Shen-hua yü shih*. Peking: Chung-hua shu-chü.

Yang K'uan. 1982. "Chung-kuo shang-shih tao-lun." In *Ku-shih pien*. Vol. 7A. Ed., Lü Ssu-mien and T'ung Shu-yeh. Reprint, Shanghai: Ku-chi ch'u-pan she. Pp. 65-421.

Yu Anthony C. 1987. "'Rest, Rest, Perturbed Spirit' Ghosts in Traditional Chinese Prose Fiction," *Harvard Journal of Asiatic Studies*, 47: 397-434.

Yü, Ying-shih. 1987. "'O Soul, Come Back!' A Study in the Changing Conceptions of the Soul and Afterlife in Pre-Buddhist China," *Harvard Journal of Asiatic Studies*, 47: 363-95.

_____. 1964-65. "Life and Immortality in the Mind of Han China," *Harvard Journal of Asiatic Studies*, 25: 80-122.

Yüan K'o, ed. *Shan-hai ching chiao-chu*. Shanghai: Ku-chi ch'u-pan she, 1983.

Yüan K'o. 1982. *Ku shen-hua hsüan-shih*. Peking: Jen-min wen-hsüeh ch'u-pan she.

THE TWENTY-ONE TĀRĀS: FEATURES OF A GODDESS PANTHEON IN MAHĀYĀNĀ BUDDHISM

Terence P. Day

Tārā is the supreme goddess in Northern Buddhism. For nearly fourteen centuries her cult has been Tibet's national religion. Tibet's Tārā-cult is also a contemporary expression of an ancient goddess devotion that is reflected in South Asia's ancient "Divine Mother" cults of Caṇḍī, Cuṇḍā-Devī, Durgā, Gaurī, Kālī, Lakṣmī (or Śrī), Pārvatī, Sītā, Sarasvatī and others, and also in Western Asia's goddess-cults of Aphrodite, Artemis (Diana), Athena, Cybele (Kybele), Hera, Ishtar, Isis and others.[1]

In India from the third century C.E. Hindu goddesses and their cults were being assimilated into Buddhism. The most popular of the goddesses was Durga, whose many names included acolyte cult figures such as Cuṇḍā (Cuntī) and Tārā. By the eighth century C.E., these and many other Hindu and Buddhist gods and goddesses had become organized into a complex Mahāyāna Buddhist pantheon. Nevertheless, within the Tibetan theistic system, the goddesses especially had become conceptually organized as a Tārā-pantheon, a hierarchical system of devis having the name "Tārā" (Tibetan "Dölma") in their titles on account of being regarded as emanations and relatives of a principal Tārā, identified as "Vajratārā" or "Mahātārā."[2] By the twelfth century, this "Tārā-pantheon" had became Tibetan Buddhism's principal theological system, with the devotional prestige of the Mahātārā (supreme Tārā) and her Tārā emanations superceding every other group of Tibetan deities. The Mahātārā has remained Tibet's sovereign deity even to the present day. She is worshipped by all ranks and classes of Tibetan, Nepalese and Sikhimese peoples. Likening her to "The Virgin Mary of Roman Catholicism", A. L. Waddell explained,

> Dölma is one of the most popular of the deities, and a large proportion of the laity can repeat her services hy heart. She is known to Northern Buddhism by the Sanskrit name of Tārā of which Dölma is a literal Tibetan translation meaning "The Unloosener (of difficulties)" or "The Saviouress." And it is to this attribute of being

> ever ready to help and easily approachable that she owes her popularity. Most of the other deities cannot be approached without the mediation of a lama; but the poorest layman or woman may secure the immediate attention of Dölma by simply appealing to her direct.[3]

The people regularly and continually recite her numerous honorific titles like a *mantra* (litugical formula). She is "Holy and noble Tārā," "Holy, blessed, noble Tārā...Long-eyed Mother of the Lord," "Venerable Tārā" and "Quick Brave Tārā". She is "Tārā our mother," and "The Lady of Great Compassion."[4] She is also the goddess whom the Buddhas and Bodhisattvas venerate, the Creatrix of the Buddhas and Bodhisattvas, the Great Mother (Tib., *sgrol-ma)* of the Tibetan peoples and the Lady with the 108 names. They call her especially *Tārāmaulakṣobhyabhūṣitā,* "The Saviour-goddess adorned by the chief of the Akṣobhyas", and "The Most Holy Devout Saviouress" (Tib., *dam-ishig sgrol-ma).*[5] She is "the goddess who lets herself be seen" especially because, in speedy answer to cries for help, she frequently appears in the vicinity of her devotees.[6] K. K. Dasgupta remarked, "The Buddhist goddess Tārā...is the most popular goddess in the Buddhist pantheon."[7] In the forward to Stephan Beyer's *The Cult of Tārā,* Kees W. Bolle stated,

> The image of the goddess Tārā...is of great importance to our understanding of Tibetan religion. Tārā is the principal superhuman being of Tibet who might be called *divine* without further qualification. She is prayed to by millions; her help in all adversity is divine... Tārā was, had always been, and still is the almighty support of her devotees who address her. In fact, she is mightier than Buddhas and Bodhisattvas...the mother who gives birth to all the Buddhas.[8]

With reference to her cult, Stephan Beyer explained,

> The worship of the goddess Tārā is one of the most widespread of Tibetan cults, undifferentiated by sect, education, class or position; from the highest to the lowest, the Tibetans find with this goddess a personal and enduring relationship unmatched by any other single deity, even among those of their gods more potent in appearance or more profound in symbolic association... Thus, to understand something of her cult is to understand something of the whole structure of Tibetan culture and religion.[9]

Singly, in her supreme form, she is Mahātārā (Great Tārā) and Āryatārā (Noble Tārā) whom all the Buddhas and Bodhisattvas venerate. She is the exalted progenitor of the "all-inclusive pantheon of Mahāyāna Buddhism."[10] As the Mahātārā (supreme Tārā) she is the embodiment of the *karuṇā* (compassion) of her sire, the Bodhisattva Avalokiteśvara, in the "family" (*kula*) of the Dhyani-Buddha Amitābha.[11] But, as the goddess with 108 names, she is both one and many, with numerous subordinate forms and manifestations. "Tārā", accordingly, has become the generic name for all Mahāyāna Buddhist goddesses, whether or not "Tārā" is stated in their written names and specific titles.[12]2

The Tārā theology reflects the assumption that all goddesses are emanational members of her extended family. The Mahātārā is the progenitor of their unique forms, their distinctive identities, their family pedigrees and conjugal lineages, and of the entire congregation which comprises this significant "Tārā pantheon" within the greater pantheon of Mahāyāna Buddhism.[13] But, D. C. Bhattacharyya inferred, from Tārā references in the *Nārāyaṇaparipṛccha* and *Dhāraṇī-Saṁgraha* manuscripts, that Mahāmāyāvijavāhinī,"the Buddhist goddess of war" is "the Supreme Form (*virādrūpa*) of the goddess Tārā." For, "She is...venerable and worshipful not only to the gods and the divine mothers...but also to Vajradhara...the Ādi-Buddha or the originator of the five Dhyānī Buddhas", and is known also as Padmapāṇiprīye *Avalokiteśvara* (Beloved of Padmani Avalokiteśvara)."[14] Moreover, like the Ādi-Buddha whose five principal "aspects" are the Dhyānī Buddhas, so also the primal Tārā has "three principal aspects", whose personal names are Ugratārā (Mahācinakramatārā), Vasudhārā-Tārā and Prajñāpāramitā-Tārā. Each of these has eight, nine or ten "aspects" or attendant goddesses. The goddess-attendants of Prajñāpāramitā-Tārā, for example, are Puspatārā, Dīpatārā, Gaudhatārā, Dhūpātārā, Vajrāṅkuśī-Tārā, Vajrapāśī-Tārā, Vajrasphoṭā-Tārā and Vajraghamtā-Tārā. But the primal Tārā is also the divine progenitor of the five protective goddesses (*Pañcarakṣā-s*), named Pratisarā, Mayūrī, Śitavatī, Sāhasrapramardinī and Mantrānusārinī.[15]

The history of the Tārā cult is the record of its progressive assimilation and transformation of Hindu and Buddhist goddess-cults in and beyond mainland India into a distinctive, heterogeneous, ideological, ritual and institutional system. It is apparent that the assimilated Hindu goddesses retained their original identities and functions, despite receiving the Buddhist names and iconographical insignia of several smaller and larger subgroups of the Mahātārās, such as "The Tārās of the five colours," "The Twenty-one Tārās" and "the 108 Tārās," under the sovereignty of the Mahātārā or "goddess with 108 names."

Given these manifold features and the apparent ubiquity and popularity of the Tārā cult among Tibet's monks as well as laity, it seems more appropriate to refer to Tibet's national religion as "Tārāism" rather than "Lāmaism", particularly since the latter is the high tradition which has never been exclusively practised by the monks who, in any case, have never comprised more than one-sixth of Tibet's adult male population.[16]

The present study of Tārāism offers a review and revision of recent scholarship on Tārā worship in Northern Buddhism, information on the ancient roots of Tārā worship in the pre-Brahmanical and Brahmanical religions of India, and insights on the origins and development of goddess worship in Eastern and Western Asia. More specifically, in this study I attempt (a) to integrate and otherwise up-date current information about the goddess Tārā and her worship found in scores of modern historical, textual, mythological, liturgical and iconographical resources, (b) to contrast the contemporary East Asian Buddhist cult of Tārā with its Hindu and non-Hindu counterparts in South and East Asia, and (c) to review and test the empirical bases and historical grounds of current theories about goddess-worship in the ancient world, particularly by considering the functions of gender symbolism in ancient theological systems.[17]

Sources for the Study of Tārāism

Many important historical and interpretational questions concerning the person and the cult of goddess Tārā have not been satisfactorily answered; hence, they remain open for new inquiries and new discoveries. The most recently discovered textual, ritual, archeological, anthropological, sociological, artistic and architectural information, new methods of literary analysis and criticism, and advances in systematic iconographical interpretation are revolutionizing the field of modern historical inquiry into religions, including goddess worship in general and the Tārā-cult in particular.

The primary sources for the historical inquiry include numerous *thangkas* (large painted scrolls adorning temple and monastery walls), painted murals and domestic paintings which have Āryatārā (The Noble Tārā) as their centrally prominent deity, holding court before numerous attendant deities. The variety and ubiquity of these paintings indicate the widespread and unshakeable popularity of Tārā worship in Mahāyāna Buddhism. The earliest surviving examples of these, in the Buddhist Cave 2 of Ellora in Western India, date from the fifth century C.E. Many thousands of illuminated manuscripts, privately held or in monastic collections, emphasize the centrality of Tārā in Tibetan Buddhist faith and devotion. These "holy pictures" have made the face of the goddess Tārā the most familiar and the most beloved of all the Tibetan deities.

The simplest instruments for realizing the intimate presence of the goddess are countless privately-owned stone icons and bronze images, which travellers carry and use as protective amulets and set up on makeshift altars and household shrines for daily worship. Images of these figurines can also be mentally conjured during informal ritual acts or through meditations which are part of the more elaborate formal procedures found in the Buddhist canonical Sanskrit, Tibetan and Chinese ritualistic texts.

The texts are indispensable sources of iconographical and other information about the identity, character and status of the goddess in Tibetan Buddhism, her relation to other Buddhist deities within the Mahāyāna Buddhist pantheon, and the popular perception of her functions as the Saviouress, Protectress and Benefactress of the Tibetan people. The most important of the ritualistic texts are the *Niṣpānnayogāvalī* (eleventh-century), the *Sādhanamala* (twelfth-century) and the *Sādhanasamuccaya* (twelfth-century).[18] The *Sādhanasaṁgraha* and the *Dharmakośa-saṁgraha* contain additional information which scholars have found essential for interpreting correctly the iconography of Tārā and other deities in the Mahāyānā theistic system.

The *Sādhanamālā* is, as its title suggests, a string-necklace (*mālā*) of formal ritual-procedures (*sādhanas*) which lead toward "visualizing" or psychically interiorizing the deities. The procedures demand the worshipper's conscious efforts toward "visualizing" or mentally introjecting the manifest forms of the principal Buddhist deities, complete with their identifying symbolic insignia, attributes, postures and colorations. Because each *sādhana* (ritual procedures) contains identifying iconographical summaries of a deity's gracious and powerful attributes, and often include references to the family *(kula)* of the deity, the user of the *sādhana* knows indubitably which deity is being invoked by its ritual. For this reason, the *sādhanas* are essential for interpreting keys to the the entire Mahāyāna pantheon and, therefore, to its component Tārā-pantheon also. Moreover, the numerous *sādhanas* in which the Tārās principally are invoked comprise a distinctive resource for retracing the Tārā-theology's complexity as well as ascertaining the character of the Māhatārā's indisputable supremacy in the "innumerable worlds of the quarters" among "innumerable Buddhas and Bodhisattvas...gods and the Tathāgatas."[19]

The kind of iconographical information which the *sādhanas* yield is illustrated by the procedure for worshipping the Red Tārā, Aṣṭabhuja-Kurukullā.

> The worshipper should think himself as goddess Kurukullā who is eight-armed, red in colour, sits in the *vajraparyaṅka* attitude [seated-meditation or *dhyānāsana* pose], on the orb of the sun over the lotus with eight petals and resides in the sanctum; she displays the *Trailokyavijayamudrā* [hand-gesture of victory over the three worlds] in

her first pair of hands, and shows in the other right hands, *ankuśa* [elephant goad], the arrow drawn up to the ear and the *varada* pose [boon-granting mudrā]. In the remaining left hands she holds the noose, the bow and the *Utpala* [blue, closed night-lotus]; she is decked in all kinds of ornaments.[20]

The eleventh-century compilation by Mahapandita Abhayakara Gupta, titled *Niṣpānnayogāvalī*, is, in B. Bhattacharyya's opinion, iconographically more informative than the *Sādhanamālā* because "the material presented...is more varied, more extensive and more prolific."[21] It is a compilation of twenty-six *maṇḍalas* or sacred "cosmograms" used in esoteric (*tāntric*) ritual and meditations.[22] These cosmograms (*maṇḍalas*) show the symbolic interrelations of gods and goddesses within the Buddhist pantheon. But, the *Niṣpannayogāvalī* additionally provides a "great volume" of iconographical information and "full descriptions" of the Buddhist deities including the twenty-one Tārās.[23] The following translated piece by B. Bhattacharyya displays this descriptive function clearly:

Goddess Vajratārā is of golden yellow colour. She is four-faced. The principal face is golden in colour, the right is white, the one behind is blue and the left red. She has eight arms. In her four right hands she shows the *vajra* [diamond/thunderbolt], the noose, the arrow and the conch. In the four left [hands] she has the yellow night lotus, the bow, the goad, and the raised *Tarjanī* [*mudrā* showing a closed fist with raised index finger in a "menacing attitude"].[24]

Numerous esoteric (*tāntric*) texts such as the Heruka, Hevajra and Vajravāharī Tantras held in libraries, monasteries and "private houses" are, in Bhattacharyya's opinion, "an inexhaustive field for research and original work on Buddhist iconography alone" but especially on the iconography of the twenty-one Tārās.[25] The more important texts are dated from as early as the third century C.E. Many have miniature drawings and paintings of Buddhist gods and goddesses showing their identifying symbolic insignia and gestures. Illuminated *Prajñāpāramitā* and *Pañcarakṣā* manuscripts which predate the *Sādhanamālā*, and privately-owned illuminated ritual texts also, reflect the widespread devotional popularity of the goddess Tārā in Nepalese and Tibetan Buddhism. Mention has already been made of countless unpainted stone images of the goddess which Tibetans use as protective talismen of Tārā in her role as the great protectress from natural and spiritual dangers and as the most bountiful benefactress.

Finally, there is a rich folklore of testimonial to Tārā's gracious appearances to her devotees in their times of need, which has been illustrated both in Tārānāth's sixteenth-century history of Buddhism in India and by modern western historians of Tārāism. This too is part of the rich primary source material on Tārā and her worship in the religion of Tibetan and Nepalese Buddhists.

The historical and interpretive study of ancient and historic goddess worship has benefitted considerably from investigative and descriptive models focussed on the cult of Tārā by western and oriental scholars. These include both essays and monographs.[26] Among them, L. A. Waddell's studies of Tibetan and Nepalese Lāmaism have long served as comprehensively reliable, scholarly introductions to the distinctive Buddhism of Tibet and Sikhim.[27] Moreover, A. Foucher's original studies of the Buddha image laid foundations for a reliable and much relied on general iconography of Buddhism and specialized iconography of Tārāism.[28] Alice Getty drew generously upon Waddell's exposition of the great "Hymn of Praises to the Twenty-one Tārās" for her own interpretation of Tārāism in *The Gods of Northern Buddhism,* where her incomplete yet systematic classifications of the Mahāyāna Buddhist pantheon, the Tārā-goddess system, and the iconography and cult of Tārā's consort, Avalokiteśvara in Tibetan, Chinese and Japanese monuments are informatively valuable.[29]

In a reference to A. K. Coomaraswamy's 1935 study, *Elements of Buddhist Iconography,* D. C. Bhattacharyya noted,

> Although he [Coomeraswamy] did not study the iconography of any particular god or goddess of *tāntric* Buddhism, his scholarly analysis of the historical and socio-psychological aspects of the various myths and symbols connected with Buddhist iconography, and his masterly exposition of the various factors leading to the origin of the image of the Buddha are veritable guidelines for subsequent scholars to follow.[30]

Benoytosh Bhattacharyya's "favourite book", *The Indian Buddhist Iconography,* is a comprehensive study of Mahāyāna Buddhist iconography in the ritual contexts of the *Sādhanamālā,* the *Sādhanasamuccaya* and the *Niṣpannayogāvalī.* In his 1968 revised edition of *The Indian Buddhist Iconography,* Bhattacharyya admitted drawing considerable and indispensable help from Walter Eugene Clark's "two sumptuous volumes of the *Two Lamaistic Pantheons,*" which included photographic reproductions of "766 preserved [Buddhist] images or inscribed pedestals" in the Pao-hsiang Lou Lama-Temple in Peiping (Beijing), and 360 plaques in "a unique [18th-century?] manuscript in the National Library in Peiping entitled *Chu Fo P'u-sa Shen Hsiang Tsan* ["Eulogy on the various Buddhas, Bodhisattvas and Saintly (sagely) Figures]. Yet, by far, the most complete reconstruction of the faith and practice of Tārāism in Tibet was titled and published in 1973 by Stephan Beyer as *The Cult of Tārā: Magic and Ritual in Tibet,* which Frank Reynolds declared to be "unquestionably the most thorough work on the cult and rituals associated with the goddess Tārā, giving full descriptions of ritual practices, explanations, interpretations and translations of cultic texts."[31] Moreover, Beyer updated Getty's bibliography of continental European and Asian writings on the history, literature, religion, art and iconography of Northern Buddhism relating to the cult of Tārā.

The History of the Buddhist Cult of Tārā

The region in which the cult of Tārā originated and from which it spread throughout mainland India and beyond remains a contentious historical issue among scholars of Buddhism. Both the etymology of the word "tārā" and the weight of archaeological, socio-anthropological, textual and historical evidence point toward its origin in the coastal region of eastern India, and probably near the Bay of Bengal. From thence, it must have spread inland throughout southern, western and northern India, and seaward along the maritime trade-routes linking the Bay of Bengal and Amrāvatī in Southeast India with mainland Southeast Asia. Its expansion in India may have been through progressive assimilations of aboriginal local and regional goddess cults. These may have even become acolyte Durgā-cults prior to being adopted into a distinctive Buddhist cult of Durgā/Tārā in northwestern India and the central Himalayan region.[32]

When retracing the history of Tārāism, it is necessary to describe not only the cultural context of goddess-cult syncretism by Brahmanism and Buddhism in ancient India, but also the interchanging of disparate religious concepts and beliefs between Hindus and Buddhists in India and in the Himalayan region, especially in Nepal and in Tibet from whence the Tārā devotion spread to Sikhim and to China, then from China to Japan. This initiative probably began with Buddhism's adoption of local Hindu and aboriginal goddess figures and their cults and, eventually, the hierarchical pattern of the Brahmanical pantheon. In a study of "The Goddess Tārā," D. C. Bhattacharyya gave cogent evidence of this Buddhist borrowing. There is strong scholarly agreement, moreover, that Tārā began her early career as a regional cult figure as a form of the goddess Durgā, centuries prior to her promotion into a distinctive Buddhist *Tārā-devī*. Caṇḍī (Cuntī), another form of Durgā, became recognized in Buddhism as the Tārā Parnaśabarī, Cunda as Mārīcī, and both Sarasvatī and Lakṣmī as Vasudhara. Bhattacharyya inferred from these and other examples,

> Almost all the manifestations of the goddess Tārā...are found to be conceptually akin to, if not derived from, some [Brahmanical] concept or form already known. The

> Buddhist iconographers, in numerous cases, only took note of the already floating concepts or forms and adapted them to Buddhist usage. The various ideologies and iconographic formulations pertaining to the Supreme Female Energy (*śakti*) as obtained in the Brahmanical pantheon, served as a veritable repertoire to derive the ingredients for the formulation of the concept and iconography of the goddess Tārā of the Buddhist pantheon. But, it has to be admitted that the concept of the Supreme Goddess, both of the Brahmanical faith as well as of Buddhism, can be traced back to a common heritage. This is true of almost all the important theologies of India.[33]

Certain brahmanical and puranic texts clearly indicate the primeval identity and mythical lineage of the goddess prior to the adoption of her cult into Hinduism. The texts represent her as the spouse of the sagely Ṛgvedic deity, Bṛhaspati, who, as lord of the creative Word, pierced the darkness of chaos and ignorance. According to a minor Hindu legend, the goddess confessed to Lord Brahmā that she became pregnant after being abducted by the ritual deity, Soma. The child born to her was Budha whose name was later adapted as Buddha.[34] Moreover, the same tradition connected the goddess Tārā with several important Hindu deities (*devīs*), including the goddess Kālī and the goddess Bhairavī, listed her among the esoteric (*tāntric*) goddess-incarnations (*devī-avatāras*), and also recognized her as one of the "ten great manifestations" (*daśa-mahā-vidyas*) of Lord Viṣṇu or of Lord Śiva. In the *Mahābhagavata-purāṇa*, for example, the goddess Tārā is the "great manifestation" (*mahāvidya*) of the goddess Sati the primary spouse of Śiva. But, in the *Devī-purāṇa* and in several *tantraśāstra* texts, which developed through Mahāyāna influences during the tenth to the twelfth centuries, the goddess Tārā is represented as a form of Umā the Goddess (Devī) of the mountains. This connection of Tārā with Umā suggests the existence of an aboriginal Himalayan Tārā-cult centuries prior to its incorporation into the cult of goddess Durgā and later transformation into the Buddhist cult of Tārā.

Nevertheless, there is no indisputable puranic and esoteric (*tāntric*) evidence that a Hindu cult of Tārā existed in India independently of and contemporaneously with the Durgā cult. Instead, evidence in the *Mahābhārata*, in the *Brāhmanda-purāṇa* whose date of composition is close to the *Mahābhārata*, and in later Puranas and Tantras strongly support K. K. Dasgupta's conclusion that a regionally popular goddess cult of Tārā thrived as an acolyte Durgā-cult prior to being separately appropriated by Mahāyāna Buddhism.[35] Moreover, the prominence of Tārā's representation as a Buddhist goddess in twenty-five Buddhist paintings in the second Buddhist cave-temple of Ellora suggests that the Buddhist transformation of the Hindu cult of Durgā/Tārā may have occurred sometime between the third and the fifth centuries C.E. in those regions of Western and Northern India and beyond where Mahāyāna Buddhist influence was dominant.

During the sixth to the eighth centuries, the primary form of Tārāism spread and flourished in the Mahāyāna Buddhist regions of central and western India as reflected in the beneficent serene-faced (*saumya*) Tārās portrayed in the Buddhist cave-temple murals of Ellora, Aurangabad and Ajanta. During the eighth to the twelfth centuries of the Pālā maritime dynasty, the cult spread from Gauda in Bengal and throughout southeast Asia as far as Java. Indeed, Pālā patronage greatly enhanced the popularity of the cult and the prestige of the goddess Tārā as Queen of the oceans, Star of the seas and Saviour-Protectress of seafaring travellers. General geographical expansion also, through cult-accretion and cultural diffusion, carried the Buddhist cult of Tārā along India's northern and southern trade-routes into Ceylon, Burma and Indonesia, throughout the Himalayan region of Nepal, Tibet and Sikhim, and eastward via China into Mongolia and Japan. This supports D. C. Sircar's opinion,

> The goddess Tārā appears to have been originally worshipped by some aboriginal people (probably of Eastern India) and was adopted in both the Brahmanical and Buddhist pantheons in the early centuries of the Christian era. Several goddesses, including a few mongoloid ones, merged in Tārā in the course of time.[36]

In his description of the Tārā cult in Tibet, Stephan Beyer followed the majority scholarly opinion that the originator of "the universal veneration for the goddess" in Tibet was the Indian Buddhist monk, Atīśa, who arrived there in 1042 C.E.[37] But, the Tibetan legend about the earlier origin of the cult of Tārā suggests that a dual "formal" or royal and "informal" or popular history of Tibetan Tārāism is needed to account for Tārāism's introduction into Tibet in different places and during different time-periods. Travellers and pilgrims may have carried along the trade routes a popular form of Tārā worship into Nepal and Tibet as early as the fifth or the sixth centuries when the cult was already strong in India. Thereafter, even more than a century later, a court-cult of Tārā was introduced into Tibet by the Nepalese princess Tri'itsun, wife of the Tibetan King Srong-btsan sgam-po (ca. 600-649 C.E.). But not before the eleventh century was an Indian monastic cult of Tārā instituted in Tibet by Atīśa. It is nevertheless said of Atīśa that, throughout his life he had been possessed by "visions of the goddess...the patron deity of his former lives" and that it was she who persuaded him to go to Tibet. There he composed four out of 117 works specifically devoted to Tārā and "on these four...was built almost the entire structure of her Tibetan cult." Atīśa moreover, translated into Tibetan seventy-seven Indian Buddhist texts of which six dealt with the goddess. But he apparently ignored certain esoteric (*tāntric*) Tārā-scriptures that describe "the appearance, mantras and rites of Green Tārā, the original form of the goddess."[38]

During the second half of the eleventh century, Darmadra introduced the great hymn of *Homages to the Twenty-one Tārās,* which all scholars agree is the most important canonical text of the Tibetan Tārā-cult. The popularization in Tibet of other esoteric (*tāntric*) scriptures of the Green Tārā appears to have been initiated by "the reverend Jñangpa" (i.e., Tāranāth, born 1575).[39] In any case, by the beginning of the fourteenth century, the Mahātārā had become supremely the Madonna of the Tibetans, and her cult a flourishing popular tradition owned by every sect and practised by the entire Buddhist monastic and lay population.

Despite the weighty empirical evidence supporting the thesis of the cult of Tārā's Brahmanical-Indian origins, some scholars in the Calcutta 1965 symposium traced its origins elsewhere. N. N. Bhattacharya, for example, cited Sylvain Levi, P. C. Bagchi, H. P. Shastri, K. H. van Gulik and Joseph Needham as supporters of his contention that both a Brahmanical esoteric cult of the *Devī* (goddess) and a Buddhist esoteric cult of the Tārā developed within a Taoist form of Chinese Tāntrism.[40] But, a simpler and more plausible argument would be that assimilation of one or more local and regional goddess cults in China with imported varieties of Indian Buddhist Tārāism produced unusual and distinctive Chinese versions of Tārā-worship such as the cult of Kuan-yin.

On the other hand, H. P. Śāstri cited a popular "Buddha-Vaśiṣṭha legend" in the *Brahmayamālā* to support his theory that a primitive, pre-Brahmanical and pre-Buddhist, aboriginal goddess cult on the China-Tibet border was transformed by the legendary Nāgārjuna into a esoteric (*tāntric*) Buddhist cult of Tārā sometime during the second or the third century C.E. Sastri also referred to a passage in the *Svatantra*-tantra which states that "Tārā-Nīlā-Saraswatī" was born in a great lake on the western slope of Mount Meru. Śāstri located this in the region of Ladakh. He concluded that "Tārā worship originated somewhere towards Ladakh," from whence it entered India, Tibet, Sikhim and China.[41]

But the relatively late date of Śāstri's textual citations have weakened his arguments. The more convincing argument by K. K. Dasgupta, which D. C. Sircar preferred, is that the Tārā cult originated in rural western India and became extensively popular prior to being "adopted into the all-India Brahmanical and Buddhist pantheons in the early centuries of the Christian era."[42] Thereafter, its expansion proceeded through assimilation with other regional goddess cults wherever Mahāyāna Buddhism was dominant. Moreover, this eclectic fusion of various goddess-cults geographically expanded her popular status, numerically multiplied her diverse names and forms, structurally complicated her manifold pantheon, and richly sophisticated the complex theology of the twenty-one Tārās.[43]

The Symbolic Structure of Tārāism

The numerous symbolic forms of the goddess Tārā's representations in Buddhist paintings and sculptures indicate her manifold functions, complex identity and exalted status within the Mahayana Buddhist pantheon.[44] Like the paintings, bronzes and other images of her "Great Mother" counterparts in India's Śaiva, Vaiṣṇava and Tāntrika pantheons, the earlier representations of the goddess Tārā portrayed her alone in either sitting or in standing postural "attitudes" (*āsanas*), while showing her beneficent and protective powers and graces through certain hand-gestures (*mudrās*) and arm-postures (*hastās*). In later representations, however, she is not alone but appears standing or sitting close to the Bodhisattva Avalokiteśvara; or else she is represented as the *yum*-reflex of a Buddha or a Bodhisattva, particularly of the green Dhyānī Buddha Amogasiddhi. Nevertheless, her diverse postural forms and numerous symbolic "attributes" reflect the ubiquitous universal presence of a complex divine figure having infinite power over the three-hundred, nine-hundred or four-thousand Buddhas, Bodhisattvas and *Lo-hans* (Chinese for *arhats* or saints) of the Mahāyāna Buddhist pantheon.

The lineages of the Tārās within the respective families (*kulas*) of the Dhyānī Buddhas determine their symbolic colors and other recognition-symbols such as the open and closed lotuses, the *vajra* (thunderbolt/diamond) and the *cakra* (*dharma*-wheel or disc). The chromatic symbolism in particular reflects her interior or spiritual powers, while the arm, hand gestures and ornaments display her beneficent and protective graces. The bodily "attitudes" (*asanas*) of the sitting, standing, kneeling, walking and dancing Tārās represent their activities in the world and in the lives of their worshipping devotees. The serene (*saumya*) facial expressions of the Green and the White Tārās display their divine benevolence, while their fierce or *mahāmayavijayavāhinī* attitudes and expressions indicate their protective guardianship of the Buddhist teachings.

As the fifth-century representations in the Ellora cave paintings show only the serene-faced Green and White Tārās, this suggests that the fierce-faced Tārās were later Buddhist tāntrika developments. The typical symbol of the serene Tārās is a closed lotus or else an open multiflowered lotus in the left hand "signifying that day or night one or the other soothes human suffering and guides people to wisdom and salvation," while the right hand exhibits the gift-bestowing gesture (*vara[da]*-mudrā).[45] These Tārās might also be represented standing, sitting, dancing and in other bodily postures (*āsanas*) but especially the in the *vajra-paryaṇkāsana* and the *lalitāsana* positions.[46] Moreover, their most repeated hand-gestures (*mudrās*) are the boon-granting *vara[da]-mudrā* and the two-handed *abhaya-mudrā*, or gesture of protection.[47] Many Tārās also display the typical insignia of a Bodhisattva: lotus, sword, whip, goad, jewel, conch and abundant wavy hair. Less frequently, a Tārā displays the typical folded-hands *mudrā* of the consort of Avalokiteśvara.

Especially in medieval representations of the tenth, eleventh and twelfth centuries, the Tārās display various supplementary sitting, standing and moving postures while holding additional emblems in four, eight, or ten hands. For example, in three of her right hands a Tārā typically holds the *vajra* (thunderbolt), an arrow and a conch shell, while her fourth right hand displays the *varada-mudrā*. In each of her left hands she holds either the blue lotus, a bow (sometimes with an arrow), and an elephant-goad, while her fourth left hand exhibits the *tarjani-mudrā*, which is a clenched fist with raised index-finger.[48]

Among her numerous emanations, the green and the white Tārās reflect her serene (*saumya*) and benevolently gracious aspect, while yellow, blue and red Tārās display her awesome protective (*mahāmayavijayavāhinī*) aspect.[49] Among these, the green Tārās are the most popular in Tibet and the white Tārās in China. The green Tārās are recognized by the image of the green Dhyāni Buddha, Amoghasiddhi, in their tiaras. The best known Tārās in this group are Khadiravanī Tārā, Mahāśrī Tārā and Dhanada Tārā. Among the yellow Tārā emanations of the Dhyānī-Buddha Ratnāsambhava is the four-faced and eight-armed Vajratārā whose images were widely dispersed throughout India and Nepal. She is popular in China as Aṣṭabhuja Vajratārā.[50] Her typical emblems are the *vajra* (thunderbolt), the arrow, conch-shell, blue lotus, bow and elephant goad held in six of her eight hands. Her remaining right hand displays her gift-bestowing *varada-mudrā* and her left hand the threatening or guarding *tarjani-mudrā*. Such standard iconographical features are essential for correctly identifying the goddess because there are exceptions to her usual blue color-symbolism, particularly in *maṇḍala*-type representations showing her in the company of eight or ten other goddesses.[51] The goddess Prasanntārā, for example, carries the symbolic yellow color of the Dhyānī Buddha Ratnāsambhava when she is alone; but when she appears in a group her symbolic color is red.[52]

Kurukullā continues to be the most widely revered of the Red Tārā emanations of the Dhyanī-Buddha Amitābha. This single-faced deity with six (or two, four or eight) arms also bears the praenomen Śukla, Tārodbhava, Uḍḍiyāna, Hevajrakrama and Kalpoktā. Among these, Kalpoktā Kurukullā is the most popular.[53] Her fierce features are outdone by the awesome blue Tārā-*devīs* who carry the symbolic color of the Dhyānī Buddha Akṣobhya. The most renowned of these protector-deities is Ugratārā also called Mahācīna Tārā, the Tārā of Great China.[54] This goddess apparently became re-incorporated into the Hindu pantheon under the name of Tārā. In later Hindu tantrika literature, she is recognized as one of the *Daśa Mahāvidyas* (Ten Great Manifestations) of the *Mahādevī* or primal Goddess. The deity named Trailokyavijaya whom S. Chattopadhyaya apparent recognized as a Blue Tārā but B. Bhattacharyya identified as a male divine emanation of the Dhyānī Buddha Amoghasiddhi, was adopted into the *Agnipurāṇa* (*Uddhajayarhave* section, chaps. 124-128) sometime between 700 C.E. and 1000 C.E. Chattopadhyaya summarized her features in this text as follows:

> ...twenty-armed, blue coloured, three-eyed and furious looking deity having a huge emaciated form as dark as the cloud, a frowning face, red eyes and fierce mouth with terrible teeth. She wears a wet skin [of a serpent or eel-like water-creature] and a garland of dead bodies and holds a thunderbolt and sword...Snakes [also] are her ornaments and a dead body is her seat. She is the embodiment of wrath and is the mother of the primary elements.[55]

These symbolic features are highlighted also in other awesome-faced indigo or blue Tārās, especially Bhṛkutī ("The Tārā with the frowning eyebrows"), whose Red Tārā counterpart is Kurukullā. Bhṛkutī, who is frequently shown in paintings with three frowning faces, is revered as the pacifier of rulers and subduer of politicians. From a distance, her face looks serene; but a closer view shows the wrathful features, vampire-like teeth and deadly ornaments of a divine protectress.[56]

Although there are many *sādhanas* for Sita-Tārās, images of them in paintings and sculptures are relatively rare. This could account for the infrequency of their illustrations in Bhattacharyya's iconographical study of the Mahāyāna Buddhist pantheon. The scarcity of the Sita-Tārā images is partly explained by the higher popularity of the green and the white Tārās in Tibet and China. L. A. Waddell noticed that, although the numerous names of the twenty-one Tārās are regularly recited by the people, all except the green Tārās and sometimes the white Tārās "are seldom depicted, except the fiendish form Bhṛkutī."[57] But the insignia of the White Tārās and their prescribed *sādhanas* (ritual procedures) indicate the respective Dhyānī Buddha families to which they belong. There are *sādhanas* for the three-eyed and four-armed Sita-Tārā which describe her as having images of all five Dhyānī Buddhas in her crown. Other *sādhanas* for the three-faced and six-armed Saḍbhuja Sitatārā indicate the image of the green Dhyānī Buddha Amoghasiddhi in her crown.[58]

The Theology of Tārā Worship

The traditional attribution of a direct relationship of the Tārās to the five Dhyānī Buddhas and to all the goddesses whom Tibetan Buddhists worship supports the supposition that a distinctive Tārā-pantheon developed within the pantheon of Mahāyāna Buddhism and placed the supreme goddess (Mahātārā, Āryatārā, Bhagavati [Blessed] Tārā, Vajratārā [Diamond Tārā]) in the highest position occupied by the Adi-Buddha in the larger pantheon. This exaltation however, was not an early development but the climax of a slow development which began with a primal local cult of Tārā, which then became popular among sea-faring merchants and travellers, before spreading inland throughout mainland India where her protective powers and prowess extended to all difficulties, dangers and calamities besetting all human beings.[59] Moreover, she became especially the protectress from eight natural dangers and calamities (*mahābhaya*): shipwreck, conflagration, enraged elephants, pirates, man-eating lions, poisonous snakes, kidnap and demons, and also, but later, from the eight corresponding, interior or psychical "dangers": pride, ignorance or stupidity, anger, jealousy, wrong views, covetousness, lust and doubt.[60]

These protective powers and graces inspired a rich folklore of popular personal testimony to her as the supreme divine Savouress and Protectress of her devotees. The sixteenth-century Tibetan historian of Indian Buddhism, Tārānāth, recounted many testimonials of monks who were saved from dangers and helped in their pilgrimage-travels by Tārā. But many more describe her gracious responses to cries for help from lay-folk also. The typical narrative form of this testimonial folklore is illustrated by Stephan Beyer as follows:

> Once there was a man...face to face with a host of demons. This man was greatly frightened, and he called out to Tārā...Again, there was once a woodcutter...He met with a mother lion, who siezed him in her mouth. The woodcutter, terrified, loudly cried out to Tārā. Suddenly he saw coming a girl, dressed in leaves, who snatched him from the lion's jaws and set him back on the road.[61]

Tārā's worshippers believed that simply crying out the Tārā's name would summon forth her presence and her aid. But sometimes a moral dimension is evident in stories describing the Tārā as rebuking an intercessor's sins and praising the devotee's virtues, vocally encouraging noble resolutions and blessing the positive purposes of those who seek her aid. She appears in response to their calls, either as standing alone in her Great Mother and Saviouress form and displaying her manifold powers and graces from eight or even one-thousand arms and hands, after the manner of her Bodhisattva-consort and thousand-armed Avalokiteśvara, or in the iconographical style of the Hindu goddess Durgā Mahādevī, as represented in the imagery of medieval times.

The worship of the goddess in Tibet is both formal and informal and frequently practiced by monks as well as laity who regard her supremely as the gracious and loving Tārā, the ever present help in time of need. Stephan Beyer explained, "To her devotees, Tārā is an abiding deity" whose "constant availability [is] perhaps best symbolized by the daily repetition of her ritual rather than by any great ceremony taking place only once a year." He added, "I have seldom seen a personal altar, monk or lay, without her picture prominently displayed somewhere, though it may be surrounded by a host of representations of other deities." But, "she is...a personal deity rather than a monastic patron, a mother to whom her devotees can take their sorrows and on whom they can rely for help."

> The popular cult of the goddess is one of trust and reverence, of self-confident reliance upon the saving capacity of the divine and upon the human capacity to set in motion the divine mechanism of protection.[62]

The regular worship of Tārā comprises a combination of informal devotions and offerings of fruits and flowers, followed by formal *mantra* recitation, propitiation, intercession and meditation, but each addressed to individually identified deities. Both B. Bhattacharyya's typical examples from the *Sādhanamālā* and Beyer's extensive descriptions of the rituals display this basic liturgical structure, which includes naming the Tārās and their associates and psychically "visualizing" their identifying iconographical insignia.[63]

The typical content is amply illustrated by "The *maṇḍala* offering to Tārā" which Beyer regarded as "the most constant form of her worship."[64] The ritual is in three stages. The first is a preliminary psychical purification of the worshipper's heart and mind and a physical purification of the requisite utensils and other ritual objects. This leads into an invocation of all the Buddhas, Bodhisattvas and Arhants and of the three jewels of the Buddha, the Dharma, and the Sangha, first on behalf of all human and non-human beings generally, then on behalf of close and distant relatives especially.

Next begins "the remainder of the ritual" comprising a series of *mantra*-recitations for "generating the chief Lady," which is a psychical reenactment of "Tārā's own primal genesis" in the consciousness of each worshipper. These psychic-generating *mantras* imaginatively reproduce the identifying iconography of a previously-named Tārā, such as her moonlike "Buddha's face," her lotus flower and her other distinctive attributes. The *mantras* also verbally declare her supreme status and supreme grace and power over her adoring subordinate "gods and demigods," because she is "the mother of all, protecting the entire world from the eight great terrors" and saving the world "from all poverty."

The *mantras* are concentrated liturgical formulas whose persistent recitation is believed to generate supernatural psycho-spiritual powers in the manner which Beyer quoted the teacher, Doje ch'opa, as describing:

> The recitation has consequences that are most great, an evocation that is most quick, and effects that are most keen; just hearing its sound has an inconceivable effect that saves from suffering...Whatever one wants to have, whatever unpleasant thing one wants to be without, she responds to it like an echo. This deity loves and protects the practitioner as if she were the moon accompanying him, never a step away.[65]

The most powerful of these recitations is the Tārā-*mantra* with eight-syllables: *Om Tāre Tuttāre Ture Svāhā*. But there is a wide variety of functionally specific Tārā mantras, each having a different appendix, such as *mama ayuh-punya-jñāna-pustim-kuru svāhā*, which is closely associated with the white Tārā. Each *mantra* is also Tārā-specific in the sense of identifying iconographically and sometimes by name the particular Tārā for whom its matrical *sādhana* (ritual procedure) is intended. In the longer *sādhanas* its repeated utterance breaks the *sādhana* into a procedural order: a preparatory self-purification, a series of verbal invocations to the Buddhas and Bodhisattvas, a series of *mantra*-recitations liberally interspersed with ritual offerings to "the field of hosts inherent in Tārā" for the purpose of an imaginative interior "acquisition" of the deity's "bodily qualities...one at a time," meditations on a standard form of the goddess, and a culminative interior visualization of the goddess through which she has supposedly taken possession of the mind and being of the worshipper.

This culmination is sustained through a continuous *mantra*-recitation during and following the final stage of the ritual for the sake of indefinitely retaining the deity's presence in the worshippers' consciousness. This form of "practicing the presence of" the Tārā keeps each worshipper's mind fully and exclusively possessed by and preoccupied with the Tārā alone. For example, toward the conclusion of the long *sādhana* 98 of the *Sādhanamālā* is the recommendation,

> He who is unable to meditate thus should mutter the Tārā's *mantra* --*Om Tāre Tuttāre Ture Svāhā*...the lord of all *mantras* endowed with great powers...saluted, worshipped and revered by all Tathāgatas.[66]

The *mantra* of the Red Tārā, Kurukullā (which is *Om Kurukulle Hum Hṛih Svāhā*), is also believed to have especially immense supernatural and natural power. Repetition of the *mantra* gives one power to bewitch: ten thousand repetitions to bewitch people in general, thirty thousand to bewitch a minister of state, one hundred thousand for bewitching a ruler, and thousands more than this gives "the power of subduing all ministers and kings."[67] But the zenith of the *mantra's* power is summoning forth a theophany of the goddess.[68]

The *sādhana* ritual is an evocation of the entire Tārā theology where sacred paintings, stone and bronze sculptures, ritual implements and all kinds of approved offerings including fruits and flowers, evince the graces and virtues of the Tārās. The ritual is the principal medium through which the Tārā-theology becomes worshipfully appropriated and symbolically experienced. The typical *sādhana* 98 states, "The worshipper after leaving the bed in the morning should wash his feet and face" and then "prepare a place for self-purifying meditation;" the devotee should proceed into "an elaborate worship of [the panoply of innumerable Buddhas and Bodhisattvas] with celestial flowers...scents, garlands...umbrellas, bells, banners and the like," starting with a confession of sins and then taking refuge in the Buddha, the Doctrine and the Sangha. Next, after finishing "the seven kinds of extra-ordinary worship the deities should be dismissed [from the worshipper's consciousness]" so that there may "begin a series of abstract meditations on Buddhist values such as Friendship, Joy, Compassion, Detachment from craving, and so on." The culmination of these will be "the visualization of the goddess, Tārā or Āryatārā."[69]

In this psychical state of "superconsciousness" the worshipper experiences the goddess and inwardly realizes whatever graces and powers are inherent in her iconographical "attributes." These supernatural sights and sensations can also be enjoyed for some time: "The worshipper should meditate on the goddess [Bhagavatī] Āryatārā as one-faced and two-armed and of deep green complexion, etc....as long as desired." Then, "after thus discovering her, she should be...worshipped with offerings of scented water, fragrant flowers, [etc. and with] various internal and external rituals." The worshipper should then deepen the meditation toward envisioning and becoming identified with the goddess, then envisioning the entire universe over which she is sovereign according to the prescription. "After finishing his meditation on the form of Tārā, he should think the world as identical with the goddess and should move about, thinking his own form as that of the goddess."

The worshipper can experience the sequence of psychical illuminations, by working with the psychical Tārā image or a material form of the deity such as a painting or stone statue "from the inside to the outside" until the entire form of the deity has become vividly visualized. When this happens, the deity may appear alone, or holding court among the subordinate members of her pantheon, or as a group of Tārās having the supreme Tārā in the centre. The goddess is experienced as having a humanlike angelic form, either in the trancelike vision which is the culmination of a prescribed ritual or as an apparition in the immediate physical vicinity of the worshipper. The visionary trance, moreover, is indefinitely sustainable during and after the ritual is completed, and this is, indeed, the climaxic objective of the ritual according to the *sādhana* 95. Indeed, the entire ritual is completed as soon as "the practitioner [has] vividly visualized himself as the Tārā" and has personally appropriated her gracious attributes and almighty life-force.

The beneficial consequences of this theophanic visualization are manifold. For, "generally speaking, to those who meditate on the Bhagavatī in this manner, all the eight supernormal powers fall at their feet, and other small powers come to them as a matter of course." Indeed, "whoever meditates on the Bhagavatī...espies her with his own eyes. The Bhagavatī herself gives him his breath, nay more, even the Buddhahood which is most difficult to attain comes to him like a plum in the palm of his hand." Moreover, even though the purest motive of the interiorization is to worship (not to control or manipulate) the goddess, nevertheless she grants requested boons to her worshippers, sometimes even casting harmful spells upon their enemies.[70]

The core ritual of Tārā-worship is "The Homages to the Twenty-one Tārās." This great prayer is even separately learned by every Tibetan child and is the habitual resort of travellers as their protection from all dangers and terrors. As Beyer noted, a person who cannot recite it entirely by heart is considered "laughingly foolish."

> It is usually chanted in a low monotone, but it may also be sung to its own melody. Families often meet together every day for its recitation, in the morning or evening. A common protection among ordinary people...is to begin the day by offering up a little milk to Tārā and reciting the *Homages* while going about one's morning tasks.[71]

The hymn is also a daily ritual in Tibetan monasteries. Its immense sacred power lies in the *mantra*-like recitation of the distinctive symbolic attributes belonging to each of the twenty-one principal Tārā emanations. But it is not the only prayerful invocation. The general population uses numerous short Tārā-*mantras* as appeals for Tārā's aid at dangerous times and in natural emergencies. Such *mantras* are also recited by more sophisticated Tibetans as powerful consciousness-raising formulae and natural health prophylactics whose potency and efficacy are most certainly guaranteed when perfectly enunciated without "the ten faults of improper recitation."[72]

The reality of Tārā-worship and its efficacy for Tibetans are nevertheless theologically problematic if the Buddhist pantheons are conceptual schema only and not communities of metaphysically "real" divine beings. But the latter appears to be B. Bhattacharyya's opinion: "the gods [and goddesses] have no independent and real existence apart from the mind of the worshipper and the manner of the worship."[73] But his opinion does not take into consideration the pantheons' *Lo-hans* or *Arhats,* who were human beings, heroes and heroines, who achieved enlightenment-salvation during their earthly life. Inasmuch as these saints were posthumously deified, they continue to live real, albeit transformed, lives in the supernatural world where they enjoy eternal felicity with the same kinds of sensory organs in transcendental bodies as the heavenly Buddhas, Bodhisattvas and lesser deities. The Lotus-sutra's heavenly vision of "myriads of *kotis* of Buddhas, Bodhisattvas, *Lo-hans, Arhats* and saints" in the Sukhāvatī heaven attributes much more than a merely conceptual identity and "existence" to the divine and heavenly beings. In this light, Bhattacharyya's opinion reflects the impression that has been made by the distinctive tāntrika interest in mental conjurations of Buddhas and Bodhisattvas through ritualized meditations and mantra recitations. On the other hand, the same tāntrika texts from which Bhattacharyya drew his theory of the Buddhist deities also explicitly refer both to physical self-manifestations of the Tārās in the natural environment of the worshippers and to her incarnations through temporary "spirit possession" in the bodies of her devotees. Hence, although the tāntrika texts appear to imply that the deity's theophanies could be mental images, the same texts also admit more concrete self-manifestations of the deity, even to the level of humanoid forms and material images. Even the *sādhana* ritual indicates both psychical and material self-manifestations of the Tārās; the deities can materialize themselves at will in the world of human experience and can adopt diverse etherial and material forms which can be conceptually arranged into the hierarchical system of divine theophanies found in the Mahāyāna Buddhist pantheon. Hence the *sādhanas* presuppose no essential distinctions between the psychical and the physical self-manifestations, since they indifferently prescribe the same offerings of bells, garlends, perfumes and umbrellas to her material and psychical images and to her other immaterial theophanies. The Tārā's forms are manifold but the worship of her, as prescribed in the *sādhanas*, is the same.

Divinity and Gender in Tārā Symbolism[74]

A crucial distinction in the *sādhana* rituals appears to be the prescription of *propitiations* toward *male* deities and *intercessions* toward *female* deities. This in turn implies a functional gender-differentiation based on a symbolic convention whereby divine transcendence, for which propitiatory offering is appropriate, is represented by maleness, and divine immanence, for which intercession is functionally appropriate, is represented by divine femaleness. This observation demands a reassessment of current Hindu and Buddhist iconology which, despite a century of modern interest, still remains rudimentary and more generally descriptive and historical than symbolically interpretive.

Modern scholars have discovered a rich resource of iconographical information in medieval ritualistic manuals; but their interpretations of gender-symbolism have usually focussed on tāntric references and tāntrika goddess-worship, without reference to recent theories and modern popular speculations about goddess worship in ancient religions. Scholars have had difficulty in explaining the symbolism of divine androgynies (deities displaying dual male and female features) beyond some tentative historical theories about the development of their cults. One difficulty is that the information which can be drawn from the standard manuals concerned with sacred-image making (such as the *Śilpaśāstra*) is sparse and imperfect. The manuals presuppose but do not explicitly prescribe and rationalize gender distinctions in their iconographical detailing of standard images of deities. In the standard bronze and stone images, as well as in the vividly detailed and colorful thangka paintings, the gender distinctions are muted and conservatively restrained, and sometimes confusingly obscured. For example, the facial features and bodily postures of many standard images of male deities appear to be feminine in respect of fair complexions, almond-shaped eyes, reddened lips, long wavy hair and lithe maidenly bodies. The gender distinctions are muted also in the iconographical prescriptions which are presented in the standard ritualistic texts. Divine attributes, powers and graces which can be regarded as either "masculine" or as "feminine" are indifferently attributed to gods and to goddesses. Even the wording of titles and ascriptions that seem in isolation to carry masculine connotations are frequently found in litanies for goddesses as well as for male deities. Accordingly, images and other representations of goddesses like the supreme Tārā, who are referred to as "The Divine Mother" (with possible connections with ancient "fertility goddesses") manifestly lack the characteristic human-fertility symbols: the wide hips, the swollen pregnant womb and milk-engorged breasts. The exquisitely sensuous, lithesome-bodied, full-breasted, broad hipped, "bursting with life" *apsaras* portrayed in the murals in the Buddhist Cave 2 at Ellora and in the decorative sculpture of the Stūpa at Sāṅcī are not goddesses, nor are they "fertility figures." Their facial and bodily postures express serene unselfconscious detachment from all sensual objects and human instinctual drives. These youthfully nubile figures, sometimes alone and sometimes in pairs, display in male and female forms the dualities of Nature and the cosmos. But, they are representations of invisible tree-spirits and spirits of mountains and rivers, etc., whose transcendental references are indicated through sky-gazing facial expressions as though they were worshipfully contemplating an ineffable transcendent Reality.

Even the diminutively sublime sculptures of sexually explicit male and female figures adorning the exterior walls of India's Hindu, Buddhist and Jain temples of Khajurāho, or vitalizing in sensuous detail the great chariot wheels of the Sun God temple at Konarak, have been incorrectly interpreted as god and goddess figures.[75] The chariot-wheel figures cannot be interpreted otherwise than as ambiguous metaphors of natural and cosmic duality signifying the fecund, cosmic, generative principle or else as representations of the sexually symbolic "twilight language" of medieval Tāntrism (Tāntricism), which is sometimes ritually enacted within tāntrika circles for the purpose of effecting the spiritual ecstacy of the *śaktā's* (devotee's) union-communion with the goddess.

Sir John Woodroffe (Arthur Avalon) noticed the essentially symbolic character of the representation of divine maleness and femaleness. "The Goddess or Devī...is God...in Its Mother aspect", although "in its strict sense neither 'Mother' nor 'Father' is applicable to the Deity as the author of forms." Woodroffe went on to note, "In the *Navaratneshvara* [manuscript] it is said: 'That Devī...should be thought of as a female or as a male, or as pure Brahman'." Later, Woodroffe comments, "The meaning of the term 'Devī' is *pṛkāshatmikā*, or that which is by its nature

Light and Manifestation" (i.e., Immanence). 'Devī' is in the feminine gender because the One...bears and nourishes all things as their Mother." That is, Woodroffe identifies the distinction as functional, not ontological. "The Devī is therefore the Brahman revealed in Its Mother aspect (*Shrīmātā*) as Creatrix and Nourisher of the worlds."[76]

All of the visual representations of maleness and femaleness indicate that the essential meaning of the gender distinction is not ontological but theological. This is also the case for other symbols by which the various attributes and family interrelations of the deities within the Hindu and Buddhist pantheons and their respective hierarchical standings and statuses have been normatively defined and distinguished. The fundamental hierarchical distinction between the deity as a "god" or as a "goddess" is transcendence (maleness) and immanence (femaleness) respectively, whose essential relationship is frequently portrayed in Hindu and Buddhist sacred art by the serene goddess (standing on the earthly plane of divine immanence) rapturously gazing upward into the face of her transcendent (heavenly) Lord, who also peers benevolently downward into the face of his consort. The male/female forms are even metaphors and messages signalling different kinds of appropriate worship (such as propitiation and intercession) for communicating with and getting help from a deity.

Alternatively, it is the unity of the two, or the duality of the godhead, which is portrayed as the god and the goddess in a conjugal embrace. In these *yab-yum* images, the symbolic transcendence/immanence gender-distinctions are unified in that "honorable father honorable mother" symbol. They theologically represent the supreme Buddha's perfection-state of *karuṇā* or infinite compassion, intimately conjoined with the perfection-state of *śūnya* or supreme transcendental wisdom. But, the *yab-yum* images also show the totally nude or nearly nude figure of the feminine being (*yum* or *śakti*) wrapped in a close conjugal embrace with the male deity (*yab*) as though indicating, expressing and emphasizing the surrender of the natural to the supernatural or the unified reabsorption of the divine immanence in the divine transcendence.[77] The two are distinctive and yet beyond the distinctions. Whenever the distinction is indicated, the forms are personalized. Hence, whenever in Hindu and Buddhist tantrism the male *yab* or *śūnya* aspect of the *yab-yum* duality is distinguished, then it is personally identified as a male deity with the preferred personal name of Heruka. But, when the female *yum* or *sakti* or *karuṇā* aspect is separately distinguished, then it is personally identified as a female deity with the preferred personal name of Goddess

Nairātmā.[78] Yet, here also, the essential point of the *yab-yum* configuration is its theological denial of an ontological divine maleness or femaleness.

The symbolic distinctions between male transcendence and female immanence in the Vajrayāna or Tāntric Buddhist metaphysics and theology are functionally significant. In the metaphysics, the Ultimate Reality is symbolically identified as the male principle *Śūnya* (The Void) with its female counterpart as *Bodhi* (Enlightenment). Next in descending order are *Śūnyatā* (Emptiness) and its female principle *Karuṇā* (Compassion). But, in the theology, the supreme Being is the Ādi-Buddha (Vajrasattva) with its consort, followed in descending order by the five Dhyānī Buddhas with their consorts, and subordinate Bodhisattvas with their consorts, who include the Tārās. In the Vajrayāna tāntrika ritual, the symbolic dualities become progressively melded into the psychic supraconscious unity of transcendental Wisdom (*prajñā*), called also Emptiness or the Void (*śūnya*).

The supreme Tārā is the primary focus of faith, devotion and worship for Tibetan Buddhists. But her popular title as "The Mother" is an honorific expression of her prestigious status over all Buddhas and Bodhisattvas and of her intimacy as the most beloved and universally adored deity of the Tibetan people. Although she is called "The Mother of the Tibetan people," no generative implication is intended since the Tibetans have not traced their physical ancestry from Tārā but from simian forebears. She is "The Mother" who protects and blesses her worshippers.[79]

The symbolic motherhood of Tārā is functionally significant in regard to Avalokitesvara. Statements in the *Sādhanamālā*, and painted and sculptured images of the goddess, represent her as either sitting or standing alone, as standing beside Avalokiteśvara, as conjugally embracing a Bodhisattva, or in a *parivara* (as the central deity surrounded by attendant deities). Each of these differently represents her relation to Avalokiteśvara and her status within the Mahāyāna Buddhist pantheon. The solitary representations emphasize her supreme status within the Tibetan Buddhist religion. Representations showing the Mahātārā standing beside Avalokiteśvara indicate the mutuality and integrality of the divine transcendence and immanence.[80] In the *yab-yum* configurations showing the Tārā as the *sakti* (power) of Avalokiteśvara, it is the integral identity of the two in the unity of a single godhead that is emphasized. The *parivara* representations, showing the seated and relatively larger Bhagavatī-Tārā holding court before the company of lesser Tārās, emphasize the Bhagavatī's supreme status within the Tibetan Buddhist pantheon.

These relational distinctions are also geometrically indicated, both in terms of their placements within circles and triangles in *thangkas* and other religious illustrations, and also in terms of their relative sizes. In representations showing the goddess Tārā in the company of Avalokiteśvara, her figure is always smaller and even dwarfed beside her male consort. This exaggerated size-difference conveys symbolic theological (not physiological) meaning, inasmuch as relative proportionality as well as gender differentiation are common iconographical conventions for representing the relation of divine transcendence (portrayed as enlarged maleness) to divine immanence (portrayed as diminutive femaleness). In most of the extant paintings and other images of the goddess and her consort, the contrasting size and gender symbolism is explicit and unambiguous. But, in representations of divine androgyny, such as Avalokiteśvara appearing to be both male and female with male *and* female features and organs, the symbolic distinctions of Avalokiteśvara and of Tārā have been melded and unified. In other words, the distinctions of divine transcendence and divine immanence are implicit even while the unity of the two is symbolically explicit. Moreover, the male side of the androgyny frequently displays some feminine features, while the female side displays some masculine features.

Heinrich Zimmer noticed this physiological ambiguity in the strikingly feminized form of a sculpture portraying Avalokiteśvara.[81] In this "fine specimen of a late, mature, Buddhist art" showing the Bodhisattva as an "embodiment at once of unending compassion and of a sublime, knowing indifference to his eternal task," Zimmer noticed "the plantlike smoothness of the limbs" and "the dreamy attitude of the Bodhisattva" displayed by "his loosely extended right arm, which is of a tender, maidenlike womanly grace," and by being generally "endowed with a charm beyond the differentiation of sex, a youthful male form and a feminine grace...perfectly fused."

Zimmer speculated that "this angelic quality" of male/female androgyny "offered a starting point for the transformation of Avalokiteśvara in the Far East into a female divinity," so that "this [dual] attitude...became a classic pattern in China and Japan, as well as in India, for the graceful form of Avalokiteśvara-Kuan-yin-Kannon."[82] In such androgynies as the extant Avalokiteśvara-Tārā images, the gender-attributes appear loosely interconnected and even interchangeable, inasmuch as the same Bodhisattva has apparently been worshipped sometimes and in certain places as male, that is, as Avalokiteśvara, and elsewhere and at other times as female, that is, as Tārā. This has proven problematic for scholarly reconstructions of the respective histories and theologies of the Avalokiteśvara and Tārā cults in medieval Tibetan, Chinese and Japanese Buddhism. For example, in certain eleventh-century West-Tibetan frescoes, the divine protector from the eight "internal dangers" is shown as the goddess Tārā, whereas in contemporaneous Chinese paintings the divine protector from those "dangers" was shown as Avalokiteśvara (*Kuan-yin*). It is probable that pragmatic as well as aesthetic considerations led the Chinese toward identifying Tibet's most popular transcendental Bodhisattva, Avalokiteśvara, with Tibet's most popular immanental Bodhisattva, Tārā, and then to developing distinctive male and female versions as well as an androgynous Kuan-yin.

The exact time-period of this Chinese transformation of Kuan-yin is an historical problem for which both Getty and D. C. Bhattacharyya offered plausible but not incontestable solutions.[83] Their supposition is that the Bodhisattva's mixed male and female attributes and features may have been acquired through a repeated amalgamation and assimilation of local god (*deva*) and goddess (*devī*) cults, or that an Indian cult of a male "god of mercy" became the Chinese cult of a male Kuan-yin late in the second half of the first century C.E. and this was later transformed into the Chinese goddess-cult of Kuan-yin. But a contrary opinion (attributed by Getty to De La Vallee Poussin) is that in Indian Buddhist theology Avalokiteśvara originally personified the female cosmic energy and "was probably worshipped in India in female form before his [sic] introduction into China."[84]

The most plausible, though most complex, historical reconstruction is that distinctive cults of Avalokiteśvara, Tārā, and of the Avalokiteśvara-Tārā androgyny became separately and locally imported into China from India during the first century C.E., and were later fused with several aboriginal Chinese cults into the Chinese cults of a male Kuan-yin, a female Kuan-yin, and an androgynous Kuan-yin. Later. these divergent cult-forms of Kuan-yin were imported into Japanese Buddhism, where Kuan-yin (Kannon) also became simultaneously represented in both male (Avalokiteśvara) and female (Tārā) forms.

John Blofield generally supported this opinion by pointing out, "When as early as the first century AD, the practice of invoking Avalokita reached China, no one thought of depicting him as female." Nor, in the fifth and the seventh centuries did the Chinese pilgrims to India, Fa Hsien and Hsuan Tsang, record finding there any female representations of the Bodhisattva. "Yet, by the twelfth century, female images of the Bodhisattva were well-nigh universal in China and Japan."[85] Blofield also invoked the authority of the Lotus Sutra (*Saddharma-puṇḍarīka Sūtra*) for his observation that "of Avalokiteśvara's 337 earthly incarnations, *all were male* and all human except for one" although apparently the Bodhisattva could "assume female form if need be."

Blofield's "private" and "unsubstantiated rationalization" was that the Chinese and Japanese preferred a serene-faced Avalokiteśvara, such as "the lovely Tārā, appearing now as a sweet-faced matron, now as a winsome maid." But it is more probable that the gender distinctions were not considered to be so fixed that they could not be conveniently interchanged. On the other hand, the assimilation of local hero and heroine cults and legends, such as the Chinese cult and legend of Kuan-yin and the Chinese incarnation legend of Princess Miao Shan, into the heterogeneous cult of Avalokiteśvara (Avalokita) may have caused gender shifts in regional cults of Avalokiteśvara and Tārā and the eventual variations in the gender of Kuan-yin (Kwan-non).[86]

It is nevertheless difficult to find an indisputable historical explanation for what Getty called "the evident confusion in art in regard to the sex of Kwan-non" and the more evident confusion in worship over the gender of Kwan-non which "has existed among worshippers even to the present day." Yet, one cannot suppose that Buddhists in general feel the confusion, when the common people pray to the deity as the "goddess of mercy," and the priests and more educated classes worship the same deity as a masculine Bodhisattva dwelling "on the right hand of Amitābha in the Western Paradise of Sukhāvatī," even while "some sects...worship Kwan-non as sexless, for it is claimed that, as objects of worship, all male and female beings should be looked upon as of no fixed sex."[87]

It is probable that the worshippers have long been comfortable with the "confusion" of genders, since it is reflected also in their ritual-manuals providing the *sādhanas* for their worship of Avalokiteśvara and Tārā. Here too, the "confusion" of Tārā with Avalokiteśvara reflects their close functional congruence in serving the needs and wishes of their worshippers for protection and material benefits. In the most pragmatical of all the rituals, the great "Hymn of Praises to the Twenty-one Tārās," the congruence of male transcendence and female immanence is plainly apparent. Tārā is a form of Avalokiteśvara, "born, like a lightning-flash from the pitying tear" of Avalokiteśvara (Avalokita) "the storehouse of pity." As L. A. Waddell summarized the tradition, Avalokiteśvara

...on looking down on the world shed tears of pity for the misery of humankind. The tear from the left eye on falling to the earth formed a lake, on which instantly, like a lightning-flash, appeared, floating on a lotus flower, the goddess Dorma, who was then commissioned by Avalokita to soothe human suffering.[88]

The congruence is indicated also by the many distinctive powers and graces of Tārā, which seem to be more "masculine" than "feminine." Among the references, "the victorious top-knot (*uṣnīṣa*)" of the fourth Tārā reminds one of the earthly or "manifest" (*nirmānakaya*) Buddha, its principal wearer. Moreover, descriptions of "That Great Lady" both as "the supremely valiant, best worker, [and] bestower of supreme power," and as "the moon-faced" and "brightly glorious one" reflect a fusion of maleness and femaleness, of transcendence and immanence, and of the identities of Avalokiteśvara and Tārā in the worship.

The unity of Tārā in Avalokiteśvara is also reflected in numerous popular stories about Tārā's aid in Tārānāth's sixteenth-century historical account of Buddhism in India. One is the legend of the *acārya*, Trīratnādasa, who took a long and perilous journey. When a great river blocked his way, "he prayed to Tārā and an old woman appeared with a boat and took him across." Next, when a mountain blocked his way, "he prayed to Avalokiteśvara" and "there came down a ladder made of canes." After this, "he climbed up [and prayed for help and] he saw the image of Tārā at the third stage of the hill and on its middle the image of Bhrikutī-[tārā]." Then, at the summit where he prayed for a month, there "appeared a woman who said, "Ārya-[tārā] has arrived. Come along." So she led him toward the highest mystical state of *samādhi* and into the presence of Avalokiteśvara.

In Tārānāth's account of the life and career of Śāntideva (Folio 82A), the goddess Āryatara appeared in the guise of a woman who took him to a forest-dwelling yogi. "The Yogi was none but Manjuśrī and this woman none but Tārā." When Avalokiteśvara is mentioned in Tārānāth's "history," the Bodhisattva's transcendence is indicated through rites of atonement and propitiation (e.g., in Folio 71B); but when Tārā is mentioned, the ritual context is intercession, drawing forth her material aid but also her help in leading upward the devotee toward the abode of Avalokiteśvara.[89]

Hence, any symbolic distinctions (especially of size and gender, form and color, and gesture and posture) in the sacred art and the sacred rituals are liturgically-contextualized, theological messages which draw attention to the heavenly and earthly locations and earth-touching graces and powers of the deities. A deity who, when seated on his heavenly lotus-throne in the yogic-posture of infinite wisdom, is Lord

Avalokiteśvara, becomes the goddess Tārā when appearing as a standing figure displaying the immanental personification of his infinite compassion. Hence, Avalokiteśvara and Tārā are not distinct deities but are transcendent and immanental aspects of a divine unity whose essential nature is beyond all finite distinctions and differentiations of number, gender and location.[90] It is on this ground, therefore, that Getty's statement, citing "Professor Lloyd," that "it is a mistake to speak of Kwan-non as a female deity" needs to be qualified, inasmuch as it is equally inappropriate to assume that Kwan-non is essentially a "male deity."[91] The Avalokiteśvara-Tārā androgyny and similar theistic dualities in Hinduism and Buddhism discredit the theory made popular by Robert Graves that religion began as Goddess-worship. Neither Tibet's supreme Buddhist goddess, nor her Hindu and Buddhist counterparts in Asia, nor any equivalent forms in the ancient Near East were supremely perceived as the primary divine Being but instead as its immanental personal manifestations. Nor is it likely that the goddess in any ancient religious system became the exclusive cultic possession of a totally male or female sect or became specially worshipped on account of having distinctively "feminine" or "womanly" functions, attributes and powers. The countless stories of the goddess Tārā's theophanies as a maiden or as an old woman yield no indications of gender preferences in her worshippers or in the recipients of her manifold blessings. Some of the Tārā's frequent theophanic appearances were responses to cries for help that had been made to the male (transcendent) Bodhisattva, Avalokiteśvara. This is consistent with her identity as the essential being or *śakti* of Avalokiteśvara.

In the Chinese images and cults of Kuan-yin, the deity is the Chinese Avalokiteśvara when represented as a male divine being, and is the Chinese Tārā when represented as a female divine being. Nevertheless, these are not two deities but are mutually interchangeable transcendental and immanental forms and aspects of one supreme Being. As the self-existent transcendent deity, Kuan-yin is male and a theophany of Avalokiteśvara. But on the earthly plane of immanental self-manifestation, Kuan-yin is female and a theophany of the goddess Tārā. Hence, since China's favorite title for the green Tārā is *Jun-tei Kwan-non*, "the feminine form of [the male deity] Kwan-non [Avalokiteśvara]," it appears possible, however surprising, that Kwan-non is the world's first, and maybe only, surviving example of a male goddess![92]

Notes

1. The connection of Tārā with Artemis and Aphrodite was made by John Blofield (*Bodhisattva of Compassion: The Mystical Tradition of Kuan Yin* [Boulder. Colorado: Shambala,1987], 14), and with Artemis and the other goddess figures by S. Bhattacharji (*The Indian Theogony* [Calcutta: Firma KLM Private Ltd., 1978], 105-177).

2. A fine example of a *Tārā-parivara* is illustrated by Alice Getty in *The Gods of Northern Buddhism* (Rutland, Vermont: Charles E. Tuttle Co., 1962 [1928]), plate 5.

3. L. A. Waddell, *Lamaism in Sikhim* (Delhi: Oriental Publishers, 1973), 73-74.

4. Stephan Beyer, *The Cult of Tārā: Magic and Ritual in Tibet* (Berkeley: University of California Press, 1973), 211-217.

5. Akṣobhya, whose symbolic colour is blue, is the second of the five Dhyānī Buddhas to whose family or *kula* some of the Tārās belong. The Mahāyāna doctrine of the Dhyānī Buddhas and their divine lineages is described below in note 11.

6. Beyer, 57.

7. K. K. Dasgupta, "The Iconography of Tārā" in *The Śakti Cult and Tārā*, ed. D. C. Sircar (Calcutta: University of Calcutta Press, 1967), 15.

8. Kees W. Bolle in Beyer, vii-viii.

9. Beyer, 3.

10. D. C. Bhattacharyya, *Studies in Buddhist Iconography* (New Delhi: Manohar Book Service, 1978), 12.

11. According to Heinrich Zimmer (*The Art of Indian Asia: Its Mythology and Transformations* [New York: Pantheon Books, 1964], 1:195, 200, 310-311), the doctrine, mythology, symbolism and iconography of the Dhyānī Buddhas (often referred to as the Tathāgatas) and their attendant Bodhisattvas are distinctive of Tibetan and Nepalese "*Vajrayāna*" Buddhism. The Dhyānī Buddhas are five in number and are emanations of the Supreme Reality or Ādi-Buddha. In Tibetan Buddhism, the Ādi-Buddha (Primal Buddha or Supreme Reality) is Vajrasattva, "he whose essence [*sattva*] is adamantine [*vajra*]." He is known also as Vajradhara, "the wielder *[dhara]* of the thunderbolt [*vajra*]. (In Sanskrit *vajra* means both "thunderbolt" and "diamond". In Tibetan, it is *dorje*.) The Dhyānī Buddhas have the names Vairocana, Akṣobhya, Ratnāsambhava, Amitābha and Amoghasiddhi. Of these, the highest place appears to be given to Aksobhya, since they carry his miniature in their crowns while he carries a miniature figure of Vajrasattva. In *tantric* literature, each is often represented in the company of his divine feminine consort or *śakti*: Vairocana with Vajradhātvīṣvari (Mārīcī), Aksobhya with Locana, Ratnāsambhava with Māmakī, Amitābha with Pāṇḍarā, and Amoghāsiddhi with Tārā. Each goddess is usually represented either standing alone close by her sire or else in the distinctive posture or "attitude" known in Tibet as *yab-yum*, that is, the standing or seated Buddha (*yab*) in whose conjugal embrace is his consort (*śakti* or *yum*). A fine, late eighteenth-century bronze of the Vajrasattva-Prajñāpāramitā *yab-yum* is illustrated by Zimmer (vol. 2, plates 610, 611) who also noted (1:115-116) that the *yab-yum* "attitude" lends itself to "an elaborate allegorical interpretation." S. B. Dasgupta (*An Introduction to Tāntric Buddhism* [Calcutta: University of Calcutta Press, 1974], 86) showed

that "each Dhyānī Buddha has...a particular consort, a particular colour, crest, *Mudrā* (posture) and *Vahana* (vehicle)...a particular Bodhisattva, a human Buddha, a *bija-mantra* [seed-syllable], a location, and each is...associated with a particular *Kula* or family, etc." From each of the Dhyani Buddhas emanate *four* Dhyānī Bodhisattvas each with attendant *śaktis* and identifiable through their distinctive iconographical symbols as described by W. Y. Evans-Wentz in *The Tibetan Book of the Dead* (3rd ed.; London: Oxford University Press, 1960), 10-15. The fullest conceptual amplification of the Dhyānī Buddha pantheon is the famous T'ang Chinese *Garbhadhātu-maṇḍala*, which has thirteen divisions comprising four hundred and five deities around the central figure of Mahāvairocana, flanked by the remaining Dhyānī Buddhas of "the four directions" (West, North, East, South) each with attendant Bodhisattvas and female consorts in the *yab-yum* attitude. It is described by Kenneth Ch'en, *Buddhism in China: A Historical Survey* (Princeton, NJ: Princeton University Press,1964), 328-329.

12. In *Two Lamaistic Pantheons* (Cambridge, Mass.: Harvard University Press, 1965), W. E. Clark photographically reproduced bronze images and wooden plaques of the principal Tārās. In his reproduction of the incomplete bronze-image collection in the Pao-Hsian Lou Lāma-Temple in Peiping (modern Beijing) one finds the following principal Tārās (in the order of Clark's listing, pp. 1-222): Tārā, Kurukullā, Māmakī, Nīlā-Tārā, Bhṛkutī, Sita-Tārā, Śyāma-Tārā, Pratisarā, Jāṅguli, Sarvarthasādhana-Tārā, Saḍbhuja-Parnasābari, Pravīra[?]-Tārā, Tzu-cha-lin [Khadiravanī?]-Tārā, Cīna-Tārā and Durgottārinī-Tārā. But, among the 310 plaques which were photographed in the eighteenth-century manuscript of the *Chu Fo P'u-sa Sheng Hsiang Tsan*, Clark (pp. 276-284) found the following principal Tārās: Pratisarā, Khadiravanī-Tārā, Pravāra[?]-Tara, Candrakānti[?]-Tārā, Kanakavarṇa-Tārā, Uṣnīsā-Tārā, Huṁsvaranādinī-Tārā, Vijaya-Tara, Aparājitā-Tārā, Mārasūdana-Tārā, Śokavinodana-Tārā, Jagadvaśī[?]-Tārā, Maṅgalotpādana-Tārā, Pācaka-Tārā, Kruddha-kāli-Tārā, Mahāśānti-Tārā, Rāganisūdana-Tārā, Sukhada-Tārā, Sita-Vijaya-Tārā, Duhkhadahana-Tārā, Siddhida-Tārā, Paripurṇa [or Parniṣpanna]-Tārā, Jaṅgulī-Tārā, Vajratara, Cīnakrama-Tārā, Cintamanicakra-Tārā, Sadbhuja-Sita-Tārā, Dhanadā-Tārā, Durgottārinī-Tārā, Sarvārthasādhana-Tārā, Ārya-Jāṅgulī, Ekajaṭa and Bhṛkutī.

13. Clark's reproductions indicate a total of at least 300 named deities and divinities (earthly humans who were canonically divinized after their death), and as many as 900 members if the different forms and versions of the deities are listed. The deities in the pantheon could number many thousands if the "host of demons, witches, fairies, heavenly musicians, serpent gods, golden birds, and household, personal and local gods" referred to by A. K. Gordon (*Tibetan Religious Art* [2nd ed., New York: Paragon Books, 1963], 12) are also included. But, Gordon's "general classification of the deities of the pantheon" (11-12) indicates the following hierarchical arrangement of the pantheon: The Supreme Reality (Vajradhara, Ādi-Buddha); the five Tathāgatas or Dhyānī Buddhas (Creation Buddhas: Akṣobhya, Amitābha, Amoghasiḍdhi, Ratnāsambhava, and Vairocana); the Mānushi (moral or earthly) Buddhas (including Dipaṅkara and the most recent historic Buddha, Śakyamuni); the Medicine or Healing Buddhas (such as Bhaiṣajyaguru); The Confession Buddhas; Maitreya (the Buddha who is to come at the end of the present cosmic era); the five Dhyānī Bodhisattvas (emanations of the Dhyānī Buddhas but principally Avalokiteśvara and his consort Tārā); the group of eight male and female Bodhisattvas; the group of independent Bodhisattvas including male and female deities such as the Tārās (Saviouresses); the Pañcharakṣās (five "Spell goddesses who protect from diseases": Mahāpratisarā, Mahāsahasrapramardinī, Mahāmāyurī, Mahāmantrānusārinī and Mahāsitavatī); Saraswatī ("Goddess of music and poetry"), Mārīchī (the Dawn-goddess) "and many others."

Next in descending order come the *Yi-dam* ("tutelary" or guardian deities including the *yab-yum* couples having the Dhyānī Buddhas in conjugal embrace with the feminine consorts (*śaktis*); the Dharmapālas (fierce-looking defenders and protectors of the Buddhist Doctrine such as Yamāntaka); and, "a host of lesser divinities" such as the Lokapālas (guardians of the cosmic quarters, east, south, west, north and northwest); Dākinīs ("skygoers or fairies" such as Makaravaktrā and Siṁhavaktrā); "Goddesses of the Bardo" ("the period between death and rebirth"); "the eighty-four Great Magicians" (being the legendary divine composers of the principal tāntrika treatises); the "Wealth gods" (such as Jambhala); the "Mountain gods" and "the Five Kings" (protector-patrons of the monasteries); and, the "divinities" ("many great historical teachers...who were deified and taken into the pantheon").

14. D. C. Bhattacharyya, *Studies in Buddhist Iconography*, 12.

15. Ibid., 67 (n. 109), 68-77.

16. The widespread worship of Tārā in Tibet is in contrast to the Tārā's relatively minor status in Chinese and Japanese Buddhism. Getty (*The Gods of Northern Buddhism*, 121-122) noticed that, in Japan, the goddess Tārā appears more frequently on temple banners and less in statues, but "is little worshipped", and "in China her worship is unknown" except for a great new year ceremony conducted "with great pomp" by China's rulers, ministers and foreign ambassadors.

17. In this essay, I argue that the gender classifications of the deities as "male" and "female" may be symbolic and theological, and were not intended primarily as physiological features nor as attributions of "sexuality."

18. A special edition of the *Sādhanamālā* in which the *sādhanas* of the *Sādhanasamuccaya* were also incorporated was edited by Benoytosh Bhattacharyya and published as Nos. 26 and 41 of the *Gaekwad Oriental Series* (Baroda: Oriental Institute, 1925-28). Bhattacharyya also edited the *Niṣpannayogāvalī* of Abhayakara Gupta for the same series as No. 109 (Baroda: Oriental Institute, 1949).

19. B. Bhattacharyya, *The Indian Buddhist Iconography*, 19-20.

20. Translated from pp. 351-352 of B. Bhattacharyya's edition of the *Sadhanamala* in B. Bhattacharyya, *The Indian Buddhist Iconography*, 151.

21. Ibid., 5-6.

22. In this essay the words *tāntra, tāntric* and Tāntrism (or Tāntricism) are used in reference to Tāntric Buddhism, which S. B. Dasgupta described (*An Introduction to Tāntric Buddhism* [3rd ed.; Calcutta: University of Calcutta, 1974], 2) as a practical esoteric or occult science having a distinctive metaphysic and theology but using "chanting and muttering of Mantras, describing [i.e.transcribing] various mystic diagrams, making of postures and gestures, worshipping various types of gods and goddesses including a host of demigods and other such beings, meditations and salutations of various types, and last, but not least, yogic practices, sometimes involving sex-relation." The word *tantra* refers to a specific kind of literature in which the esoteric philosophy and practice (*sādhana*) is taught and illustrated but which also frequently has this word in its titles. Tāntrism (or Tāntricism) is sometimes called *Mantrayāna* (The Mantra Vehicle) which is a relatively late development in Northern (Mahāyāna) Buddhism but which became institutionalized principally by Nāgārjuna (ca. 150-250 C.E.) and Asaṅga (ca. 4th-century C.E.).

23. B. Bhattacharyya (*The Indian Buddhist Iconography*, 3) indicated the indispensable value which Professor Clark of Harvard University found in the *Nispānnayogāvalī* for identifying and labelling a collection of bronze statuettes of a Lāmaist pantheon discovered by Staal Holstein in Peiping (modern Beijing) in 1926.

24. B. Bhattacharyya, *Nispannayogvālī of Abhayakara Gupta*, 38, translated in B. Bhattacharyya, *The Indian Buddhist Iconography*, 240.

25. Ibid., 4-5.

26. Among the major essays are: L. A. Waddell on "The Indian Buddhist Cult of Avalokita and his consort Tārā, the Saviouress" (1898); Hiranand Śāstri's historical explanation of "The origin and the cult of Tārā" (1925) which appears to have been reassessed in M, K, Dhavalikar's essay on "The origin of Tārā" (1963-4); M. T. de Mallmann's *Introduction a l'etude d'Avalokiteśvara* (1948) and *Etude Iconographique sur Manjuśrī* (1964); E. Conze on "The Iconography of the [goddess] Prajñāpāramitā" (1949 and 1950); D. Mitra's study of "Aṣṭamahābhaya Tārā" (1957); J.E. van Lohuizen-de Leeuw on the goddess Cundā and her image (1966) and Dipak Chandra Bhattacharyya's two essays on "The Goddess Tārā" and the *Pañcarakṣā-Tārās* (the five protective goddesses) (1978).

Seven fundamental and highly instructive introductions to the history and structure of Tārāism are, in the order of their first editions: L. A. Waddell, *The Buddhism of Tibet or Lamaism* (1895); A. Foucher's two-volume *Etude sur l'iconographie bouddhique de l'Inde (1900-1905)*; Alice Getty, *The Gods of Northern Buddhism: Their History, Iconography and Progressive Evolution through the Northern Buddhist Countries* (1914, rev. 1928 and 1962); Benoytosh Bhattacharyya, *The Indian Buddhist Iconography* (1924, 2nd edn.1958, rev. 1968); A. K. Coomaraswamy, *Elements of Buddhist Iconography* (1935); Walter Eugene Clark, *Two Lamaistic Pantheons* (1937, reprint 1965); and Stephen Beyer, *The Cult of Tārā: Magic and Ritual in Tibet* (1973).

27. See, esp., L. A. Waddell, "The Indian Buddhist Cult of Avalokita and his Consort Tārā 'the Saviouress,' Illustrated from the Remains at Magadha," *Journal of the Royal Asiatic Society* (1894); *id.*, *The Buddhism of Tibet, or Lamaism* (London: W. H. Allen, 1895); *id.*, *Tibetan Buddhism* (2nd ed.; N.Y.: Dover, 1972); and *id.*, *Lamaism in Sikhim* (Delhi: Oriental Publishers, 1973).

28. Alfred Charles Auguste Foucher, *Etude sur l'iconographie bouddhique de l'Inde* (2 vols.; Paris: A. Leroux, 1900-1905).

29. Alice Getty, *The Gods of Northern Buddhism* (Rutland, Vermont & Tokyo: Charles E. Tuttle Co., 1962). In this work, Getty has mentioned banners showing the goddess "surrounded by a double rainbow glory in which are represented the group of twenty-one Tārās of which ten are white, five are red, five are yellow and in the centre is the green Tārā." No "blue Tārās" are mentioned. Moreover, although images of the green Tārā and the white Tārā are common, representations of the others are less frequent, even rare, so that is is difficult to make a complete illustrated presentation of the Tārā-pantheon. Numerous variations in the representational forms of the Tārās also complicate the system. There are serene-faced (*saumya*) and fierce-faced (*ghora*) classes of Tārās. Some Tārās appear alone and seated, thereby indicating their supreme distinction from other deities; others are seated in yogic postures or are shown in various different modes as attendant figures or consorts, either standing beside their seated partners, or else in the esoteric (*guhya*) mode of a conjugal embrace with the standing or sitting Bodhisattva, or else in the distinctive tantrika *yab-yum* or unified "honorable father honorable mother" configuration by which the Tārā is shown as the *śakti* or spiritual self or personalized energy of the seated Bodhisattva who is usually Avalokiteśvara.

Moreover, according to their respective lineages as emanations of different Tathāgatas (Dhyānī Buddhas), the titles, colors and other symbolic insignia of the Tārās are different. For example, the symbolic color of the Tārā consort of Avalokiteśvara is white when she also bears such titles as Sita-Tārā, Kurukullā and Parṇaśabarī. But, as the *śakti* or *yum* of this Bodhisattva, her symbolic color is usually green in which mode she also bears different insignia and also different names such as Jāṅgulī-Tārā and Śyāmatārā. But the colors are interchangeable. Accordingly, there are white, blue and yellow forms of Jāṅgulī and also yellow and green forms of Parnaśabarī and also white and red forms of Kurukullā.

30. D. C. Bhattacharyya, *Studies in Buddhist Iconography,* 2.

31. Frank E. Reynolds et al., *Guide to Buddhist Religion* (Boston: G. K. Hall, 1981), 258.

32. The supposition that the cult of the goddess Tārā developed from a local and regional aboriginal cult into a pan-Asian religious system is supported by Sukumari Bhattacharji's account of the growth of the cult of Durgā in India (*The Indian Theogony. A Comparative Study of Indian Mythology from the Vedas to the Purāṇas* [Calcutta: Firma KLM Private Ltd., 1978], 174). "The process of Durgā's growth in stature was long and steady. One by one she absorbed the main traits of regional mother-goddesses, household deities who were worshipped for different things by different tribes. Some were fierce and awe-inspiring, others were mild, benign and motherly, yet others were embodiments of lofty ideas--all these were fused into one composite supreme goddess--Durgā. Each of the component deities brought with her a special ritual, specific cultic practices and a different mythological and religious significance to the devotee. A supreme goddess who commanded the whole-hearted allegiance of various types of people, had to combine in her personality all the different traits that would satisfy these manifold demands."

33. D. C. Bhattacharyya, *Studies in Buddhist Iconography,* 24.

34. The story of Soma including his elopement with Bṛhaspati's wife, Tārā, and her pregnancy and bearing of Soma's son, Budha, occurs in the Rāmāyaṇa in sections III.3.11, V.31.5; VI.86.4 and VII.88.9 (see Bhattacharji, *The Indian Theogony,* 155-56). In Hindu mythology, *Budha* was the name of the planet Mercury; this planetary deity's "mother" was *Tārā.* L. A. Waddell (*Lamaism in Sikhim* [Delhi: Oriential Publishers, 1973], 74) remarked, "Either by wilful or accidental confusion the idea got transferred to *Buddha,* who about this time also received a place in the Hindu Pantheon."

35. K. K. Dasgupta, "Iconography of Tārā." in *The Śakti Cult and Tārā,* ed. D. C. Sircar, 115-133.

36. D. C. Sircar, "The Tārā of Candradvīpa," Sircar, *The Śakti Cult and Tārā,* 133.

37. Beyer, 4-5.

38. Ibid., 12.

39. Ibid., 13.

40. N. N. Bhattacharya ("The Chinese Origin of the Cult of Tārā," in *The Śakti Cult and Tārā,* ed. Sircar, 143-146) strongly supported the theory of the Chinese Taoist origin of the cult of Tārā. But, his arguments for the assumption that Taoism was the original source of the Buddhist cult of Tārā lack a sufficient empirical grounding.

41. K. K. Dasgupta ("The Iconography of Tārā," esp. 118-19) discusses H. P. Śāstri's opinion on the Nepalese Buddhist origins of the Tārā-cult.

42. Sircar's presentation was titled "Tārā" and this part of his argument appears in *The Śakti Cult and Tārā,* 133.

43. The contradictory viewpoints of contributors in Sircar, *The Śakti Cult and Tārā,* concerning the spacial and temporal origins of the Tārā-cult reflect the historic persistence of the same eclectic religious outlook and behaviour which enabled the ancient Aryans easily to

assimilate with their ancestral religion whatever local aboriginal cults were discovered during their eastward and southward migrations into mainland India. The evidence upon which the Calcutta scholars variously traced the cult's origins at different times and places of eastern and western India, the Himalayan region, Nepal, China and Tibet indicates a simultaneous expansion over a long period of time of several local goddess cults through which they eventually became regionally-extensive heterogeneous cult systems. This syncretism allowed aboriginal deities and local cult practices to become assimilated into systems of generic deities and their cults to become regional and national religious systems such as Tibetan Tārāism. The geographical factors supporting this kind of religious syncretism were illustrated and explained by William Kirk, "The Role of India in the Diffusion of Cultures," *The Geographical Journal*, 141(1975): 19-33. The probability that the Tārā cult expanded geographically by absorbing regional and local goddess cults is supported by contemporary evidence of parallel growth in the goddess cult of Durgā, who in Buddhist mythology and iconography became Ekajaṭā, Nīla [Blue] Sarasvati, Tāriṇi, Ugratārā, and others who may have formerly been local aboriginal goddess-figures. On the other hand, there is insufficient empirical evidence for ascertaining certainly when and how the name Tārā or Tārinī became exclusively a "Buddhist" property in northwest India while keeping the ancient name of Durgā within Hinduism throughout most of east and southern India. The lavishly detailed Tārā representations in the painted murals of the Buddhist cave-temples in central and western India indicate the zenith of the cult's regional popularity in India between the third and the fifth centuries C.E., but do not prove that the Buddhist cult of Tārā must have historically originated in Western India sometime prior to the fifth century C.E.

44. D. C. Bhattacharyya (*Studies of Buddhist Iconography*, 101-105) in particular believed that scientifically interpreting the complex Buddhist iconographical symbolism demands specialized iconographical and iconological expertise as well as advanced historical knowledge of Buddhism.

45. A. C. Moore, *Iconography of Religions* (London: SCM Press, 1977), 200. A fine illustration of the Green Tārā holding the open lily is presented as figure 3 in Beyer (p. 9).

46. In the Brahmanical and the Buddhist iconographical symbolism, the various hand-gestures (*mudrās*) of the deities represent their beneficent graces, their diverse arm-postures (*hasta*s) their interior and yogic powers (*siddhis*), and their respective body-gestures (*āsanas*) their cosmic and divine activities.B. Bhattacharyya indicated in *The Indian Buddhist Iconography*, 433, both the general and the technical meanings of the Sanskrit word *āsana*.In its general sense it means "a seat, a mystic [*sic*] or any attitude exhibited in the lower limbs." In this general sense, the word *padmāsana* means "the lotus seat" or lotus-throne. Moreover, *sukhāsana* means any relaxed or comfortable sitting posture. But, its technical meaning applies to various "attitudes" of sitting, standing, walking or dancing. The *paryaṅkāsana*, which is also known as the *dhyānāsana*, the *vajraparyankāsana*, or as the *vajrasana* is depicted by Bhattacharyya in Figs. 29A, 30A, and 39A-44A (pp. 408, 410-411), is "the meditative pose [and] characteristic sitting attitude of the Dhyānī Buddhas" who are shown in this posture in Figs. 6A, 8A, (p. 402) and elsewhere. The *ardhaparyankāsana* has two varieties.The "ordinary" variety, called *ardhaparyaṅkena mahārājalīla*, shows the deity seated with one leg in the typical yogic lotus-posture and the other leg with its knee raised (as in Fig. 4A, p.401); and the "dancing" variety, called *ardhaparyaṅkene natyastha* (mentioned by Bhattacharyya, 134, and as "a dancing in *ardhaparyaṅika* pose," 199, 390, with illustrations from Lokesvara forms of Avalokiteśvara in Figs. 35A, 105A and 107A).

The "attitude" or posture which shows the image with one of the legs pendant instead of with the raised knee is the *lalitāsana*, which is illustrated in Figs. 3A, 13A and 18A on pp. 401, 404, 405; but, the posture in which both legs are pendant is called *bhadrāsana* as in Fig. 20A, p. 405.

A frequently presented "attitude" is the *ālidhāsana* (Fig. 15A, p. 402).This is a standing-posture having "the right leg outstretched while the left is slightly bent" as for "drawing a bow charged with an arrow."The converse of this standing posture is the *pratyālidhāsana* (Fig.15A, p. 404) having the left leg outstretched and the right slightly bent.
Bhattacharyya pointed out (390-391) that the standard postures or "attitudes" in which the Buddhist deities are represented have "spiritual significance".The *vajraparyaṅkāsana* and its equivalents signify meditation and introspection, and the seated *ardhaparyaṅkāsana* shows serenity.The *ālidhāsana* signifies "heroism" and the *pratyālidhāsana* indicates "destruction and disgust" while the "dancing in *ardhaparyaṅka* displays wrath and horror."

47. In the Mahāyāna Buddhist iconographical system, each deity has its distinctive identifying hand-gesture (*mudrā*), which is supposed to be imitated by the worshipper. But different rites to different deities are accompanied by different signs of the hands and fingers. Kenneth Ch'en explained (*Buddhism in China,* [Princeton, NJ: Princeton University Press, 1964], 328-329) that, "just as the *mantras* [ritual utterances] contain all the secrets of sounds, so the *mudrās* contain all the secrets of touch." The Buddhist hand-gestures may have been acquired from sectarian Hinduism before distinctive Buddhist variants were developed. But six types of *mudrās* became basic in Buddhist iconography particularly in relation to the principal Buddhist divine families. Splendid reproductions of images showing the six typical *mudrās* are found in Benjamin Rowland, *The Evolution of the Buddha Image* (New York: Asia Society Press, 1963); E. B. Havell, *The Art Heritage of India* (Bombay: D.B. Taraporevala, 1964); Heinrich Zimmer, *The Art of Indian Asia* (2 vols.; New York: Pantheon, 1964); and David L. Snellgrove, ed., *The Image of the Buddha* (New York/Paris: Kodansha International/UNESCO, 1978).

The *abhaya-mudrā* of divine blessing shows the right hand raised with its palm facing outward toward the worshipper and the left hand resting in the lap of the seated figure with the palm turned upward.

The *bhūmisparśa-mudrā* is the "earth-touching" gesture, the right hand turned downward with finger-tips touching the ground or else hanging over the deity's right knee.

The *dharmacakra-mudrā* is "the turning of the Wheel of the Law (Dharma) gesture," the forefingers and thumbs of each hand joined at the tips in a circle while the hands are held close to the chest.

The *dhyāna-mudrā* is the "meditation gesture", both hands resting palm upwards in the lap of the seated Buddha, with the right hand under and supporting the left.

The *vara(da)-mudrā* is the gesture of "charity", the right hand held downward with the palm outward toward the worshipper for the compassionate granting of divine favours and/or fulfilling vows of compassion such as the great "Bodhisattva Vow".

The *vitarka-mudrā* is the gesture of reasoning, teaching and sometimes of serenity, the fingers of the right hand bent into its cupped but outward-turned palm and the bent forefinger of the left hand.

48. The *tarjanī-mudrā,* showing the raised index finger of a clenched fist with palm facing the worshipper and held close to the chest, is typical in representations of Vajrayāna deities, who have fearsome facial expressions and ornaments such as necklaces of shrunken heads or of skulls. In The Indian Buddhist Iconography (310-12), B. Bhattacharyya explicitly connected this *mudrā* with the "*Gauri*" group of Vajrayana goddesses (i.e., goddesses having the name *Gauri* in their titles). In the Tārā group of goddesses, this *mudrā* is typical for the four-faced and eight-armed goddess Vajratārā, who is an emanation of the yellow Dhyānī Buddha, Ratnāsambhava.

49. The most important fearsome (*mahāmāyāvijayavāhinī*) Tārās are shown in B. Bhattacharyya (ibid., 307-308) as follows:
(a) the Yellow Tārās (of the *kula*-family of the Dhyānī-Buddha Ratnāsambhava), Jāṅgulī, Parṇasabari, Bhṛkutī and Vajratārā; (b) the Blue Tārās (of the *kula*-family of the Dhyānī-

Buddha Akṣobhya), Ekajatā and Mahācīna Tārā; and (c) the Red Tara (of the *kula*-family of the Dhyānī-Buddha Amitābha), Kurukullā.

50. The iconography of Aṣṭabhuja Vajratārā is illustrated by B. Bhattacharyya (ibid.) in figures 180, 181 and 182.

51. A bronze image of the blue Vajratārā emanation of Akṣobhya in the Indian Museum is mentioned (but not illustrated) by Bhattacharyya (ibid., 243).

52. Bhattacharyya (ibid., 250) has provided an illustration (fig. 192) of the eight-headed and sixteen-armed deity Prasannatārā.

53. The typical insignia of the Red Tara Kurukullā are the bow and arrow, thong and elephant goad. Beyer has presented a fine drawing of this Tārā. See also B.Bhattacharyya, *The Indian Buddhist Iconography* (fig. 121); and Heather Karmay, *Early Sino-Tibetan Art* (London: Aris and Phillips, 1975), fig. 35.

54. The fan and the sword of this one-faced and two-armed Blue Ugratārā or Mahācīna Tārā are shown by B. Bhattacharyya, *The Indian Buddhist Iconography*, fig. 135.

55. See S. Chattopadhyaya, "Trailokyavijaya" in *The Śakti Cult and Tārā*, ed. Sircar, 147-148; but cf. B. Bhattacharyya, *The Indian Buddhist Iconography*, 184-185.

56. B. Bhattacharyya (ibid., 152-53) also provided a description of Bhṛkutī, although he also admitted that sculptured and painted images of this deity are rare.

57. L. A. Waddell, *The Buddhism of Tibet, or Lamaism* (London: W. H. Allen, 1939 [1895]), 359.

58. An illustration of the three-faced, six-arm Saḍbhuja-Sitatārā holding an arrow, rosary and two lotuses, also showing the earth-touching and protective *mudrās*, appears as fig. 171 in B. Bhattacharyya, *The Indian Buddhist Iconography*.

59. K. K. Dasgupta (in *The Śakti Cult and Tārā*, ed. Sircar, 115) drew this inference from etymological roots of the word "Tārā" meaning "across the ocean." But most scholars apparently prefer the translation of "Tārā" as "star", and the inference that the goddess may have been a planetary deity having oceanic and coastal-seaboard connections in a cult which gradually exalted her status as Queen of the oceans, Star of the sea, and protectress-saviouress of navigators and sea-faring merchant-travellers.

60. Karmay, 104.

61. Beyer, 233-236.

62. Beyer, 55.

63. B. Bhattacharyya, *The Indian Buddhist Iconography*, 20-23; and Beyer, 170-226.

64. Beyer, 195-199. The identification of the *mantra* (ritual recitation) with a *maṇḍala* (cosmogram) is indicated by certain ritual texts which describe and illustrate a *Daśatārā-maṇḍala* in which each of the ten syllables of the Tārā-*mantra* is depicted as one of ten iconographically similar Tārās. D. C. Bhattacharyya (*Studies in Buddhist Iconography*, 63-64) also mentioned a *Navatārā-maṇḍala*. in which the principal Tārā is accompanied by eight other Tārās. Photographic reproductions of several horizontal and vertical Tārā-maṇḍalas are shown in the same work as plates 23-25.

65. Beyer, 231.

66. B. Bhattacharyya, *The Indian Buddhist Iconography*, 21, 23.

67. Ibid., 142.

68. B. Bhattacharyya (ibid., 368) drew attention to eight female figures on the aureole (celestial crown) on an image of Khadiravanī Tārā. The iconographical forms of these eight figures are identical with the form of the principal Tārā, and "obviously represent...the eight syllables of her *mantra*: *Om Tāre Tuttāre Ture*. This may be contrasted with representations showing the goddess Vajratārā surrounded by *ten* identical goddesses who apparently are theophanies of the ten syllables of the longer Tārā-*mantra*: *Om Tāre Tuttāre Ture Svāhā*. Bhattacharyya also explained (29-30) that any *mantra* is a mystic power-syllable or verbal formula. The *mantras* must be "applied according to rules" and repeatedly muttered for generating psychic powers which "can astonish the whole world...even to confer Buddhahood or omniscience." On the other hand, the *mantra* has to be repeatedly uttered with great care, neither too quickly nor too slowly, with the mind free from evil thoughts, and never when one is overly tired or fatigued. Its pure repetition day and night causes "the *mantra* person or deity sacred to the *mantra*" to become visualized as forms generated by each syllable's vibrations. The visualization produces psychical identification with the deity, the worshipper perceives himself as the deity with "the same complexion, forms and limbs" described in the *sādhana* for the *mantra*. The wide variety of Tārā *mantras*, and their marvellous and miraculous powers, are fully explained and richly illustrated by Beyer (208-211, 231-236).

69. These quotations and those in subsequent paragraphs are from B. Bhattacharyya, *The Indian Buddhist Iconography*, 20-23.

70. Beyer, 447-450, 460.

71. Beyer, 232.

72. Beyer, 224-225.

73. B. Bhattacharyya, *The Indian Buddhist Iconography*, 23.

74. In this section certain new theological hypotheses are developed from Bhattacharyya's indications of the symbolic significance of gender distinctions in the deities of the Mahayana Buddhist pantheon. The word "thealogy" is contrasted with "theology" in an essay by Naomi R. Goldenberg ("The shift from theology to thealogy," *SR* 16[1987], 37-52), where it is defined as the use of "female symbols to refer to God." The discussion calls into question a recently resurrected popular theory (as reflected, e.g., in *The Goddess Remembered*, by the Canadian National Film Board) that, in the earliest primeval form of religion, the deity was only known as the benevolent Earth Mother without a "divine Father" counterpart. This empirically unsound and historically doubtful hypothesis has drawn on Robert Graves' studies of Greek mythology in *The White Goddess*; Merlin Stone in *When God was a Woman* (New York: Dial Press, 1976); Savina Teubal, *Sarah the Priestess* (Cleveland: University of Ohio Press, 1984); and Charlene Spretnak, *Lost Goddesses of Early Greece: A Collection of Pre-Hellenic Myths* (Boston: Beacon Press, 1981). In Goldenberg's opinion, "the real significance" of the "Goddess movement...from theology to thealogy" is the restoration of the divine immanence against the dominance of divine transcendence whereby "the metaphysical comes home to the physical" (see esp. 49-52). Cf. J. Townsend's critique of the historical foundations of the modern goddess movement elsewhere in this volume.

75. See, e.g., David Knipe in "The Goddess and Her Worship" of the Wisconsin South Asian educational film series.

76. Sir John Woodroffe (Arthur Avalon), *Hymns to the Goddess* (Madras: Ganesh & Co., 1973), v, vi.

77. B. Bhattacharyya (*The Indian Buddhist Iconography*, 30, 390-391) explains that in Tibetan *yab* signifies "the honorable father" and *yum* signifies "the honorable mother." Moreover, the *yab-yum* form of the deities, like the *asanas*, has "a deep spiritual significance." On the one hand, "when the deity is single, it means that the female counterpart has merged into the deity even as salt melts in water." The message of the *yab-yum* image is the union of *Sunya*, the ultimate reality in Vajrayāna Buddhism with "the female principle" of *Bodhi* or the Buddha-Mind and the male principle of *Karuṇā* (compassion). The union of *Bodhi* and *Karuṇā* in *Śūnya* has been represented in Indian, Nepalese, Chinese and Tibetan *tāntric* paintings and images by the *yab-yum* duality of the Dhyānī Buddhas with their consorts, and other *yab-yum* dualities such as Heruka (or Hevajra) in the embrace of Nairātmā (or Vajravārahī), and of Tārā in the embrace of Avalokiteśvara. The various designs of these numerous dualistic representations, which visually immanentalize the transcendent supreme Reality (*Śūnya*), are governed by explicit sacred functions. Following Bhattacharyya (331-35), the particular functions of the principal personal forms of *Śūnya* appear to be as follows:

Function	*Form of Śūnya*	*Identity*
Disease cured	Simhanāda	Male deity, form of Avalokiteśvara
Snake-bite cured	Jāṅgulī	Female emanation of Akṣobhya
The wicked destroyed	Mahākāla	Male Hindu-Buddhist deity
Protection from dangers	Parṇaśabarī	Female emanation of Amoghasiddhi
Emotional burdens	Kurukullā	Female emanation of Amitābha
Success in Love	Vajrānaṅga	Female emanation of Akṣobhya
Freedom from bondage	Heruka	Male emanation of Akṣobhya

Furthermore, just as the male forms are mainly transcendent deities and emanations of the supreme Reality, so the female forms are its immanental forms. Accordingly, in Tibetan Buddhism, propitiation is offered to the male form of Karuṇā (Compassion), that is, to Avalokiteśvara; but intercessory cries for help cause his theophany in a female form, that is, as Tārā. Moreover, while meditation can cause a conceptual visualization in the worshipper of the male deity, Avalokiteśvara, it can also cause the divine respondent to appear as Tārā.

78. In *yab-yum*, Heruka is popularly known as Hevajra.

79. The legend of the simian origins of the Tibetan people and of "the monkey-Bodhisattva" Avalokiteśvara is briefly explained and discussed by Beyer, 4.

80. Getty (121) explained that, in Tibetan representations of the goddess, "the Tārās are almost always seated, but if they accompany Avalokiteśvara, or any other important god, they are usually standing." The non-*tāntric* forms, moreover, show a serene countenance and a mass of wavy hair while the *tāntric* forms display a fierce or *ghora* aspect, dishevelled hair and a third eye. Moreover, "Tārā may be represented in the company of other self-manifestations and by other gods."

81. Zimmer, *The Art of Indian Asia*, 1:183; 2:plate 321.

82. Ibid., 1:183.

83. D. C. Bhattacharyya, *Studies of Buddhist Iconography*, especially in the chapter on "The goddess Tārā"; and Getty, *The Gods of Northern Buddhism*, especially in connection with the dual gender of Kuan-yin (Kannon).

84. Getty, 79.

85. Blofield, 38-40.

86. Getty (118) made the point that Kuan-yin was "not worshipped as the consort of Avalokiteśvara, but as a feminine manifestation of the god himself *for a specific purpose* [emphasis added] as was also the goddess Kwan-non in Japan."

87. Getty, 90.

88. Waddell, *Lamaism in Sikhim*, 77, n. 1.

89. These references are found in D. Chattopadhyaya (ed.), *Tārānāth's History of Buddhism in India* (Simla: Institute of Advanced Studies, 1970), 192-193, 215-216.

90. B. Bhattacharyya (*The Indian Buddhist Iconography*, 29-30) discussed only the psychic origination of the Vajrayāna deities, without exploring also the psychical symbolism of their gender distinctions and other iconographical features.

91. Getty (90) quoted "Professor A. Lloyd" (*The Creed of Half Japan*, 1911): "It is a mistake to speak of Kwan-non as a female deity. Kwan-non, the son of Amitābha is capable of appearing in many forms, male or female, human or animal, according to circumstances. But he is never manifested except as a means of practically demonstrating the divine compassion for a suffering creation."

92. Of the seven *tāntric* forms of Avalokiteśvara which were introduced into Japan from China (probably by Kukai [Kobo Daishi] in the ninth century), only the one known as Juntei-Kwan-non was feminine (i.e., a Tārā). Her Sanskrit name may have been Cuntī-devī, who was worshipped in India as a form of the goddess Durgā. Getty (93) pointed out that "Jun-tei is sometimes represented as an angry goddess, but is usually pacific. She has the third eye and eighteen arms, all the hands holding different symbols." Androgynous deities may not, however, be peculiar to oriential religious traditions. E. A. Wallace Budge (*Gods of the Egyptians* [New York: Dover Books, 1969], 1:287-88) has drawn attention to "the male and female elements of the four elements": Nu/Nut, Heh/Hehut, Kakui/Kakui, and Ker/Kerhet. *The Oxford Classical Dictionary* ([Oxford: Oxford University Press, 1968], 987) refers to Carmenta (Gr.=Nicostrata), daughter of Mercury, who in Greek authors is more commonly referred to as a goddess, but in Latin authors more commonly as a male deity under the name of Carmentis. Other male-female variants were Prorsa/Prorsus and Post-Verta/Post Vertis, being water-nymphs when female and water-gods when male. Perdix, the sister of Daedalus, had many shrines in Athens but was frequently confused with here son Talos when she was worshipped (still under the name Perdix) as a male deity.

ISIS: GODDESS OF THE OIKOUMENE

Rory B. Egan

For about two centuries before the time of Christ and for more than three centuries afterwards, Isis, a goddess who had been worshipped for centuries in Egypt, attracted and held the loyal devotion of thousands of people from every stratum of society in the Mediterranean world and in other parts of the world as far apart as India and Britain into which the cultural influence of the Greeks and Romans had extended. Devotion to Isis in the Greek and Roman world involved a ritual initiation into the mysteries of her cult, as did devotion to several other gods in the Greco-Roman pantheon, whether they were indigenous to Greece or Rome or were imported from areas to the east of the Mediterranean. Although secret initiatory rituals for such divinities as Dionysus and Demeter were practiced by the Greeks for many centuries before that, they seem to have gained in number and popularity during the Hellenistic period, that is, during the centuries following the conquests of Alexander the Great (died 323 B.C.E.) which had opened vast tracts of the Near East to Greek cultural influences and which had profoundly changed the geo-political and cultural context in which the Greeks lived. After Alexander, the Greeks became part of a much larger world of experience in which they became receptive to new customs and ideas, including religious ones, from the Near East (although cultural and religious interchanges between the Greeks and their eastern neighbours had in fact been going on for centuries by this time). It was the Hellenistic period that saw in the Mediterranean basin the development of the social and religious milieu into which Christianity was to be born, and the mystery cults of the pagan gods were an important element in that milieu. Those cults continued to flourish as a prominent part of Mediterranean paganism throughout the early centuries of the Christian era until they eventually shared the demise of paganism in general, although not without having had some degree of influence on Christianity itself. In that regard, for instance, there are plausible signs that Isis herself, in her iconography and her multifarious attributes, is a precursor of the Virgin Mary, the mother of Christ.

In any case the cult of Isis outside of Egypt is a creature of the same phase of Greco-Roman history that set the stage for Christianity and witnessed its eventual triumph over paganism. It is in fact difficult to imagine how the Egyptian divinity would have found the widespread acceptance that she did among the populations of the Mediterranean had it not been for the changed social and political environment brought about by Alexander. He introduced an environment that was necessarily cosmopolitan in nature, blurring the traditional boundaries that had existed between states, even within the Greek world itself, and also those that distinguished the Greeks from other ethnic groups. While the Hellenistic world was cosmopolitan and diverse, the military successes of Alexander and the administrative efforts of his successors had imposed on that world a precarious unity of sorts that survived even after most of the world that Alexander controlled had been subsumed into the even larger political entity that was the Roman Empire. This latter process had been virtually completed with the annexation of Isis' homeland to the Empire following the death of Alexander's last successor, Cleopatra, some three decades before the birth of Christ. By this time the cult of Isis had already spread to Rome and to most other corners of the oikoumene (i.e., "the inhabited earth"), as Greeks of the Hellenistic and Roman Imperial periods called the world as they knew it.

It is obvious to anyone with the slightest knowledge of the traditional pantheons of the Greeks and Romans that they included a plethora of female divinities, both anthropomorphic and numinous, covering a diversity of areas of human concern and responsibility, most of them having to do with characteristically female functions such as fertility, maternity, nurturing and domestic concerns, but some, such as those associated with Athena, encroaching into such traditionally male realms as warfare and politics. It is perhaps a less obvious fact that the multiplicity of goddesses in the respective pantheons of Greece and Rome reflects a complicated process of borrowing and assimilation that goes back into the prehistory of those peoples. Still it must be asked why, given an apparent overabundance of goddesses covering so many different facets of human life, did the Greeks and the Romans, at a relatively late stage in the development of their own pantheons, prove so receptive to another goddess who, moreover, duplicated many of the functions of established goddesses. Part of the answer might be that the transformation of the oikoumene, and the changed world view that came with it, almost demanded a new goddess whose relevance would not be restricted to the particular age group or gender of her devotees, their modes of livelihood, individual ethnic or kinship groups, distinct political entities or geographical areas, special types of human crisis or aspiration, isolated functions or phenomena of the natural world or to permanently-fixed cult locales. Some or all of these limitations applied to most of the members, male or female, of the traditional Greek pantheon, even those who were almost universally known and worshipped within the Greek world, and some of them applied as well to several of the other "foreign" gods who entered the Greek or Roman world at about the same time that Isis did. None of those limitations, however, pertained to Isis herself as the Greeks and Romans knew her. No doubt the fundamental importance which the Egyptians accorded Isis as the agent of the annual revitalization of her brother and consort Osiris, a revitalization which was identified with the flooding of the Nile, the sine-qua-non of life itself in Egypt, preconditioned her for the new role which she was to play in Greco-Roman paganism. But the fragmented, provincial, or compartmentalized functions of the Greek and Roman goddesses left a vacuum to be filled by a goddess of ecumenical functions and relevance who, without replacing the established goddesses, would functionally comprehend several of them and transcend the differences that separated them.

The goddess Isis and the phenomenon of her cult in the Greco-Roman world almost defy succinct description, and certainly comprehensive treatment, in an essay of this nature. Not only is she the product of three great and complex civilizations--Egyptian, Greek and Roman--each of which has its own idiosyncratic religious history, but her cult is copiously documented in literary works and, particularly, in archaeological records, mostly iconographic and inscriptional. These latter are still being collected from areas in three of the world's continents, and in their modern published form already fill a large number of volumes. Yet, even in the face of such a wealth of documentation, we are left tantalizingly in the dark about some features of her cult, due to the simple fact that mystery rituals were involved. As in the case of all of the mystery cults of antiquity, we are left to speculate on the basis of fragmentary evidence. Given the formidable store of evidence of one kind, and the virtual absence of evidence of another kind, this essay will have the modest aim of trying to form a picture of Isis herself in relation to her cult and its practitioners, by presenting a sampling of salient facts and features pertaining to the Greek and Roman Isis while ignoring for the most part her earlier phase as an Egyptian divinity.

Isis and the Greeks

While it was in the Hellenistic period that the cult of Isis really began to spread and flourish outside of Egypt, the arrival of the goddess in the Greek world should actually be viewed in a rather larger chronological and historical context. Egyptian and Greek, or at least Aegean, culture had been in contact for many centuries before the visit of Alexander to Egypt and the establishment of his successors, the Ptolemies, as rulers of Egypt. There had in fact been contact between Egyptians and the Aegean antecedents of the Greeks as early as the third millennium B.C.E., and between Egyptians and Greeks from the second millennium on. The Greek historian Herodotus, writing in the fifth century before Christ, offers his Greek readers an extensive account of the civilization, history and religion of the Egyptians. We hear of bilingual interpreters and guides among the Greek mercenaries and merchants in Egypt from well before the Hellenistic period, and we know of at least one permanent enclave of Greeks and Greek culture, the trading depot of Naucratis, which was established in the late seventh century B.C.E. and featured temples dedicated to Greek divinities. So too, while the establishment of temples in honor of Egyptian deities in Greek cities becomes a common practice in the Hellenistic period, that practice was already underway in cities such as Athens as early as the fifth century B.C.E. The intermingling of Greeks with Egyptians on Egyptian soil led Greeks to attempt to identify Greek divinities with Egyptian ones. The Greeks in fact, in apparent capitulation to the claims of the older civilization, acknowledged the seniority of the Egyptian deities from whom they supposed their own to have derived. Herodotus says that Isis is in Greek Demeter, and goes so far as to conclude that Greek religion and the Greek gods were derived from Egypt (with the exceptions of Hera and Poseidon for whom no Egyptian counterparts could be found). Herodotus is in fact given to seeing the Greek gods as models who are universally valid by whatever name they might be known elsewhere, and he identifies their counterparts, not only in Egypt, but also among most of the other nations that he investigated as well.

Where Isis is concerned, we can see, amid a number of obvious differences, several analogies which would prompt an identification with the Greek Demeter. The Greek goddess is concerned with the fertility of crops, particularly cereal crops, a concern which she shares with Isis who is responsible for the flooding of the Nile and hence for the fertility of Egypt. As the consort of Osiris, Isis is a power to be reckoned with in the world of the dead, while Demeter's daughter Persephone, possibly just a younger version of Demeter herself, is the bride of Hades, the divine king of the Greek underworld. Both Demeter and Isis go on a search for a lost relative, Isis for her deceased husband, Osiris, Demeter for her daughter who has been carried off to the realm of Hades. And in each case the search is of vital consequence for the agricultural fertility of the country. One difference between the two goddesses is in the identity of their consorts. Several male divinities, including Zeus and Poseidon, were consorts of Demeter; but the Greeks thought of Dionysus when they considered Osiris, who was the consort of Isis. Like Osiris, Dionysus recurrently dies, through dismemberment, and comes back to life; but, unlike Osiris, Dionysus has nothing more to do with the realm of the dead. That notwithstanding, the Greeks had Demeter and Dionysus married to each other in Egypt as early as the fifth century B.C.E. At that time, though, to judge from Herodotus, there is no sign of the later identification of Isis with any of the other goddesses of the Greek pantheon. The early linking of the Isis and Demeter might well have had significant influence on the eventual development of Isis as the object of a mystery cult, since Demeter had been for centuries the Greek divinity preeminently associated with mystery rituals and there is no evidence of anything of that nature in the native Egyptian cult of Isis.

In the two centuries between Herodotus and Alexander we have very little information about Isis, her purported connections with the Greek pantheon, and the way she was perceived by Greeks, although it might reasonably be assumed that the process of assimilation and identification continued. In any case, when Alexander founded Alexandria in Egypt, he established sacred precincts, as the historian Arrian tells us, not just for the Greek gods but for Isis as well. After the death of Alexander one of his generals named Ptolemy acquired control of Egypt and founded a dynasty that was not to end until the death of Cleopatra almost two hundred years later. The first Ptolemy had as one of his paramount concerns the establishment of some mode of accommodation between the Hellenized Macedonians, who were governing Egypt, and the subject population of indigenous Egyptians. This problem had its manifestations in many cultural spheres, including religion. In an attempt to reconcile at least some aspects of Greek and Egyptian religion, Ptolemy commissioned two religious experts, an Egyptian priest named Manetho and a Greek named Timotheus who belonged to one of the priestly families in charge of the Eleusinian mysteries, the famous and popular cult in honor of Demeter and Persephone located near Athens. One consequence of this conjunction of religious experts might well have been the corroboration of the identity of Isis with Demeter, and, in particular, the establishment of Isis in a role comparable to that of Demeter in the mysteries of Eleusis. All of this was no doubt an important factor in giving impetus to the diffusion of Isis' cult in the Greek world outside of Egypt. Another product of the theological engineering of Manetho and Timotheus was a new Egyptian god, designed largely for foreign consumption, and named Sarapis. Among the Greeks, Sarapis largely replaced Osiris, who never caught on among them in the same way that his sister-consort did. Sarapis was sometimes worshipped in the same temple with Isis, sometimes in adjacent temples, and on one occasion he is even said to be the consort of Isis.

We have a good idea of the sort of goddess that Isis became in the Hellenistic world outside of Egypt from a number of documents known as "aretalogies", which her devotees have left for us, usually in the form of inscribed stones, but in one instance in literary form in the Latin novel of Apuleius. These aretalogies are in effect catalogues of the glorious attributes and accomplishments of the goddess, presented in the first person, as if Isis herself is listing them. The several versions, or fragments, that survive show a rather consistent pattern with only minor variations evident from different time periods and locations. This has led to some speculation that there might have been a sort of master copy or archetype located in Egypt from which all the others were made. But if there was such a copy it has yet to come to light. A sort of cento of several of the known aretalogies would contain the following information about Isis. She has set up laws that no human can undo. She was the first who discovered fruits for human use. She invented writing, with both sacred letters and profane ones so that everything would not be written in the same way. She invented navigation. She established justice. She brought men and women together. She has determined that women would bear children for nine months. She established a law to the effect that parents are to be treated with affection and kindness by their children, and she prescribed punishment for those children who are not kind to their parents. She and her brother Osiris have put an end to cannibalism. She has established for humans initiation in sacred mysteries. She has taught humans to honor the images of the gods. She has set up sacred precincts. She has ended tyrannical rule. She has ended murder. She has compelled women to be loved by their husbands. She has made justice stronger than gold or silver. She has established a rule that truth is to be regarded as a noble thing. She has devised marriage contracts. She has established different languages for the Greeks and those who are not Greek. She is also, in some aretalogies, responsible for various celestial or cosmological functions and phenomena.

After digesting several of these aretalogies we are prompted to ask if they conform to the profile of the characteristics and accomplishments of the native Egyptian version of Isis. Did the personality of Egyptian Isis lend itself to all of these various creative and civilizing functions? The simple answer is negative. Many of these functions must be drawn from the attributes of a number of other members of the Greek pantheon, to which she was herself newly admitted. One of the claims put into her mouth was, "I am the oldest daughter of Cronus the youngest," that is, that she is taking the place of Hestia, the eldest daughter of Cronus, who was the youngest son in his own family. Despite her seniority, Hestia is a goddess virtually devoid of personality or mythic associations and therefore easily ousted from the pantheon, to be replaced by the parvenue from abroad. What Isis or her devotees claimed for her in the aretalogies, however, is not merely a position in the Greek pantheon, but rather a predominant position in which her functions overshadow those of all the other divinities.

Another glimpse of the image which her adherents had of Isis may be had from a group of four poetic hymns by one Isidoros (whose name, coincidentally or not, can be construed to mean "gift of Isis") which were inscribed on stone and found at a site near Cairo earlier in this century. As poetry, these hymns are pedestrian efforts, written in a very flawed type of Greek, a consideration which does not diminish their interest as documents for the cult of Isis. One of the hymns is divided into three parts: the bios or biography of Isis, her thesmoi or ordinances, and her technai or skills. In the second part the poet tells us that all of the people in the world--the Greeks, the Thracians, and all foreigners--invoke the noble and honored name of Isis, but that each people has a different name for her. The Syrians call her Astarte, the Lycians Leto, the Greeks call her Hera, Aphrodite and Demeter, the Egyptians Thiouis (a name which means "the only one"), because she alone is all of them. All of this is to say in effect that Isis is the single and universal female divinity, while all of the others are simply variant names or avatars of Isis. We shall see that the Latin novelist Apuleius says much the same thing.

The third part of Isidorus' hymn describes the various ways in which Isis works as a savior goddess. She "saves" those who are at sea in a storm or in a shipwreck, those who are wandering in foreign countries far away from home, those who are afflicted with disease or with sleeplessness. She saves cities and those who live in them along with their wives, children and possessions in time of war. This catalogue of her saving activities reinforces the notion that Isis is "the only one," and it suggests that her devotees saw her as appropriating attributes and functions of the female members of the traditional Greek pantheon, as well as functions of some of the male gods, including Zeus, Poseidon and Apollo, all of whom are known to have functioned as "saviors" in one sense or another.

Isis and the Romans

The Romans will have had their awareness of all things Egyptian, including religion, heightened once they took over the administration of the country near the end of the first century B.C.E., but for several generations before that time Rome had been involved in many other parts of the Hellenistic world and had been assimilating numerous features of Hellenistic culture. We know that the Greeks of the Hellenistic period had a significant role in shaping the version of Isis whose cult had been introduced into Rome, albeit not without resistance from some quarters, by at least the middle of the first century B.C.E. Isis was in fact only one of several "oriental" deities to gain a measure of popularity in Rome. Some of them, such as Yahweh, were brought there by their immigrant adherents, whereas at least one, the Iranian Mithras, was brought back by Roman soldiers who returned from the eastern regions of the Empire. Among the others were the Phrygian Cybele and that eastern mother goddess whom the Romans called Magna Mater. Several of these gods and goddesses, including Isis, once established in Rome, were carried wherever Roman power and influence spread, and that included Northern Europe and the island of Britain.

We see evidence that Isis was accepted, or opposed, at Rome with varying degrees of enthusiasm. As might be expected, the conservative element in Roman society led the resistance, sometimes in a striking and dramatic manner, as when the consul Aemilius Paulus personally took an axe to a Roman temple of the goddess in 50 B.C.E., when no other Roman (so the story has it) would undertake to execute a senatorial decree for the destruction of the Iseum. By contrast, less than a hundred years later, the emperor Caligula accorded the cult of Isis official recognition at Rome. Once having found imperial approbation, Isis seems to have retained it successfully, for her image appears on coins along with emperors and their relatives in the second, third and fourth centuries after Christ. The fact of official acceptance and the indications that the imperial families actually cultivated the goddess do not in themselves tell us much about how she was regarded in the eyes of society at large, and there continued to be complaints about her and her devotees. Instances, whether real or only alleged, of sexual prodigality in her precinct, even involving her clergy, circulated in Rome. Her precincts were said to be used for lovers' assignations and there was a tradition that the goddess herself had played a whore. This latter charge is not necessarily as wholly irreligious as it might seem, if only we recall that one of the goddesses whose attributes Isis appropriated was Aphrodite-Venus, the goddess of sexuality in whose honor "sacred prostitution" (to use what is admittedly an inadequate term for the custom) was practiced in some of her temples in the eastern Mediterranean.

The merger, under Roman administration, of Greece and Egypt and all of the rest of the Hellenized world did not ever bring about a complete cultural homogeneity throughout the Empire. The cultural diversity that flourished under the umbrella of Roman political control had its reflexes in the cult of Isis no less than in other aspects of Mediterranean civilization. Thus there are differences to be observed in the reception of Isis, not only among Greeks and Romans but among Greeks of different social strata and intellectual bents, to say nothing of religious predilections. On the Roman side, the variety of the attitudes towards Isis can be illustrated by letting a sampling of Roman writers speak for themselves and, in whatever limited way, for their society. Before doing that, though, we might consider a couple of pieces of evidence which belong to the Roman Imperial period but which are written in Greek.

The first of these is a papyrus document belonging to the large and varied collection of papyri recovered from the sands of Egypt at a place called Oxyrhyncus. It is a catalogue of the geographical locations throughout the world where Isis is worshipped and of the various names by which she is known. Among other things this document claims that the cult of Isis was known not only as far east as the Indus river, but even on the banks of the Ganges which she is said to cause to swell (much as in her native Egypt she was responsible for the flooding of the Nile). A selection from the large catalogue includes the information that in Chalcedon Isis was Themis (a Greek divine personification of "Law" or "Ordinance"), in Thessaly she was Selene (a Greek moon goddess), in Bithynia she was Helen (presumably the Helen of Trojan fame who was worshipped as a goddess in parts of the Greek world, being sometimes identified with Artemis), in Caria Hecate, in Persia the "Latin Goddess," and among the Indians she was Maia. It is impossible of course to know whether the Greek names associated with Isis at some of those Asiatic locations represent the Greek divinities that I suggest or whether they might be merely our anonymous author's Greek equivalents of oriental goddesses. The list, in any case, goes on, and we are told that in the eastern Mediterranean she is also known as Tyche Agathe (Good Fortune), Praxidike ("Exactor of Penalties," sometimes an epithet of Persephone, daughter of Demeter and Queen of the Underworld), Lotophore (Lotus-Bearer), Potnia ("Mistress," which is also an epithet of Hera and Artemis), the Holy One, the All-Seeing one, Aletheia (Truth personified), Phronesis (i.e., "Prudence" or "Good Judgement"), Pronoia (i.e., "Providence" or "Forethought"), Mistress of the Sea, leader of the Muses, Charitomorphos (She of the Gracious Form) and Kallimorphos (She of the Beautiful Form).

Many of these epithets are redundant or at least overlap semantically with one another. And so they tend to the same conclusion that Isidorus' hymn expresses--that Isis is the only one. However thorough the list of titles on the now fragmentary papyrus must have been when it was complete, it can be augmented by numerous inscriptions in Greek or Latin which tell us that there was an Isis Aphrodite, even an Isis Aphrodite Anadyomene, with the third element in this name being an epithet applied to the Greek goddess of love as she is "rising up" from the sea at the time of her birth. There was an Isis Pelagia, that is, Isis of the Sea, an Isis Astarte, and an Isis Aphrodite Astarte, a title which embraces both the Hellenic and the Semitic pantheons, for Astarte (also known as Ishtar) was an oriental goddess in some ways analogous to Aphrodite and in fact seems to have lent some of her attributes to that Greek goddess during a much earlier phase of religious syncretism. There was an Isis Great Mother of the Gods, and so on.

The other Greek document of the Roman period is of quite a different nature, being a formal essay entitled On Isis and Osiris and written early in the second century after Christ by the moral essayist, Plutarch. Plutarch focuses, not on the current state of Isiac worship in the Greco-Roman world, however much that phenomenon might have inspired him to pursue his topic, but rather on the Egyptian perception of Isis and on the Egyptian myth of Isis and Osiris, with the latter being much more prominent in Egypt than he ever was elsewhere. Plutarch stresses the universality of Isis as a goddess for all human beings, something which we have seen to be one of her more striking characteristics in Plutarch's own time and milieu. Noting the diversity of her deeds and attributes, he searches for the unity that underlies it. Thus, for Plutarch, Isis is the material substrate which assumes all the manifold and varied surface forms and attributes of the feminine. He also sees her as the personification of the good that, with a hint of Persian dualism, stands in opposition to evil, which is personified by the villainous Seth, who recurrently murders Osiris and whom the Greeks identified with Typhon, the archenemy of Zeus, the father and ruler of their gods.

With one notable exception, whom we shall later consider at some length, the Latin writers of the generations surrounding Plutarch's who mention Isis make no such attempts at philosophical, theological or psychological analysis of the significance of her myth and cult. Still, various poets of the Augustan Age and the following century do provide us with occasional glimpses of how the goddess was perceived in at least some segments of Roman society. It must of course be remembered that poets have a variety of motives for saying what they do, and that the Roman poets in question have vastly different objectives from those of the Isiac panegyrist, Isidorus. In interpreting what they say, moreover, we must be alert to the presence of such elusive elements as irony, sarcasm, invective, license, or indifference regarding the literal truth and so on.

Tibullus, a writer of love elegies, addresses his beloved Delia (a fictionalized version of a real lover?) in a poem (1.3) which has him absent from Rome and grievously ill. He thinks of his mistress Delia who had urged him not to leave Rome and he thinks also of her devotion to Isis. He asks of what benefit Isis is to him now and of what use were the bronze instruments that she had so often clashed (as devotees of Isis customarily did). He asks Delia what are the benefits of her having assiduously observed the rites of Isis by bathing in clean water and, as he clearly remembers, sleeping alone in a chaste bed. He then addresses Isis directly and asks her for assistance, reminding her that her past successes as a healer are attested to by pictures painted in her temple. He promises Isis that if she cures him Delia will fulfill a vow which she has made, and that she will sit amid a crowd of Egyptians before the door of the goddess's temple, dressed in linen, with her hair let down, and singing Isis' praises twice a day.

Another writer of love elegies, the versatile and prolific poet Ovid, in a collection of poems known as the Amores, has several references to Isis. In one of them (1.8) he quotes a witch who is advising his mistress on amorous tactics. She suggests withholding her favors from time to time, sometimes by feigning a headache, at other times by citing religious obligations to Isis. In another one (2.2) the poet urges his mistress' guardian not to be overly vigilant and excessively suspicious during her absences from home, and specifically not to be too inquisitive about what might have taken place at the temple of Isis. The latter is doubtless an allusion to the reputation that the temples of Isis had as locations for sexual encounters. Ovid is in fact more specific on that point in his Ars Amatoria (1.77), ostensibly a poetic handbook for the entrepreneurial lover, where he groups the synagogue with the temple of Isis as places for amatory encounters. In still another of the Amores (2.13) the poet's mistress, Corinna, is pregnant and the poet invokes both Ilithyia (the classical goddess of childbirth) and Isis, making abundant references to her Egyptian associations (the topography of Egypt and other Egyptian gods such as Anubis, Osiris, and Apis) and asking her to save both Corinna and him, her lover, by one and the same salutary action. He reminds Isis that Corinna has often in the past sat in worship of Isis on the appointed days.

In the collection of poetic letters known as the Tristia (2.297-98), Ovid cites the connection of Isis with the figure of Io, a heroine of Greek mythology who constituted a mythical link between Greece and Egypt, whither she had been pursued from her native Greece by the amorous Zeus after she had been transformed into a heifer. Once there, she became pregnant by Zeus and gave birth to Epaphus. The identification of Isis with Io is not exclusively, or even originally, Ovidian although Ovid might very well be at least partially motivated to introduce it because it represents the erotic associations which Isis had in the minds of some Romans. Whatever justification such associations might have had in fact, they appear to have been poetic commonplaces from the Augustan period on through the next century.

Yet another love elegist, Propertius, expresses his own jealous resentment at the attention which his mistress devotes to Isis at his expense. At the beginning of the poem, which is addressed to his semi-fictional lover Cynthia, the poet presents an anti-Isiac diatribe inspired by the goddess' interference with his amorous activities.

> Now again the dismal solemnities have returned to us and Cynthia has already been engaged with them for ten nights. How I wish that they would be done away with--those rites which the daughter of Inachus [i.e. Io] has sent to Italian women from the tepid Nile. That goddess, whoever she was, who so often has separated such eager lovers, was always a harsh one. But certainly you, Io, in your clandestine amours with Jupiter, became aware of what it is like to set out on the hard journey when Juno ordered you, as a girl, to assume horns and to surrender your speech for the harsh sound of cattle. How frequently you abused your mouth with oak leaves and, while in your stable, you chewed the cud of arbutus on which you had pastured!

> Have you, once Jupiter removed the wild appearances from your visage, become for that reason a disdainful goddess? Was Egypt with its swarthy brood not enough for you? Why has Rome become the goal of such a long journey of yours? What good does it do you to have girls sleeping like widows? But believe you me, your horns will return and we will chase you, cruel one, from our city; since there has never been any good feelings on the part of Rome for Egypt.

Early in the second century after Christ, the harsh and conservative Roman satirist, Juvenal, used what were, to traditional Roman eyes at any rate, peculiar aspects of the Egyptian goddess' cult to point up the irrational and eccentric conduct of the Roman matrons of the poet's own generation. According to him, their immorality is unbounded and they are given to ludicrous acts of credulity when, at the order of Isis, they go on expeditions all the way to Egypt to fetch the goddess's holy water from a place called Meroe. Juvenal's expressed attitude to the devotees of Isis must have been representative of a certain constituency in Rome at the time. For that element of society, the cult of Isis would only have been one among several oriental cults which, along with other aspects of eastern culture, served as convenient symbols of the unhealthy contamination of native Roman customs and values by foreign influences.

The next Latin writer to be considered is quite different from the elegists and the satirist in his attitude towards Isis. He is Lucius Apuleius, a native of Roman North Africa and, among other things, a Platonist philosopher. He is the author of the earliest Latin novel that is completely extant, the Metamorphoses or Golden Ass. As it happens, this novel is also one of the more important and extensive documents we have that is connected with the worship of Isis, whose devotee and initiate Apuleius apparently was in real life. This novel, belonging to the type frequently termed "picaresque," is at first appearances a most unlikely piece of religious propaganda; but one of its aims does seem to have been evangelistic. Utilizing the plot of a traditional story of a man who gets changed into an ass and back again, and interweaving with it a number of other pre-existing elements of fiction and folklore, often of a rather Rabelaisian flavor, the Metamorphoses traces the vicissitudes of its "hero" and narrator, a certain Lucius. The bulk of the novel deals with the tribulations of Lucius during a protracted phase of his life which he spent in asinine form. This phase began when he enlisted the services of a witch who was to transform him into a bird. When the wrong ointment was applied, he became an ass instead. In that form, he was subjected to a long series of unpleasant first-hand experiences, as well as being witness to a number of others which he narrates for the reader. He is aware that the antidote to the ointment, the substance that will turn him back into human form, is fresh roses, but he is repeatedly frustrated in his attempts to eat any of them. At last, when he is in a situation in which, as part of a public entertainment, he is supposed to copulate with a condemned women in the Greek city of Corinth, which had a colony of Isis-worshippers, he is visited by Isis in a dream. The goddess advises him to escape from his handlers and to watch for her cult procession in which her priest will be carrying some of the required roses. Lucius acts on her advice and, upon nibbling some of the roses which the priest is holding, is transformed back into a man. After finding salvation from his predicament with the help of Isis, he becomes an enthusiastic devotee and initiate.

While it is in the culmination of the novel, in the salvation and conversion of the ass, that the Isiac content is most evident, some of its interpreters have seen religious, and indeed specifically Isiac, import in several of the episodes leading up to the culmination. In particular, it should be remarked that the ass is inimical to Isis in her native Egypt, being the animal associated with Seth-Typhon, the god responsible for the death of Osiris. It might well be that this is what prompted Apuleius to meld the story of the conversion of Lucius to that traditional tale of transformation to and from an ass. At any rate, we have in the author of the Metamorphoses, not only a learned philosopher and an imaginative literary master, but also someone who, in his own life as a Roman and an African steeped in Greek philosophy, was associated with the three most important of the geographical and cultural realms to which Isis herself belonged. Apuleius, coy and cautious as he is about revealing specific details, is, of all the known initiates of Isis, the one who is most informative about the phenomenology of her cult. It will be well, therefore, to let Apuleius himself speak to the subject on a couple of points.

Near the beginning of the eleventh book of the Metamorphoses, the "Isis book," Apuleius has the still asiniform Lucius, after viewing the shining orb of the moon, utter a prayer to the moon goddess, whom he does not explicitly name as Isis but whom he regards as an all-powerful and universal divinity. He begins with what afterwards became a well known Marian invocation--Regina Coeli.

> O Queen of Heaven, whether you are Ceres, the original nurturing mother of the harvests, who, joyful at the recovery of your daughter [i.e., Proserpina], did away with the wild and primitive diet of acorns and demonstrated the gentle food for which you now cultivate the soil of Eleusis; or you are heavenly Venus, who at the very beginning of things brought the sexes into association by giving birth to Love and who implanted in the human race the root of perpetual propagation, and who

> are worshipped now at Paphos in your temple around which water flows; or you are the sister of Phoebus [i.e., Artemis/Diana], who, effecting the birth of children by your gentle ministrations, have brought forth numerous peoples and are now worshipped in your famous sanctuary at Ephesus; or you are Proserpina of the horrendous nocturnal howlings, the one who appears in three different forms and controls the force of ghosts and holds tight the fastenings of the earth, who wanders through many groves and is worshipped in a variety of cults--that one who with feminine light illuminates all the city walls and nourishes with moist fires the happy seeds and, during the wanderings of the sun, dispenses irregular light; by whatever name, with whatever ritual, under whatever guise it is proper to call upon you--stand by me now in my direst tribulations, restore my broken luck to strength, grant peace and cessation to the cruel misfortunes that have afflicted me.

Shortly after Lucius has delivered his plea to the unknown goddess, he sees a vision of Isis rising from the sea. In a passage which can, for most of its details, be matched by the surviving iconographical record, Apuleius offers, through the mouth of Lucius, a description of the goddess as she appeared to Lucius in his dream. His description is prefaced by a protest that he is unable to do justice to her impressive apparition; but he proceeds anyway, after asking the goddess herself to lend him the necessary eloquence.

> To begin with, rich and plentiful hair, nicely divided up into ringlets, flowed down softly over the goddess's neck. A crown with flowers of many shapes and types was drawn over the very top of her head. In the middle of it, above the brow, there was a flat disc like a mirror, or rather like the moon, that sparkled with a white light; and on the left and right side it was held up by coils of rising vipers, while it was adorned with ears of grain that extended above. Her multicolored dress, woven from fine linen, was bright with the brilliance of white in one place, yellow like the flower of the crocus in another, and aflame with roseate redness in another, and, what for a great length of time held me spellbound as I observed her, was her cloak of darkest black, resplendent with its ebony gleam. This was deployed around about her and ran from below her right side to her left shoulder where it was gathered into a kind of a knob. Part of it hung down in a pattern of multiple pleats and flowed into a fringe of little knots at the very edges. All over the border and on the broad surface as well, scattered stars were sparkling and in their midst a full moon emitted its flaming fires. Wherever that remarkable cloak flowed in its movement around her, a wreath composed of every type of flower and fruit clung to it by a special binding. She had a great variety of accessories. Her right hand carried a brass rattle whose metal edge was curved in the manner of a sword belt and had several little rods drawn across the middle of it. When she shook these triplicate chords it emitted a shrill sound. From her left hand hung a golden vessel. From the outer surface of its handle there arose an asp which, with its neck puffed out wide, raised its gravid head. Slippers woven from the leaves of the palm of victory covered her immortal feet. That is the way she appeared and, as she breathed out the rich spices of Arabia, she deigned to speak with her godly voice.

This description of the goddess is followed immediately by her response to Lucius, which takes the form of an aretalogy in which she identifies and defines herself.

> Here I am, Lucius, moved by your prayers, the mother of nature, the mistress of all the elements, the first offspring of the eons, the greatest of the spiritual powers, the queen of the dead, the leader of the heavenly ones, the manifestation in one form of all the gods and goddesses. I control by my nod the bright and lofty reaches of the sky, the salubrious breezes of the sea and the lamentable silences of the infernal regions. My single divine immanence is honored under a variety of forms and guises, in diverse rituals and by many names throughout the world. Hence the Phrygians of primeval origin call me Pessinuntia, mother of the gods, while the Athenians, sprung from the soil of their own counter, call me Cecropian Minerva (=Athena), and then the sea-girt Cyprians call me Venus of Paphos, the Cretans, skilled at archery, call me Diana (=Artemis) Dictynna, the trilingual Sicilians call me Stygian Proserpina, the Eleusinians call me the primeval goddess Ceres, others call me Juno, others Bellona, some Hecate and some Rhamnusia, and the Ethiopians, who are illumined by the first rays of the rising sun god, as well as the Arii and the Egyptians, preeminent in ancient learning, worship me with the approprite ceremonies and call me by my true name--Queen Isis.

Isis goes on to tell Lucius that she is answering his prayers for deliverance from his asinine state, but she also advises him that this deliverance will entail an obligation to become her votary and to follow various ritual and ascetic practices for the rest of his life. The prescribed regimen will also assure him of a place in the Elysian fields, the happy part of the underworld, when he departs this life, but that departure might itself be delayed beyond the normal time if he is faithful in the observance of her cult. She tells him that on the next day, while observing a procession of her priests and devotees, he will notice that her high priest is carrying a bunch of roses, and that he is to go forward and partake of the roses from the priest's hand. Lucius does so and is transformed back into human form. The prelude to this central event and the sequel to it provide Apuleius with an opportunity to describe more of the visible manifestations of the cult of Isis and the people who observe it. The parade demonstrates the distinctive costume and accoutrements of her followers: women clad in white spreading flowers or fragrant balm along the procession route, and others with mirrors in their hair reflecting the image of the goddess who was coming along behind them in the parade; men and women carrying candles or torches; a group of musicians with a variety of instruments accompanying a choir of youths; a large contingent of initiates, male and female, dressed in white linen, the women with their hair anointed and veiled with silk and the men shaven bald, and all of them creating a constant din with their brass or golden rattles; the priests in their vestments carrying various relics and symbols having to do with Isis and other gods; the actors dressed up as the Egyptian gods themselves as the final contingent in the procession.

When Lucius has regained his human form, the high priest, in the presence of the marvelling crowd, addresses to him a homily which not only congratulates him on his being favored by Isis, after the lust and folly of his youth had brought such prolonged misfortune on him, but also urges upon him the importance of joining the service of the goddess. Lucius joins the procession as a participant and as an observer of the rest of the ceremonies. He describes the ritual launching of the "ship of Isis," a vessel that was set out on the sea to mark the beginning of the new sailing season, and a number of other observances in honor of the goddess. In the ensuing day, Lucius is repeatedly urged in dreams to be initiated into the priesthood of Isis and he tells the reader that he only hesitated to take that step because of the daunting requirements of chastity and other ascetic restrictions and obligations. Eventually, though, he does join the ranks of her priests, and describes only those parts of the initiation that he was permitted to divulge. Even that much gives us a rather vivid picture of some of the Isiac liturgy, and the actual initiation is followed by another prayer to the goddess, this one an expression of gratitude, and in effect another aretalogy, albeit in the second person this time.

> You, holy and constant savior of the human race, ever generous with your favors to mortals, grant your sweet maternal affection to wretched people in their misfortunes. There is no day, no night, nor indeed any slight instant of time, that passes devoid of your beneficence, when you are not protecting humans on land or sea and extending your right hand of salvation to those driven along by the storms of life. You unravel the inextricably twisted strands of the fates, and soften the gales of Fortune, and curb the harmful courses of the stars. The powers above revere you and those below respect you. You turn the sphere, you light the sun, you govern the world, you place your heel on Tartarus. To you the stars respond, the seasons recur for you, supernatural powers take joy in you, and the elements are in your service. At your nod the breezes blow, the clouds grow up, the seeds germinate and buds grow the birds who make their way through the sky are in awe of your majesty, as are the beasts who roam the mountains, the serpents hidden in the ground and monsters that swim in the sea.

Lucius concludes this prayer with another protestation of his inadequacy to describe all the power and goodness of the goddess, thereby suggesting that the ineffability of her nature was a standard ingredient of prayers to Isis or of catalogues of her attributes.

While there are those who claim that other ancient novelists used their literary medium as a means of espousing the worship of Isis, Apuleius remains the most eloquent literary advocate of Isis. Still the archaeological record testifies with a different sort of eloquence to the vast expanses of time and geography over which the cult of Isis was observed. Isis devotion had its beginnings millennia before Apuleius and was not finally suppressed until several centuries after the passing of that author. The documentation is so strong that there is a risk of distortion in focusing on it without due regard to the overall social and religious context in which Isiac worship flourished. For, despite the claims of her devotees, Isis was never the "only one," even if some modern commentators have engaged in romantic hyperbole based on the impressive testimony of literature and archaeology. One reason that this happens is that there is a natural tendency to retroject into antiquity some of the conditions and characteristics of more recent phases in the history of European religions.

Perhaps the most effective antidote to such a tendency is to delineate some of the things that the worship of Isis was not. The cult of Isis in itself never amounted to anything like a national religion--not in Egypt any more than in the Greek or Roman world--certainly not in the sense that it was the exclusive outlet for the religious instincts and activities of the majority of the population, or even of a predominant minority. In fact, it should not properly be called a "religion" at all, anymore than any of the other pagan cults involving mystery rituals should be. Even the approbation of Roman Emperors must not be construed as giving Isis-worship anything resembling establishment status, for the same rulers would patronize any number of other divinities of diverse origin. The same goes for most of the devotees of Isis of more humble stature in the community. The whole phenomenon of Isiac devotion, therefore, is not to be defined or demarcated within paganism by setting it against, say, the cult of Mithras or that of Dionysus or Demeter, or any of the so-called Olympian divinities, particularly since it often merges or overlaps with such cults. Consequently, the worship of Isis cannot be defined as an entity by setting it against Judaism or Christianity either. It forms an inseparable part of the larger and complex reality of ancient Mediterranean paganism during some of the more volatile and complicated centuries of the pagan era, the same centuries that happen to be the final ones in the history of paganism.

Conclusion

The final centuries of paganism were, of course, the formative centuries of Christianity as well. And so, to the disinterested observer, it should not be too surprising if some of the phenomenology of the pagan cults should resemble some of that belonging to Christianity. In fact, the Isiac cult, in its externals at least, bears a number of features in common with Christianity in such areas as liturgy, iconography, material appurtenances, ascetic regimen and popular pieties. This means that for students of the history of Christianity its affinities with the cult of the multivalent goddess of the pagan oikoumene must continue to excite curiosity and fuel speculation, as it has in the past. But the very complexity, the protean diversity, of Hellenistic and Greco-Roman religious practices and spirituality, dictate against our forming any firm conclusions on questions of possible Isiac influences in the early phases of Christianity, or on the common effects of the same socio-cultural matrix on Isiac cult and creed and on Christianity.

In the strictest sense, of course, Christian theology has made no allowance for female divinity, whether her powers and prerogatives be restricted and specialized, or broad and comprehensive like those of Isis. That notwithstanding, the Virgin Mary, as many have observed, bears many a point of resemblance to Isis in iconography, her rituals, her titles and, perhaps most notably, in her role as the mother of a deity. That role was admittedly underplayed in the reception of Isis in the world of the Greeks and Romans, but it is a role with foundations in the earliest Egyptian strata of her development. There are those who have seen a prototype of the Pieta in Egyptian representations of Isis holding the corpse of Osiris, and a prototype of the nursing Madonna in representations of the lactating Isis nursing the infant god Horus. If these associations are correct, then we are confronted with an interesting irony. After centuries of adaptation and evolution in the Mediterranean world outside of Egypt, some of the more striking vestiges of the worship of Isis in the post-pagan world reflect, not the developments in her cult that were concurrent with the emergence of Christianity, but features that go back to a time and place remote from both Christianity and Greco-Roman paganism.

Bibliographical Note

The published documentation and scholarly literature on Isis is so vast as to preclude succinct description, or even orderly selection of a representative sample. This note will, therefore, simply provide the reader with several points of entry into the morass. Among the several English translations of Golden Ass, the one by Robert Graves is most accessible (*The Transformations of Lucius, Otherwise Known as The Golden Ass by Lucius Apuleius* [Harmondsworth/New York: Penguin, 1950]. For an English translation of Book XI accompanied by the Latin Text and with a scholarly introduction and commentary, see J. Gwynn Griffiths, *Apuleius of Madauros: the Isis Book* (Leiden: Brill, 1975). Griffiths has also produced an essay entitled, "Isis in the Metamorphoses of Apuleius," in *Aspects of Apuleius' Golden Ass*, ed.B. L. Hijmans Jr. and R. T. van der Paardt (Groningen: Bouma's Boekhuis, 1978), 141-166. Those wishing to pursue an interest in the Egyptian, as opposed to the Greco-Roman, Isis might begin with C.J. Bleeker, "Isis and Hathor, Two Ancient Egyptian Goddesses," in *The Book of the Goddess Past and Present*, ed. C. Olson (New York: Crossroad, 1983), 29-48. The focus is on the Greco-Roman Isis in R.E. Witt, *Isis in the Graceo-Roman World*, (Ithaca: Cornell University Press, 1971); and F. Solmsen, *Isis Among the Greeks and Romans* (Cambridge, Mass./London: Harvard University Press, 1979). The cult of Isis is treated as part of the larger phenomenon of the mystery cults by W. Burkert, *Ancient Mystery Cults* (Cambridge, Mass./London: Harvard University Press, 1987). All of the works cited here contain references to other literature.

ŚAKTI: HINDU IMAGES AND CONCEPTS OF THE GODDESS

Klaus K. Klostermaier

Introduction

The images of *śakti*, expressed in visual art and the concepts of *śakti* embodied in words are parallel and interchangeable, and one may begin such a presentation as this one either with images or with words. For the uninitiated, the words about the goddess may be more easily accessible than the often terrifying images.[1]

The literary sources of the *śakti* tradition are numerous and to be found throughout the long history of Hinduism. The Ṛgveda contains the famous *Vāk Sūkta* (X,125): a hymn to the Word through whom everything is created and everything is understood. Not only is the noun *vāk* of feminine gender; the Word is addressed as goddess. The *Mahābhārata*, besides other references to *śakti*, contains a description of, and hymn to, Kālī, the bloodthirsty goddess of war, who appears to Arjuna in a nightly vision immediately before the outbreak of the Great War (*Sauptikaparvan* 8,64 ff). An entire Purāṇa, a bible-like scripture is devoted to the mythology and theology of the goddess: the *Devī Bhāgavatam* is accepted by many Hindus as a revelation by the goddess and as supreme truth. In addition, there are numerous lengthy treatises known as *Tantras* which are held to be scriptures by the Śāktas, those Hindus for whom *brahman* is the Great Mother. *Śakti* literature continued to be created throughout the middle ages and the modern period: a great many medieval poets and singers poured out their love and devotion to Devī in beautiful popular hymns, and thinkers such as Aurobindo Ghose and Gopinath Kaviraj wrote extensive philosophical treatises on the goddess in the twentieth century.

The artistic representations of *Śakti* are, if anything, even older and richer. Prehistoric and protohistoric female statuettes (mostly made of terracotta) have been recovered in great numbers from the areas associated with the Indus-civilisation. Their striking resemblance to goddess figurines worshipped in present day village India leaves little doubt that these were meant to be images of the goddess. Female figures, divine and semi-divine, are ubiquitous throughout classical Indian art. Not only are the great gods, Brahmā, Viṣṇu and Śiva shown in the company of their consorts, independent representations of the goddess in metal, stone and wood are testimonies to a flourishing goddess worship throughout the ages. The motives represented have changed but little through the centuries. The important myths connected with the goddess and her salvific interventions are the major subject of artistic representations. During the Indian middle-ages, when religious emotion was expressed in an often sensuous and erotic manner, representations of the goddess in the guise of Rādhā, the lover of Kṛṣṇa were the favourite motif of miniature painters. There will be hardly a Hindu home without an image of the goddess, and all forms of Hinduism are permeated with an element of Śāktism, excepting perhaps some of the neo-reformist movements like the Ārya Samāj.

The role of women in Śāktism and the place which Śāktism assigns to women is quite different in its varying expressions. Historically, no doubt, matriarchs dominated life; the proto-historic statuettes of mature women with prominent secondary sexual attributes seem to confirm and document this. In some areas of Eastern and Southern India matriarchy[2] survived into our time: these are also the areas where the identification of the Supreme with the goddess[3] as an independent and all-powerful deity was maintained, while in the rest of India the goddess was reduced to being the consort of the Supreme (Male) God, not rarely finding herself in a polygynic family, thus reflecting the status of women in society. Throughout the early history of India, however, much emotion and fervor was devoted to the worship of the (female) consort of God, be she Śrī (Lakṣmī) or Pārvatī (Gaurī), or one of her incarnations like Rādhā. This again may reflect Indian social reality, which in spite of the legal disadvantage of women over against men maintained a high level of respect and affection for women as mothers and wives. Certain family rituals, like the *āratī* which is performed in every pious Hindu home at evening, were exclusively reserved to the mother of the home and most activities in connection with the worship of the domestic deities again were carried out by women. Women, too have traditionally formed the most loyal vistors of temples and shrines. While not acting as *pūjāris* (performers of rituals in temples) women have gained status as *gurus* (spiritual leaders and teachers) in Śāktism. *Pūjāris* rank rather lowly on the social religious ladder, whereas the *guru* is on the very top. Thus the acceptance, also by men, of women-*gurus* and the belief that *dīkṣā* (initiation) performed by a woman-guru is preferable to *dīksā* by a male puts women into a position of considerable authority.

For many Hindus the exercise of the highest political power as Prime Minister of India by Indira Gandhi had religious (*śākta*) overtones. As "Mother India" is worshipped as goddess, so Indira Gandhi was seen as an embodiment of *Śakti* by some of her admirers. Although not formally associated with any of the traditional Śākta sects and often quite idiosyncratic in the use of scriptural texts and forms of worship, contemporary women-saints such as Ānandamāyī Mā and Śārada Devī, or the "Mother" at the Aurobindo Ashram, have been considered by their followers as embodiments of Śakti and, frequently, worshipped as living goddesses.[4] Their following consists fairly equally of men and women; men, too, consider initiation by such women-*gurus* as more efficacious than by a male-*guru*. It would be incorrect, however, to attribute any modern feminist thrust to such religious groups; on the one hand they continue, what had always been an important goddess-tradition within Hinduism, on the other hand they often are quite conservative as far as social matters are concerned. They would hardly figure as protagonists of contemporary Western women's issues, although through their presence and influence they raise the position and prestige of women in the Indian milieu.

Aspects of Goddess Theology

Śakti means power: for the Hindu, power is the criterion of divinity, and consequently everything that exhibits power is revered and worshipped. The *devas* [deities] appear as powers, that is the reason why they are worthy of veneration.

Hinduism does not have a central authority to regulate belief and worship. Thus we should not conceive of the Devī-religion as a homogenous phenomenon. Throughout the ages there have been, and there still are, a number of parallel religions with a focus on Devī. *Śakti* as virgin/mother appears to have been the oldest and most prominent of the goddess traditions. It may have originated in tribal cults and entered Hinduism at a later date. Its range is deep and wide. It reaches from fertility cults and the worship of crude mother images to sublime philosophical discussions of the goddess as brahman and to a metaphysics of Śāktism.

Śakti as a consort of the Great God is an indispensable element of all major Hindu denominations. Her role can range from companion and servant to mistress and life-principle. As Śrī and Bhū she is attending on Viṣṇu; as *Śakti*, she is the energy of Śiva, who without her (embodied in the "i" of *Śiva*) would be *śava*, a corpse. The *ardhanarīśvara* image, the representation of the Highest God as half woman and half man, expresses in a unique way the Hindu belief that male and female are equally represented in the deity and that worship of God entails also worship of the goddess.

In the following, three major aspects of the goddess will be dealt with: Cosmological, theological/soteriological and socio-political. While not exhaustive, these aspects are representative enough to gain an understanding of the role of *Śakti* in Hinduism. A section on "Cult and Iconography" is added to provide information on visual representations of the various aspects of *Śakti*.

I. Cosmological Aspects

1. *Śakti* as the inherent power of creation. It is a peculiarity of all religions known under the name of Hinduism to associate the function of creator, maintainer and destroyer of the universe with the specific *īśvara* or Lord it worships, be it Viṣṇu, Śiva or Devī. Thus the goddess is addressed in the *Devī Māhātmyam* (I,7f):

> By you this universe is borne, by you this world has been created. By you it is protected and you, O Devī, shall consume it at the end.

Goddess-religion identifies Devī with *prakṛti*, matter, rather than with *puruṣa*, spirit. It takes the reality of this world very seriously and resists all attempts of more idealistic systems such as Advaita Vedānta, to consider the world as illusion. As the *Tripurā Rahasya* declares:

> Do not conclude that there is no such thing as the world. Such thinking is imperfect and defective. Such a belief is impossible. One who tries to negate the whole world by the mere act of thought brings it into existence by that very act of negation. Just as a city reflected in a mirror is not a reality but exists as a reflection, so also this world is not a reality in itself but is consciousness all the same. This is self-evident. This is perfect knowledge.[5]

In the Indian context this is a very important position. It not only insists on accepting the visible world as reality, it also locates, as we shall see, the means to ultimate fulfillment within this world.

2. *Śakti* as the power of maintaining the world. The second major function of the *īśvara* of Indian tradition is the maintenance of the world in existence. Here again the theistic systems take up a position both against the momentariness teaching of the Buddhists and the unreality-teaching

of the Advaitins. The world, to fulfill its purpose, must not only be brought into being but also sustained and maintained. Thus Devī-religion identified the goddess, not only with the principle that brought the universe as a whole into existence but also with the power which maintains it, both in general and in very specific ways. The goddess is particularised into the mistress of the animals, as the one who makes vegetables grow and fruits ripen. The ambivalence of her power is manifest in her fierce and propitious forms. She is singularly connected with life: childless women implore her power to conceive. In times of epidemics, it is the goddess who is implored to grant health and relief. Even today many Indian mothers refuse to get their children inoculated against smallpox in order not to offend the goddess Mariamma, who, amongst other things, is also invoked as saviour from smallpox.

3. *Śakti* as the power of destruction. Some of the oldest texts dealing with the goddess describe her as the goddess of war and destruction.

Durgā is mentioned as a war-goddess in the *Mahābhārata*.[6] It seems that she superseded Indra in this function at a comparatively early time. The goddess of war played a great role in Tamilnādu. The goddess was known as Ayai (Mother), Kottavai (Victorious Mother), and Kotti (Slaughterer). She was predominantly the goddess of the Maravar tribe. Among the hosts of dread figures in the battlefield the goddess is the principal one. She was worshipped by the Maravars with offerings of palm wine, fried rice, the blood and marrow and entrails of the victims, and thus she became protector of the Maravars, marching in terrible majesty at the head of their ranks. She is described as moving about the battlefield, with garlands of the entrails of victims on her person, dreadfully laughing at the sight of fallen enemies swimming in their blood. On her flag there is a lion.[7]

This seems to be the same tribal goddess of war which is described in late Tamil works that celebrate the then-accepted cult of Devī:[8]

> Shaking her giant shoulders and dancing to her own song of triumph in the battlefield in the presence of her son Murugan, with dishevelled hair and irregular teeth which adorn an abnormally large mouth, with eyes rolling through rage and with a frightful look, with ears having an owl and a snake as pendants and an awkward large belly, and with an awe-inspiring gait, while she picks out the eyes from a black stinking head, which she is in the act of eating, her mouth dripping with blood.[9]

While describing one of the many cruel battle scenes, the narrator includes without further introduction a vision of "Death-Night in her embodied form":

A black image, a bloody mouth and bloody eyes, wearing crimson garlands and smeared with crimson unguents, attired in a single piece of red cloth, with a noose in hand, and resembling an elderly lady, employed in chanting a dismal note and standing full before their eyes and about to lead away men and steeds and elephants all tied in a stout cord. She seemed to take away diverse kinds of spirits, with dishevelled hair and tied together in a cord, as also many mighty car-warriors divested of their weapons.[10]

An interesting detail is added: The Pāṇḍava soldiers had seen in their dreams this dread figure of the goddess every night since the battle between them and the Kurus had begun: "The brave warriors of the Paṇḍava camp, recollecting the sight they had seen in their dreams, identified it with what they now witnessed."[11] As companions on the battlefield, the Rāksasas and Piśācas are mentioned "gorging upon human flesh and quaffing the blood."

They were fierce, tawny in hue, terrible, of adamantine teeth and dyed with blood. With matted locks on their heads ... endued with five feet and large stomachs. Their fingers were set backwards. Of harsh temper and ugly features, their voice was loud and terrible. They had rows of tinkling bells, tied to their bodies. Possessed of blue throats, they looked very frightful.[12]

If we understand this clue rightly, the goddess has now become the deity of war and battleground: Indra, the youthful conqueror of the early Āryans has been displaced by Durgā, the nightmarish embodiment of senseless murder.

II. Theological Soteriological Aspects

The theology of *Śakti* appears fully developed in the Devī Purānas and Tantras, numerous and voluminous texts from the Indian middle-ages, a time when Hinduism was flourishing after the downfall of Buddhism and Jainism again and when a number of Vedāntic schools competed with each other. A certain vocabulary connected with salvation had developed by then, used by all sects, but used also in such a way as to make deep differences of opinion manifest. As before, we see *Śakti* theology in opposition to the nihilistic-idealistic trends of both Buddhist and Vedāntic schools of thought.

1. *Śukli* as *māyā*: delusion and bondage. As John Woodroffe has it:

The goddess is the great *śakti*. She is *Māyā*, for of her the *māyā* [delusion] which produced the *samsāra* [universe] is. As Lord of *Māyā* she is *Mahāmāya*. Devī is *avidyā* [ignorance] because she binds, and *vidyā* [knowledge] because she liberates and destroys the *samsāra*. She is *prakṛti* [matter; nature] and as existing before creation is the *Adyā śakti* [primal power]. Devī is the *vācaka śakti* [power to speak], the manifestation of *Cit* [consciousness] in *Prakṛti*, and the *vācya śakti* [word power] or *Cit* itself. The *Ātma* [self] should be contemplated as Devī. *Śakti* or Devī is thus the Brahman revealed in its mother aspect (*Śrīmātā*) as creatrix and nourisher of the worlds. Kālī says of herself in Yoginī Tantra: "*Saccidānānda rūpāham brahmaivaham sphuraṭ-brahman*."[13] [I am the form of being, consciousness, bliss; I am brahman, the pulsating brahman.]

Māyā for the Śāktas is not an illusion, a non-reality, a fiction which reveals its non-existence to the eye of realization; she is real and she really binds the person into her life-situation. Śāktas are convinced that *śakti* as *māyā* fulfills a soteriological function insofar as it challenges a person and makes her mobilize her own powers. As Swami Pratyagatmananda observes:

> The imperfections or fetters have their place and function in the descent of the universe from its ultimate perfect source and have therefore got to be resolved and not simply "by-passed" when ascent is sought from cosmic limitations to the purity, freedom and perfections of the ultimate source. *Jīva* [individual person] has to work out his salvation not by simply negating his limitations and his evil, but by so working them up that they become his allies, his helpers, and ultimately his liberation.[14]

2. *Śakti* as *mukti*: emancipation and freedom. Śāktism on the whole appears to have developed as a parallel to Vaiṣṇavism and Śaivism, i.e., as a theistic religion with a realistic theory of salvation, the deity being *mukti-dātā,* bringer of emancipation to a living being incapable of finding freedom without help. The most famous Devī-myth, the one entitled "The goddess slaying the buffalo-demon", offers an excellent model for this. The goddess, who comes into existence in consequence of the pooling of all the powers (*śaktis*) of the major gods (who find themselves helpless facing the buffalo-headed demon who had usurped control of the earth) takes on the enemy and vanquishes him, thus liberating humankind and restoring order to the earth. Many other, less famous and less popular stories about the goddess depict her similarly as saviour and giver of boons to her devotees. As with the texts associated with Viṣṇu and Siva, texts relating the exploits of the goddess also have salvific effects:

> The chanting and hearing of the story of my manifestations remove sins, and grant perfect health and protect one from evil spirits...He who is on a lonely spot in a forest, or is surrounded by forest fire, or who is surrounded by robbers in a desolate spot, or who is captured by enemies, or who is pursued by a lion, or tiger, or by wild elephants in a forest, or who under the orders of a wrathful king is sentenced to death, or has been imprisoned, or who is tossed about in his boat by a tempest in the vast sea, or who is in the most terrible battle under a shower of weapons, or who is amidst all kinds of dreadful troubles, or who is afflicted with pain--such a man on remembering this story of mine will be saved from his straits.[15]

The most characteristic teaching of Śāktism, however, comes close to Advaita Vedānta: *Śakti* is considered to be identical with Brahman.[16] *Śakti* is the creative force which creates the world and the creation is one with the force which pervades it.[17] The earliest evidence for *śakti*-Advaita can be found in some Purāṇas, in which Devī is explaining her own identity with Brahman.[18]2 The *Śākta Upanisads,* which belong to the period from the twelfth century onwards, teach unmistakably *śakti*-Advaita[19] and liberation throug Śrīmahāvidyā.[20] Quite significant are also the narrations in the *Purāṇas* where Devī is described as imparting *jñāna* [wisdom] as a means to liberation.[21] The *Tantras* are built on a basis of *śakti*-Advaita, considering the world (which is seen as real) as an expression of *śakti. Śakti* as *Cit-śakti* [consciousness - power] has two basic powers: *prakāśa* [revealing] and *vimarṣa-śakti* [reflection]. The latter makes self-experience possible through the manifestations of the world.[22]

Since *śakti* is both *avidyā* [ignorance] and *vidyā* [knowledge], matter and spirit, the *sādhana* [spiritual practice] taught by Śāktas often emphasizes the oneness of *bhukti* [enjoyment] and *mukti* [liberation], the merging of matter and spirit, instead of their separation as advocated by other systems. The perfection of the *jīva* [individual person] is achieved through an assumption of all the different forms of *śakti* into his own subtle body, thus becoming one with the force that sustains the universe.[23]

3. *Śakti* as *hlādinī*: the inner-divine bliss-relationship. The school of Caitanya, known as Gauḍīa-Vaiṣṇavism, in which the divine couple Rādhā-Kṛṣṇa is celebrated as the embodiment of the deity and the expression of its blissfull love, speaks of *śakti,* in the form of *hlādinī-śakti,* power of bliss, as a principle innate in Kṛṣṇa, and to a lesser degree, in all persons. As A.K. Majumdar observes:

> Rādhā is Kṛṣṇa's *hlādinī-śakti,* but she is neither a part or even the representation of *śakti;* she is the *śakti* herself in its fullest amplitude. Rādhā is the *pūrna* [full] *śakti*... Rādhā is the realization of the principal emotion being the concretized form of the ideal *hlādinī śakti*...in the *rasa mandala* [dance platform]... the dance of duality ends in ultimate unity... From this unity of Rādhā-Kṛṣṇa emerges the ultimate *rasa* [feeling, enjoyment]....[24]

Here, something very deep is touched, something of fairly universal significance. Religions which are no longer able to perceive the *īśvara śakti,* the *dynamis tou theou,* the inner-divine power of love and bliss, become sterile and petrified in a set of formulae.

III. Political Aspects

In addition to cosmological and theological aspects, Śaktism also has important political dimensions which deserve to be highlighted. In ancient and medieval times, when monarchies flourished in most of today's India, kings (in addition to other justifications) required the authorization of the local temple of the goddess before they could exercise their royal power. According to Gombrich and Gupta:

> while [*śakti*] *has* no authority, she *is* authority, concretised or personified as god's *ajñā* [command].... The sign of royal authority is the *mūdrā* or seal which the king gives to his officers. *Śakti* is called *mudrā*. To have god's *mudra* is thus to have his authority, to be empowered to act on his behalf. A person thus empowered is called *ajñādhāra* "bearer of authority," "wielder of the mandate"; the term is common to [tantric] religion and politics.[25]

The connection with actual political power becomes evident also in the writings of some prominent contemporary Indian thinkers. Aurobindo Ghose, who was prepared to risk his life on behalf of the Indian freedom movement early in the century, discovered, after a vision of Kṛṣṇa, that his calling was to devote his life to the development of the *śakti* within, waiting for the great moment of the *śakti-nipāta*, the descent of power, which would transform him into the *avatāra* of the 20th century. Like Aurobindo, for V.S. Agrawala, life and matter become the vehicles of divine power and the true revelation of deity. Thus he wrote,

> Mother Earth is the deity of the new age. The *kalpa* [age] of Indra-Agni and Śiva-Viṣṇu are no more. The modern age offers its salutations to Mother Earth whom it adores as the super-goddess. The physical boundaries of the Mother Land stretch before our eyes but her real self is her cultural being which has taken shape in the course of centuries through the efforts of her people. Mother Earth is born of contemplation. Let the people devote themselves truthfully to the Mother Land whose legacy they have received from the ancients. Each one of us has to seek refuge with her. Mother Earth is the presiding deity of the age, let us worship her. Mother Earth lives by the achievements of her distinguished sons.[26]

IV. Cult and Iconography

The earliest texts regarding Devī-Durgā are hymns to the goddess, and the bulk of later Devī religious literature again consists of hymns, *mantras*, description of rituals, feasts, and ceremonies. Whereas Devī mythology is comparatively uniform, Devī worship takes innumerable forms. The worship of Devī is usually connected with some material object that represents Devī; she is *prakṛti*, never "pure spirit".[27]

This material object may be a *yantra*--either drawn on the ground, or on a piece of paper, or engraved in metal or stone[28]--or it may be a *ghaṭa* [vessel] covered with red coth, or a sculpted or painted image of the Devī. These again are much more diversified than the images of any other deity. According to the various forms of Śāktism, Devī is represented either as the consort of Śiva, the consort of Viṣṇu, as the Great Mother, as *śakti* of Śiva, Visnu, etc., as Virgin, or in any other of the many form under which she is invoked by Śāktas.

As the consort of Śiva, she is represented with two, four, six, or ten arms--holding lotus, *pāśa* [noose], *aṅkuśa* [dagger], *śaṅkha* [conch], *cakra* [discus], and showing *varadā* [boon-giving] and *abhaya* [do-not-fear] *mudrā,* while one hand may be hanging free.[29] Sometimes she is represented as having three eyes.[30] She is portrayed standing at the side of Śiva, sitting at his side, or sitting on his left thigh.[31]

There is another representation of Devī in which she is still associated with Śiva but not subordinated. As Durgā she has nine forms: in all of them she has four, eight, or more arms, three eyes, a dark complexion and she is standing either on a *padmāsana* [Lotus-seat] or on the head of a buffalo or seated on the back of a lion.[32] Her breast is bound with a snake. She is the "dear younger sister of Viṣṇu who came out of the Adiśakti."[33] Her attributes are: *śaṅkha* [conch], *cakra* [discus], *śula* [spear], *dhanuṣ* [bow], *bana* [arrow], *khadga* [two-edged sword], *kheṭaka* [club], and *pāśa* [noose].[34] Her nine forms are worshipped for various ends: as Nīlakāṇṭhī she is the bestower of wealth and happiness, and as Kṣemankarī she gives health. Harasiddhī is worshipped for the "attainment of desired ends," but as Rudrāṁśa Durgā, Vana Durgā, Agni Durgā, Vindhyavāsinī Durgā, and Ripumārī Durgā she has a predominantlya terrific aspect. One of the most popular images is that of Devī Mahiṣamārdinī or Kātyāyanī. She has usually three eyes, and has ten hands[35] carrying an assortment of weapons. At her feet should be a buffalo, decapitated, with blood gushing from its neck. The *asura* [demon] emerging from it in human form should be half visible, pinned down by the noose of the goddess. The right foot of the Devī is on the back of the lion, the left one on the head of *mahiṣa*.[36] There is also an image of Navadurgā, depicting Devī with eighteen hands, that is "capable of granting all powers."[37]

Many of the manifestations of Devī mentioned in the myths are represented in figures too: Bhadrakālī, Mahākālī, Ambā, Ambikā, Maṅgalā, Sarvamangalā, Kālaratrī, Lalitā, Gaurī, Umā, Pārvatī, Rambhā, and so forth.[38] Totalā is said to be able to destroy all sins.[39] As Trīpurā she is the object of worship of the Tantrikas, often represented as residing in *maṇi-dvīpa* [jewel-island], also combined with the Śiva-Śava.[40]

As Bhūtamātā Devī, she is worshipped by *bhūtas* [ghosts], *pretas* [spirits of deceased], and *piśācas* [goblins], by Indra, *yaksas* [tree spirits], and *gandharvas* [heavenly musicians].

There is a group of eight Devīs with a predominantly terrific function who are worshipped for the destruction of enemies and the removal of fear from devotees: they are Jyeṣṭhā,[41] Raudrī,[42] Kālī,[43] Kalavikarṇikā, Balavikarṇikā, Sarvabhūtadamanī, Balapramathanī, Manonmanī.

The various *avātaras* of Devī mentioned in the *Devī Purāṇas* are also represented figuratively: Thus we find statues of Vāruṇī-Cāmuṇḍā[44], Rakta-Cāmundā, Śiva-dūtī, Yogeśvari, Bhairavī, of Śivā, Kīrti, Siddhi, Riddhi, Kṣamā, Dīpti, Rati, Śvetā, Bhadrā, Ghantākarnī, Diti, Arundhati, Aparājita, Surabhi,[45] of Kṛṣṇā, Indrākṣī, Annapūrṇā, Tulasīdevī, Aśvārudhadevī, Bhuvaneśvarī, Balā, and Rājamātaṅgī.[46] Of special importance is the image of Kālī.[47] Associated with Viṣṇu, Devī is represented as Lakṣmī,[48] Bhūmī,[49] Sītā, Rukmiṇī, Satyabhāma, and Rādhā.[50] With Brahmā she is associated as Sarasvatī.[51] The Saptamātṛkās[52] are usually represented as a group in the temples of South India.[53]

The hymns by which Devī is addressed consist in an enumeration of her titles, qualities, and achievements.[54] Again we have differences stemming from the various conceptions of Devī: as consort of Śiva or Viṣṇu she is praised as faithful wife;[55] as "Great Mother" she is identified with *brahman*, with *prakṛti*, and with *ātman*. The five functions of creation, preservation, attraction, liberation, and destruction are ascribed to her.[56] In Tantric worship she is identified with certain *mantras*,[57] and letters and the worship of the *yantra* play a great role.[58] In other forms of worship she is seen incorporated in a woman who receives worship as Devī.[59] Some of the most popular and profound hymns to Devī are ascribed to Śaṅkarācārya.[60] She is praised as Mother, as Eternal, as granting both enjoyment and liberation,[61] as the body of Śambhu, identified with the material universe and with the subtle elements.[62]

> O mother, may all my speech, howsoever idle, be recitation of *mantra*; may all my actions with my hand be the making of *mudrā*; may all my walking be *pradākṣina* [circumambulation of sacred object]; may all my eating and other functions be *homa* rites; may my act of lying down be prostration before thee; may all my pleasures be an offering to the *ātman*. Whatsoever I do may it be counted for the worship of thee.[63]

Much of *Tantra* hymnology is written in the *sāmdhya* ["twilight"] style, that is, with a double meaning: one gross and sensual, the other sublime and spiritual. Only the initiated will discover the true sense. Promises are usually attached to the recitation of Devī hymns: the devotee is assured of the forgiveness of his sins, of *mukti*, of all sorts of blessings, of an appearance of Devī.[64] The same blessing is usually attached to the listening to, and recitation of, texts related to Devī worship as, for example, the *Devī-Bhāgavata Purāṇa*.[65]

Devī worship consists largely of the same acts as those employed in the worship of Viṣṇu or Śiva. But a few peculiar features are worth mentioning. One of them is bloody sacrifice. The proper worship of Devī is done through the killing of a victim. In former times human sacrifice was connected with several important centres of Devī worship, and assuredly a large number of people met their death as offerings to Devī.[66] Now, usually the sacrifice of fowls and goats takes the place of human sacrifice. Sexual promiscuity also often formed part of Devī worship at certain places.[67] Black magic and sorcery are also closely connected with several centres of Devī worship.[68] Tāntrikas in former times did not attribute any importance to pilgrimage since the union of Devī and Śiva could be found in one's own body. But later on, fifty-one *śakti-pīṭhās* came to be recognized as centres of *śakti* pilgrimage, according to legend they were the places where the parts of Sati fell to the earth.[69] Every one of these places has its own legends and promises of merits and gain in this world and in the next.[70]

Assam has been the centre of Śāktism as far back as our knowledge of Śāktism goes. The most famous of the Assamese temples, Kāmākhyā, near Gauhati, is the most important of the *śakti-pīthās*, being the place where the *yoni* fell down, which is worshipped in the form of a cleft rock.[71] She is worshipped there under the title Kāmeśvarī. According to the *Kālikā Purāṇa* the mountain upon which it fell is Śiva's body.

Thus Kāmākhyā is both a cemetery and the place of the activity of Śiva *śakti*. Both these aspects, death and life, seem to be essential for Śāktism.[72] Reportedly, even now both right-hand (exoteric, orthodox)and left-hand (esoteric, unorthodox) practices are performed in this temple and animals are slaughtered at its altars.[73]

The main feast in honour of Devī is Devī-nava-rātra, popularly known as Dūrga-Pūjā in Bengal, where it is the greatest festival of the year.[74] It is celebrated to commemorate the visit of Pārvatī at her parents' home after her marriage to Śiva, and even now the married daughters return for this occasion to their parents' homes.[75] Numerous images of Devī-Mahiṣamārdinī are put up in houses and public places; at the end of the festival these images are immersed in the Gaṅgā or the sea. Often worship of Devī is performed before earthen vessels draped in red cloth, symbols of Devī. The major centres of Devī worship have their own peculiar feasts.[76] One of these is Ambuvācī, when Mother Earth is supposed to have her menses and the temple remains closed for three days.[77] Only red flowers are used in worship then, and the devotees receive red cloth.

Devī worship is particularly intense in times of epidemics, which are signs of her wrath, because she had been neglected. Then she is appeased by the sacrifice of buffaloes, pigeons, and goats.[78] Similarly, Devī is invoked when somebody has been bitten by a snake or shows signs of poisoning.[79] Usually, it is Devī herself who in the *Purāṇas* and *Tantras* exhorts people to worship her and also gives instructions as to how people should do it.[80]

The cult and iconography of Devī show unmistakably that Devī is saviour. The most popular representation depicts her as saving the world from the demon, a feat which is commemorated in her annual feast. All the hymns invoke her as saviour from various evils, and the sacrifices again are meant to move her to use her power to save the devotee.

Conclusion

Hindu images and concepts of the goddess are historically and phenomenologically related to images and concepts of goddesses in other parts of the world and for almost every individual feature mentioned, parallels could be found in other traditions as well. However, it can be argued, that nowhere do we find such a richness and diversity of concepts and such an exuberance of images of the goddess. This then makes it impossible to establish a coherent, all-embracing Hindu theory of *śakti*. *Śakti* has contradictory features; *śakti* means many different things to different people; *śakti* is seen in a dialectic rather than in a linear logic. *śakti* is unmistakeably female; *śakti* disrupts the order created by the male spirit, *śakti* is concrete, in contrast to much abstract male speculation about things divine. Philosophers like Aurobindo and scholars like Agrawala may be right when they identify the temper of the present time as one that is shaped by *śakti*: not only is power the prevalent criterion of everything, the profound irrationality of the age of science, the inner contradictions inherent in our technological progress, the affirmation of life in the face of mass-extermination of humans, the ambivalence of technology which promises to transform the world into a heaven and also threatens its total annihilation, dominate not only the thoughts of an elite but profoundly shape the fate of all.

The Indian people, who encountered *śakti* in the excesses of a tropical nature and in the tragedies of their eventful history, nevertheless maintained their hope, that ultimately *śakti* would save and not destroy, liberate and not enslave, bless and not condemn humankind for ever.

Notes

1. The presentation of this topic in the Symposium was accompanied by a series of slides showing artistic renderings of the goddess in sculpture and painting. This publication cannot include the illustrations and concentrates on the literary evidence; however, references to *Śakti* images are mentioned for those readers who wish to follow up some suggestions in the text.

2. Matriarchy means "a form of social organisation...in which the mother is head of the family, and in which descent is reckoned in the female line, the children belonging to the mother's clan" (*The Random House College Dictionary*, Revised Edition 1984, p. 825). It is not to be confused with "rule of women" on account of their being women, as also patriarchy is not simply male-rule but rule of the father of the family or clan. Patriarchy can go together with suppression of males other than heads of families, as matriarchy does not mean universal female emancipation. Matriarchy, as defined above, is and has been, a fact in the social life of South Indian society. [Ed. note: cf. Townsend's comments on "matriarchy" and her definition in her essay in this volume.]

3. In spite of the great variety of "goddesses" worshippped in India throughout the ages, there appears to be an understanding that all of these are but manifestations of an unmanifest Supreme Goddess, appearing in various giuses and exercising a variety of functions.

4. Short sketches of the lives of these and other *śākta*-women (together with ample bibliographical references) saints and gurus are found in June McDaniel, *The Madness of the Saints: Ecstatic Religion in Bengal*. (Chicago: Chicago University Press 1989) 191-240.6

5. *Tripurā Rahasya* (Jñānakhanda), English translation, A.U. Vasavada (Varanasi: Chowkhamba, 1965) 156.

6. *Mahābhārata*, Virāṭaparvan 6; Bhīṣmaparvan 23 (Critical Ed. IV, App. I, 4D; VI, App. I, 1).

7. Jnana Prakasar, *Siddhānta Śaivism*, 99 (quoted by A.P. Karmarkar, *The Religions of India* (Lonavla: Mira Publishing House, 1950), 105.

8. *Pattupāṭṭu*, I: 370-31.

9. A.P. Karmarkar, *The Religions of India*, 152.

10. *Mahābhārata*, X, 8, 64-65.

11. Ibid., 8, 82.

12. Ibid.

13. J. Woodroffe, *Introduction to Tantra Śāstra* 4, 1963 (Madras: Ganesh & Co.), 12; quoting *Yoginī Tantra* I, 10.

14. Swami Pratyagatmananda, "Tantra-Philosophy," in *The Cultural Heritage of India*, ed. H. Bhattacharya, (1965), III: 437-39.

15. *Devī Māhātmyam*, XII, 20-30

16. Swami Pratyagatmananda, 437-448. According to the *Mahānirvānatantra śakti*-reality is neither *advaita* [Non-Duality] nor *dvaita* [Duality] but *dvaitādvaitavivarjita* [Beyond-Duality-and-Non Duality].

17. *Tripurā Rahasya*, 154: "The omnipotent Goddess who is consciousness, who is truly the 'I-consciousness,' creates appearances of the world upon its own essence like reflections in a mirror by her willpower or the power of *māyā* known as freedom."

18. E.g. *Kūrma Purāṇa* I, 1 (6th Century C.E.).

19. See *Devī Upaniṣad* I, 2; *Saubhāgya-Lakṣmī Upaniṣad* I, 11.

20. *Devī Upaniṣad* I.

21. E.g., *Devī Bhāgavata Purāna* V, 35; VII, 33-37; XII, 8.

22. *Tripurā Rahasya*, Chap. 4.

23. J. Woodroff, *Introduction to Tantra Śāstra*, 48-51.

24. A.K. Majumdar, *Caitanya: His Life and Doctrine*, (Bombay: Bharatiya Vidya Bhavan, 1969) 290.

25. Gupta and Gombrich, "Kings, Power and the Goddess", *South Asia Research* 6/2 (1986), 127.

26. V.S. Agrawala, "Mother Earth", in *Nehru Abhinandan Granth*, (Calcutta: Nehru Abhinandan Sabhā, 1949), 490.

27. Cf. J. Woodroffe, *Introduction to Tantra Śāstra*, 74-122.

28. The most famous *yantra* is the Śrīcakra consisting of forty-three triangles. Regular *pūjā* [worship] is offered to it twice daily in South-India Śakti *pīthālayas* [places of Devī worship]. Other *yantras* are engraved upon gold, silver or copper plates, which are rolled into a cylinder and then put into a golden or other metallic case so that they may be worn on the body of a person with a view to avoid diseases, possession of devils and other such evils, which, it is supposed they have the power to ward off. Occasional worship is also offered to this case containing the magical *yantra* and the wearer's faith in this efficacy may well affect cures in many cases. (T.A.G. Rao, *Elements of Hindu Iconography* (Reprint; New York: Paragon, 1968), 332, vols. I-II. Cf. Moti Chandra, "Our Lady of Beauty and Abundance: Padmaśrī," in *Nehru Abhinandan Granth*, 497-513 (with illustration).

29. See T.A.G. Rao, *Iconography*, vols. I-II, 320ff.

30. Ibid. Illustrations.

31. Ibid. Illustrations of Pārvatī and Śiva standing are in the Elephanta caves (H. Zimmer, *The Art of Indian Asia* [New York: Bollingen Foundation, 1955], vol. 2, plate 257). For Pārvatī sitting at the side of Śiva in Ellora, Kailāśanātha temple, see B. Rowland, *The Art and Architecture of India* (Baltimore: Penguin Books, 1967) pl. 119. For Devī sitting on the left thigh of Śiva in Bengal, see H. Zimmer, *Myths and Symbols in Indian Art & Civilization* (New York: Harper & Row, 1963), pl. 34.

32. Illustrations in Rao, *Iconography*, pl. 99-102. For Devī standing on the head of a buffalo, see Rowland, *The Art and Architecture of India*, pl. 116 and seated on the back of a lion, see J.N. Banerjea, *The Development of Hindu Iconography* (Calcutta: The University of Calcutta, 1956), pl. XLIII, 4; Devī seated in *padmasana*, see Rao, *Iconography*, pl. XV).

33. *Suprabhedāgama*, cited by Rao, *Iconography*, vol. I-II, 340.

34. All of these attributes can be associated with salvific activities of Devī.

35. For illustrations, see Rao, *Iconography*, pl. 102-105 (especially Ellora and Mahabalipuram); Banerjea, *Development*, pl. XLI, No. 2 and 4; XLII, No. 1-3; Zimmer, *Myths*, pl. 58 and 59; Zimmer, *Art*, vol. II, pl. 117, 210, 284-85; 288, 326, 434.

36. This model is not followed universally. In the representation at Mahabalipuram, the goddess is riding on her lion, aiming at the demon who has a human body with a buffalo head. The *Viṣṇudharmottara* describes a Mahiṣamardinī with twenty arms.

37. An interesting representation of the origin of Durgā with eighteen arms is given in Zimmer, *Myths*, pl. 56.

38. Bhadrakālī: illustrations in Rao, *Iconography*, pl. 106 (a bronze from Tiruppalattur), and Zimmer, *Myths*, pl. 57 (a Rājput painting). Mahākālī: illustrations in Rao, *Iconography*, pl. 108.

39. Rao, *Iconography*, pl. 361.

40. A Rājput painting of the Devī seated in *mani-dvīpa*, in Zimmer, *Myths*, pl. 66 (cf. his commentary, 197-216).

41. Jyeṣṭhādevī seems to be a very important goddess and her worship appears to be very old. See Rao, *Iconography*, pp. 390-396. The *Bodhāyana-Gṛhya-Sūtras* contain a chapter dealing with the worship of this goddess. The Ālvār Tondar Adippodi derides the worshippers of this goddess. Rao says that in several temples Jyeṣṭhādevī occupies a corner, from others she had been thrown out, in some temples she is mistaken for another god. She has a crow in her banner and an ass as her *vahana* [mount] and is flanked by a bull and a youthful female figure. The *Liṅga Purāna* has a long account in which it is saiḍ that Jyeṣṭhādevī came out from the milk-ocean after the poison Kālakūtā. In Tamilnādu she has many names: Mugadi, Tauvai, Kaladi, Mūdevī, Kettai, Ēkavēni. She is said to be happy at all places where inauspicious acts are being done or inauspicious words are being uttered. Illustrations: Rao, *Iconography*, pl. 121-123.

42. Illustrations: ibid.

43. Kālī is represented in many forms: Kālī on Śiva-Śava (Zimmer, *Myths*, pl. 67) dancing on Śiva (ibid., pl. 69); devouring Śiva (ibid., pl. 68).

44. Rao, *Iconography*, 364; illustrations in Banerjea, *Development*, pl. XLIV, no. 5.

45. Rao, *Iconography*, 366.

46. Rao, *Iconography*, 368-71.

47. Illustrations in Zimmer, *Myths*, pl. 67-69.

48. Illustrations in Rao, *Iconography*, pl. VI.

49. Ibid.

50. The female counterparts to some Viṣṇu-*avatāras* find their representation as Narasinhī, Varāhī, etc. See Banerjea, *Development*, pl. XLIV, No. 2 and 3.

51. A recent illustration in *Devī Bhāgavata Purāṇa* 580, Gorakhpur: Gītā-press 1960), shows a parallel representation of Sarasvatī, Lakṣmī and Durgā. But there is also a four-faced Brāhmanī, see Banerjea, *Development*, pl. XLIII, No. 1), a Vaisnavī and a Śivā.

52. Illustrations of the Saptamātrikās in Rao, *Iconography*, pl. 118, No. 1 and 2 (Ellora and Belur) and pl. 119 (Kumbhakonam). Usually the Seven Mothers are flanked by Bhairava and Gaṇeśa. H. Zimmer, *Art*, vol. II, 230; vol. I, B4c.

53. Rao, *Iconography*, 379-381. The *Vārāha Purāṇa* brings an eulogy to the eight *mātras* who represent eight qualities: *Kāma* [desire] (=Yogesvari), *Krodha* [anger] (=*Maheśvarī*), *Lobha* [greed] (=*Vaiṣṇavī*), *Mada* [intoxication] (=*Brāhmaṇī*), *Moha* [delusion] (=*Kāmadevī*), *Matsārya* [jealousy] (=Indrāṇī), Paiśunya [slander] (=Yamī), and *Āsuya* [envy] (=*Vārahī*). The *Kūrma Purāna* I,11 contains a legend according to which Śiva sends Bhairava and the Mātrikās after the killing of Andhaka, to *pātāla loka* [a nether-world], the abode of Nrsinha. Bhairava merges again into Śiva. "The Mātrikās began to destroy everything in the universe for the purpose of feeding themselves, *Bhairava* then prayed to Nṛsinha to abstract from the *Mātrikās* their destructive nature and it was thereupon withdrawn from them." On worship of *Mātrikās*, see P.V. Kane, *History of Dharmaśāstra* (Pune: Bhandarkar Oriental Research Institute, 1933-1978) II/I, pp. 217ff.

54. Durgāstotras, in which Devī is praised as saviour, are found in *Mahābhārata* IV, 6; VI, 23; *Harivamśa* III, 3; II, 2-4, 22; *Mārkaṇḍeya Purāṇa* 81-93 (78-90); *Vāmana Purāna* 17-21; 51-56; 32-33; *Kūrma Purāna* I, 11-12; *Varāha Purāna* 27-28; 90-96.

55. *Bṛhadstotraratnakāra*, Devīstotra No. 4; *Devī Bhāgavata* IX, 4. *Brahmavaivarta Purāṇa*, Kṛṣṇajanmakhaṇḍha 34, 17.

56. *Devī Bhāgavata* III, 4; Hymn to Gaṅgā and other rivers *Bṛhadrstotraratnākara*, 255-270.

57. *Agni Purāṇa*, Chap. 309 contains a *mantra* for worshipping the goddess Tvaritā who "grants enjoyment of earthly comfort and salvation after death."

58. The hymn in *Devī Bhāgavata* XI, 1f. shows strong Tantric influence. Representation of a Yantra in Zimmer, *Myths*, pl. 36. Various Yantras depicted and described in D.N. Bose, *Tantras* (3rd ed.; Calcutta: Oriental Publishing Co., 1956), Chap. XIV.

59. As, for example, in the famous Bhairavī Cakra (described in *Mahānirvāṇa Tantra* VIII): also in other *cakras* described by Bose, *Tantras*, Chap. XI.

60. Thus, for example, the famous *Ānandalaharī*, *Sandaryalaharī*, *Tripurasundarī*, etc. (*Bṛhadstotraratnākara* No. 5). About their authenticity, cf. S.K. Belvalkar, *Lectures on Vedānta* (Pune: Bilvakunja 1929), Lecture six.

61. *Ānandalaharī*, vv. 14-18.

62. Ibid., vv. 11-13.

63. Ibid., v. 28. The recitation of a litany of names and titles of Devī is a very common practice. The following puranic texts contain the one hundred and eight names of Devī: *Matsya Purāna* 13, 26-53; *Devī Bhāgavata Purāṇa* VII, 30, 55-83; *Padma Purāṇa*, Sṛstikhaṇḍa 17, 185-211; *Skanda Purāṇa*, Āranyakanda 98, 6-92; *Varāha Purāṇa* 90-95; *Kūrma Purāna* I, 11-12 (1000 names of Devī).

64. Thus already in the two Durgāstotras in the *Mahābhārata* (see supra). Also: *Devī Bhāgavata Purāṇa* VII, 39.

65. A long description with quotations from various scriptures is given in the Hindi *Devī Bhāgavata Purāṇa* (Gorakhpur: Gita Press, 1960), 35-38.

66. A description of a human sacrifice to Devī is found in *Bhāgavata Purāṇa* V, 9, 12-20. The *Kālikā Purāṇa* (fourteenth century) contains a so-called "blood-chapter," (*rudhirādhyāya*) describing the various bloody sacrifices in honour of the goddess, "Om. Aim Hrim Śrim. Kauśikī, thou are gratified with blood." Karmakar (*The Religions of India*, 213) cites many historic instances of human sacrifice. Up to the nineteenth century, every Friday one human sacrifice was offered in the Kālī temple at Tanjor. Marathas were keen observers of this cult. The head was placed on a golden plate before Kālī; the lungs were cooked and eaten by Kandra Yogis; the royal family ate rice cooked in the blood of the victim. Many tribes, for example, Khonds, Nāgas, Bhumji, Bhuviyayas knew the practice of human sacrifice. Guru Gobind Singh offered a disciple to Durgā. About the practice of human sacrifice at the notorious Tamreśvari temple in Sasya (Assam), see Barua-Srinivasa-Murthy in *Temples and Legends of Assam* (Bombay: Bharatiya Vidya Bhavan, 1963), 86. The human sacrifice was an annual feature there. In 1565, Nāra Nārāyan, a ruler of Kuch, rebuilt the temple of Kāmākṣī. For its consecration, one hundred and forty men are said to have been sacrificed. Also, in Bhavabhūti's *Mālatī-Mādhava* we find the description of a human sacrifice before the image of the Devī. D.C. Sirkar (*Sakti-Pithas*, [Delhi: Motilal Banarsidass, 1948], 16) brings ample historical evidence of regular human sacrifice to Devī. Even now the papers report from time to time cases of human sacrifice and self-immolation to Devī.

67. Cf. B.K. Barua-H.V.S. Murthy, *Temples and Legends of Assam*, 14.

68. Ibid., pp. 15-18.

69. Ibid., 23-29. According to Sirkar, *The Śakti-Pīṭhas*, the origin of the Śakti Pīṭhas is due to a further evolution of the *Daksa-yajña* story at the beginning of the Middle Ages (see also *Devī Bhāgavata Purāṇa* VII, 30 and *Kālikā Purāṇa* 18). There are two different versions. According to the first, Brahmā, Viṣṇu and Śiva enter Sati's body. According to the other, Viṣṇu cuts Sati's body into pieces by means of his *cakra*. Sirkar suggests a possible connection with Buddhist relic-worship. "Both the Father god (*lingam*) and the Mother Goddess (*yoni*) were worshipped by the pre-Āryan peoples of India" (7). Bhāgavatī may have meant originally the deity having a *bhāga* (being the source of all beings) and Bhāgavat could be a secondary derivation for the male Supreme-God. There is an interesting ceremony called *Hiraṇya-garbha-mahādāna* which signifies the rebirth from the Golden Womb of the Goddess. The earliest mention of Śakti Pīṭhās with *yoni* and *stana* are in *Mahābhārata* III, 82, 83-85. Bhīmāsthāna is mentioned associated with the *yoni*, in III, 84, 93-95; Gaurīśikhara associated with *stana*, in III, 84, 151-153. Early Tantras (eighth century? C.E.) mention four *pīṭhās*: Ātmapīṭha, Parapīṭha, Yogapīṭha, and Guhyapīṭha. Later texts mention eight, ten, eighteen, forty-two, fifty-one and even one hundred and eight *pīṭhas*.

70. Ibid., passim. Bāna in *Harṣacarita*, Chap. V recounts how different people implored the goddess for the recovery of the sick king: "Young nobles were burning themselves with lamps to propitiate the Mothers. A Dradividan solicited the Vampire with the offering of a skull. An Andhra man was holding up his arms to conciliate Caṇḍī. Distressed young servants were pacifying Mahākālī by holding melting gums on their heads. A group of relations were about to offer their own flesh. Young courtiers resorted openly to the sale of human flesh."

71. Barua-Murthy, *Temples and Legends of Assam*, 19-44. F. Pratt, *Hindu Culture and Personality* (Bombay: Asia, 1962), 234 calls Devī worship "worship of the Terrible for its own sake." He thinks that Devī worship is connected with the urge to self-castration, suicide, murder. There

are many instances in literature of people cutting their own throat in honour of Kālī in Durgā temples.

72. Barua--Srinivasa--Murthy, *Temples and Legends of Assam*, 26.

73. See Bani Kanta Kakati, *The Mother Goddess Kāmākhyā* (Gauhati: Lawyers' Book Stall, 1948).

74. In *Devī Bhāgavata Purāṇa* III, 26ff., the Devī-navarātra-vrata is explained. Kane, *History of Dharma-Śāstra*, V/I, describes some other common Devī feasts: *Mānasapūjā* (125, worship against snakebite); *Haritālikā* (144-46); *Śrīpañcamī* (432-3); *Sartī-devī* (434); *Sambhayuga* (455); *Sabavotsara* (105). For the history of present-day worship of Devī during Dūrga-Pūjā in a mud-image cf. D.C. Sirkar, *The Śaktī-Pīthas*, 74, note 1.

75. Batuknath Bhattacharya, "Festivals and Sacred Days," in *Cultural Heritage of India*, vol. IV, 486 tries to connect Dūrgā-puja with the Ṛgvedic *Devīsūkta*.

76. See the volumes on *Temples and Legends of Assam*, Bengal, Bihar, and Andhra Pradesh, published by Bharatiya Vidya Bhavan, Bombay.

77. Barua-Murthy, *Temples and Legends of Assam*, 37.

78. The Purāṇas contain a large number of chapters on the mode of worship of Devī. The bulk of Tantras also consists of rituals and ceremonies. See *Devī Bhāgavata Purāṇa* VIII, 24-26; V, 32-33; IX, 4-6; IX, 15, 25; XII, 13-16; and *Kalyāṇa Upāsanānka* (1968), 350-357.

79. H. Whitehead, *Village Gods* (2nd ed.; Calcutta: Association Press, 1921), 112-138.

80. *Devī Bhāgavata Purāṇa* VII, 38; *Mahānirvāṇa Tantra*, passim; *Lakṣmī Tantra* 34; *Bhaviṣya Purāṇa* IV, 138.

PART TWO:
THE MODERN DISCUSSION

UNDERSTANDINGS OF "THE GODDESS" IN CONTEMPORARY FEMINIST SCHOLARSHIP

Dawne McCance

In her essay, "Mapmaking: A Survey of Feminist Criticism," which opens the 1985 collection *Gynocritics/La Gynocritique: Feminist Approaches To Writing By Canadian And Québécoise Women*, Barbara Godard suggests that since the late 1960s, the focus of North American feminist criticism has changes "from denouncing men's works to exploring women's writing". Identifying and denouncing sexist stereotypes in patriarchal texts has gradually given way to feminist criticism focused on the exploration of women's texts, "re-evaluating the canon of received texts to include non-canonical genres where women excelled, and attempting to define a female tradition in writing." In this second phase, as Godard points out, feminist criticism often involves a search for "lost" women, lost stories and rituals, different conceptual and cultural spaces.[1]

The same transition has occurred, I think, in religious feminist criticism. Works directed to the delineation of androcentrism and misogyny in male-authored religious texts have been followed by works more explorative of positive traditions for women.[2] In its second phase, religious feminist criticism is marked by the theme of quest. Most notably, the search for lost voices, for myths and symbols excluded from patriarchal tradition, manifests itself as a "quest for the goddess."

It is the purpose of this paper to outline a number of different understandings of this "quest for the goddess" on the part of contemporary religious feminists. Let me say at the outset that much of this work is transitional, tentative, some of it assertive, all of it committed. In intellectual range, it extends from the scholarly to the popular, catering to a developing audience. As I think this paper suggests, "the goddess" means different things to different writers. Perhaps for all such writers, however, the growing interest in goddess thematics has been stimulated by recent work on the prehistoric and ancient Mother Goddess, particularly by documentation of archaeological findings such as those of James Mellaart at Catal Huyuk, as well as by such studies as Marija Gimbutas's *The Goddesses And Gods of Old Europe 6500-3500 B.C.* (1982), E.O. Jame's *The Cult Of The Mother Goddess* (1959), and Erich Neumann's *The Great Mother* (1955).[3] Because most academic religious feminism has emanated thus far from the religious traditions of the west, this paper will focus on biblically-based feminists, including so-called "post-biblical" feminists, introducing some cross-cultural perspectives in the concluding section. I am applying the problematic label "feminist" to writers who so describe themselves.

The "quest for the goddess" poses particular problems for feminist scholars within the theistic traditions of the West, precisely because these traditions generally lack feminine symbolism of the divine. As Rita Gross observes, these religions stress the personal dimension of their symbols of the divine, and stress that the divine should be conceived of and related to as if a personal being in relationship with other persons. "But this personal god is always symbolized and addressed as a male person in the three major traditions of the West, and male forms of symbolism and address are adamantly maintained."[4] Given this obvious difficulty, how biblically-based feminists seek and appropriate "the goddess" raises central questions of feminist methodology.

In order to distinguish the methodological approaches of western religious feminists, a threefold typology has often been suggested. For example, in her essay, "Symbols of Goddess and God in Feminist Theology," Carol Christ suggests that biblically-based feminists fall into three main types: at the one extreme, if you will, those for whom biblical traditions are essentially nonsexist, and therefore, for whom feminist reform does not touch core substance; at the other end of the spectrum, those for whom biblical traditions are so fundamentally sexist as to be nonreformable; and finally, those who fall somewhere between these two poles, those for whom tradition is sexist, yet reformable.[5] In this paper, I will adopt such a threefold typology in relation to feminist understandings of "the goddess".

Type One: Translating Biblical Androgeny

For type-one feminists, biblical tradition is essentially nonsexist. I am not sure that these writers can be related to a religion of "the goddess" as such; if they can, it is through their exegesis of a biblical androgyny. Here, the "quest for the goddess" becomes a search for "forgotten" names and images of the divine, which can be found through a "proper" exegesis of Old and New Testament scriptures. Consider Phyllis Trible, Letty Russell, and Rita Gross as examples.

Trible's *God And The Rhetoric Of Sexuality* attempts to read the Old Testament as intrinsically nonsexist.[6] That is, according to Trible, the Old Testament has *within it* an equalitarian image of God as male and female. Trible attempts to "disclose" this basic image through her investigation of female metaphors for God in such passages as Psalm 22:9-10, Genesis 49:25, and Hosea 9:11-14. "Now," writes Trible,

> a close reading of these verses underscores further connections between the deity and the female...Each occurrence links God with psychophysical aspects of birth. In the first line [of Psalm 22:9-10], the divine you receives the infant from the womb and places it safely upon the breasts of the mother...Although the poetry never explicitly calls God midwife and mother, its form and content disclose these metaphors...In Genesis 49:25, breasts and womb occur together again...though the verse combines two partial metaphors, the explicit father and the implicit mother, we accent here the female dimension of the God *sadday*, who give the blessings of the breasts and the womb...For Hosea, signs of female infertility have become symbols of corporate sterility. In response to sin, the God of the womb and breasts aborts fetuses and dries up milk. This link between the divine and the maternal speaks death, not life. Yet even in judgment these symbols are for us points of departure in a continuing journey to explore the image of God female.[7]

Letty Russell's *Human Liberation In A Feminist Perspective* applies a similar "hermeneutics of disclosure" to the New Testament.[8] In order to undertake what she calls the "search for a usable past," Russell distinguishes between tradition and Tradition, between script and Scripture: small-t "tradition" and "script" refer to historical-patriarchal formulations of biblical teaching, while capital-T "Tradition" and "Scripture" refer to the liberating (nonsexist) kerygma. It is not necessary for feminist Christians to develop a new religion and create new gods (or goddesses) in order to liberate themselves, Russel argues; one need only recover the true meaning of Tradition.[9] Among other things, this recovery involves inclusion of female attributes in the Godhead.[10] Intrigued by the suggestion that "elements from the Canaanite worship of the Mother Goddess...may have been incorporated into the Hebrew concept of God," Russell argues that the search for a usable past includes the search for "forgotten names of God": characteristics of God which were considered to be feminine in pre-biblical traditions, and which, she thinks, can also be found in Old and New Testament scriptures.

> It is not necessary to think of God primarily as having masculine characteristics of domination and lordship, a practice that has served to legitimate aggression and domination in androcentric cultures. It is also possible to think of God as having characteristics frequently thought of as feminine...[One] forgotten name or image of God which mirrors the cultural and biological role of women is seen in the use of

> *bird imagery* in the Scriptures. Here God's concern for humanity is expressed in imagery that possibly is drawn from the representation of female goddesses with *sheltering wings*. Yahweh is described by an analogy to the action of a female bird protecting her young (Ps. 17:8; 36:7; 57:1; 91:1,4; Isa. 31:5, etc.) The sustaining care of Yahweh for Israel is represented in Deut. 32:11-12 by the words: "Like an eagle that stirs up its nest, that flutters over its young, spreading out its wings, catching them, bearing them on its pinions, the LORD alone did lead him, and there was no foreign god with him" In a similar reference in Matt. 23:37 (Luke 13:34) Jesus says: "O Jerusalem, Jerusalem..! How often would I have gathered your children together as a hen gathers her brood under her wings, and you would not!"[11]

In her essay, "Female God Language in a Jewish Context," Rita Gross appears similar to Trible and Russell in proposing a move beyond God the Father,

> to an imagery of bisexual androgynous deity by reintroducing the image of God as female to complement the image of God as male. I wish to argue for this option because I am convinced that Judaism is theistic through and through and that theism-the view that the absolute can be imaged as a person entering into relationships of love and responsibility with humans-requires anthropomorphism. But I am equally convinced that images of God as a male person without complementing images of God as a female person are both a mirror and a legitimation of the oppression and eclipsing of women.[12]

Gross argues that "'God-She' is not some new construct added onto the present resource of Jewish God language." Rather, "'the Holy One, blessed be He' is also...'the holy One, blessed be She' and always has been. Only the poverty of our religious imagination and the repressiveness of our social forms prevented that realization."[13] The images are already "there," in other words, awaiting "proper" exegesis. For these type-one feminists, then, biblical texts contain liberating bisexual androgynous imagery, which needs only to be disclosed. The change for traditional history of religions implied by this approach is, to use the words of Rita Gross, "the transition from an androcentric methodology to an androgynous methodology. The resulting transformation," she observes, "would be subtle and overwhelming, though not total."[14]

Type Two: Post-Biblical Witchcraft or Thealogy

Quite the opposite conclusion is reached by those feminists whom I am placing at the other end of the methodological spectrum, those for whom biblical tradition is so fundamentally sexist as to be beyond reform. For example, Naomi Goldenberg argues in *Changing Of The Gods: Feminism And The End Of Traditional Religion*, that the retranslation of Jewish and Christian scriptures is a "self-deceptive enterprise." "In order to develop a theology of women's liberation, feminists have to leave Christ and Bible behind them."[15] It is this group of radical or post-biblical feminists which has been most closely associated with an alternative religion of the Mother Goddess. For some writers at this end of the methodological spectrum, the "quest for the goddess" becomes an archaeological search for origins. For others of the radical type, "the goddess" signifies a feminist archetypalism. For others still, "the goddess" seems to function as metaphor of the experience and empowerment of contemporary women. By way of illustrating understandings of "the goddess" at this end of the spectrum, I will refer to Starhawk, Naomi Goldenberg and Carol Christ.

The writings of Starhawk present us with an understanding of "the goddess" as seen through contemporary witchcraft, or wicca. As Starhawk portrays it in the first chapter of *The Spiral Dance: A Rebirth Of The Ancient Religion Of The Great Goddess*, contemporary witchcraft is a revival of Palaeolithic Goddess religions.[16] She defines witchcraft as the oldest of the world's religions, characterized by the worship of a Mother Goddess perceived as birth-giver, nurturer and protector of life. Not unlike other writers at this end of the spectrum, Starhawk situates prehistoric Goddess religion in a sedentary, peaceful and matrifocal culture which she contrasts sharply with the invading cultures which swept over Europe from the Bronze Age onward. Under invading patriarchies, she suggests, the Mother Goddess splintered into many new figurations, "married" male gods, and, under Judeo-Christian tradition, was slowly driven underground.[17] Starhawk considers Mary of Nazareth, Joan of Arc, and the European witchcraze of the fifteenth to eighteenth centuries, as instances of either revival or suppression of the prehistoric Mother Goddess.[18] Such arguments are now common in so-called "radical" religious feminism.[19]

Starhawk describes contemporary witchcraft as a religion of poetry, not theology: its "myths, legends, and teachings," she says, "are recognized as metaphors for 'That-Which-Cannot-Be-Told,' the absolute reality our limited minds can never completely know...The primary symbol for That-Which-Cannot-Be-Told is the Goddess."[20] In Starhawk's view, "the Goddess" is not conceived anthropomorphically as a deity external to the world; "She is the world. Manifest in each of us."[21] It follows, for Starhawk, that witchcraft is a religion of ecology: its goal is harmony with nature, recovery of the body and the sacredness of sexuality, tolerance, and survival. This means, she points out, that "the goddess" has political implications: "The symbol of the Goddess conveys the spiritual power both to challenge systems of oppression and to create new, life-oriented cultures."[22] The following gives Starhawk's understanding of "the Goddess":

> The symbolism of the Goddess has taken on an electrifying power for modern women. The rediscovery of the ancient matrifocal civilizations has given us a deep sense of pride in woman's ability to create and sustain culture. It has exposed the falsehoods of patriarchal history, and given us models of female strength and authority. The Goddess-ancient and primeval; the first of deities; patronness of the Stone Age hunt and of the first sowers of seeds; under whose guidance the herds were tamed, the healing herbs first discovered; in whose image the first works of art were created; for whom the standing stones were raised; who was the inspiration of song and poetry-is recognized once again in today's world. She is the bridge on which we can cross the chasms within ourselves, which were created by our social conditioning, and reconnect with our lost potentials. She is the ship, on which we sail the waters of the deep self, exploring the uncharted seas within. She is the door, through which we pass into the future. She is the cauldron, in which we who have been wrenched apart simmer until we again become whole. She is the vaginal passage, through which we are reborn.[23]

In a recent article, Naomi Goldenberg writes that eventually "theology and each disciplinary speciality within Religious Studies-history of religion, sociology of religion, philosophy of religion and psychology of religion-will have to face 'the Goddess' and to encounter the *thealogy* which reflection on 'Her' is creating."[24] *Thealogy*, from the Greek, thea, goddess, is a word coined by Goldenberg in reference to "the logic of witches and scholars of goddess religion." For Goldenberg, "the Goddess" is alive within us, and therefore, is best understood through the perspective of psychoanalytic theory. In *Changing Of The Gods*, Goldenberg's approach is primarily Jungian; more recently, she has suggested that object relations theory is most relevant to feminist thealogy.[25] In either case, she argues that both psychoanalysis and contemporary Goddess religion involve a feminist archetypalism which grants centrality to the figure of the mother. "Like the Goddess movement in religion," Goldenberg writs, "object relations theory places a woman at the beginning of the universe and thus champions a shift from an interest in male symbols to a focus on female ones. Both ways of thinking pose a challenge to the importance of the father."[26]

Goldenberg is certainly not alone in basing her understanding of "the Goddess" on an psychoanalytic appeal to feminine archetypes. From a host of sources, I mention as example only Joan Chamberlain Engelsman's *The Feminine Dimension Of The Divine*, which analyses Christian tradition as a repression of the feminine dimension of the divine (focusing on Sophia and the Virgin Mary), and which argues that the contemporary feminist movement represents the return of the repressed;[27] the often-cited *Return Of The Goddess* by Edward Whitmont, which appeals to Ishtar, Inanna, Anath, Kali and others as manifestations of "the Goddess" who is today arising in the depths of the unconscious psyche;[28] Jean Shinoda Bolen's *Goddesses In Everywoman,* which presents a Jungian perspective of women based on seven images or archetypes provided by Greek goddesses, and used by Bolen as an analytic tool for bringing women to "self-knowledge."[29]

An emphasis on creating new religious traditions marks the writing of Carol Christ. Like that of Mary Daly, Carol Christ's writing has moved from traditional Roman Catholic and Christian theology to what she refers to as "post-Christian post-Jewish thealogy." In *Laughter Of Aphrodite,* Christ points out that neither biblical traditions nor prehistoric and ancient Goddess traditions is normative for her thealogy. She argues that contemporary "Goddess traditions" must today be created anew. In the end, her thealogy is not "about the Goddess" any more than it is "about God"; her "Goddess religion" is about the experience of contemporary women.[30] As Naomi Goldenberg has observed, Carol Christ treats contemporary women's writings "as sacred texts".[31] It seems to me that in Christ's writing, the "quest for the goddess" functions as metaphor of the affirmation of female experience and female power. Christ makes a decisive statement to that effect in her landmark essay, "Why Women Need the Goddess":

> The simplest and most basic meaning of the symbol of Goddess is the acknowledgement of the legitimacy of female power as a beneficent and independent power. A woman who echoes Ntosake Shange's dramatic statement, "I found God in myself and I loved her fiercely," is saying, "Female power is strong and creative." She is saying that the divine principle, the saving and sustaining power, is in herself, that she will no longer look to men or male figures as saviors. The strength and independence of female power can be intuited by contemplating ancient and modern images of the Goddess. This meaning of the symbol of Goddess is simple and obvious, and yet it is difficult for many to comprehend. It stands in sharp contrast to the paradigms of female dependence on males that have been predominant in Western religion and culture.[32]

Type Three:
Biblical Transformation/Reconstruction

Somewhere between the two methodological types which I have portrayed here as biblical androgyny and post-biblical witchcraft or thealogy, fall the approaches of several other religious feminists, more "radical" than type-one, perhaps, but nevertheless committed to a reform position. Roman Catholic theologian Rosemary Ruether serves as an illustration. She departs from type-one feminism in at least two ways.

First, Ruether argues that women should not settle for androgynous imagery or gender complementarity, since this approach falls too easily into an androcentric or male-dominant perspective, with the female side of God subordinate to the dominant image of male divine sovereignty.[33] Second, Ruether's approach differs from type-one in involving a much more extensive process of rewriting and revising biblical tradition. In *Womanguides*, for example, she argues that feminist theology cannot be done solely from the existing base of the Christian Bible. "The Old and New Testaments," she says, "have been shaped in their formation, their transmission, and, finally, their canonization to sacralize patriarchy" such that "the doing of feminist theology demands a new collection of texts."[34]

Yet she does not seek this collection through the revival of witchcraft or ancient Mother Goddess religion. Ruether has dismissed, and with some impatience, what she sees as the nostalgia of radical post-biblical feminists who invoke an original matriarchal society dominated by the cult of the Mother Goddess. "If there ever was an autonomous women's religion," she writes,

> it has not survived as an existing independent tradition. It is doubtful that the goddess worship of antiquity was such a religion. And even if it should hold clues to some alternative, it has not come down as living tradition. To pretend that it has and to construct an imaginary line of descent for feminist religion indicates a false understanding of origins. To a large extent this means that instead of creating a more holistic alternative, such feminist spiritualities succumb to the suppressed animus of patriarchal religious culture.[35]

For Ruether, feminist theology draws from the following sources: the Bible, read in new light (again, a hermeneutics of disclosure: "We can read these patriarchal texts from the underside and note their hidden message..."); marginal or heretical texts in which women's speech and presence are normative; and new texts written by contemporary women.[36] "It is possible to start something new," she writes, "using images from the past but transforming their meaning and imbuing them with contemporary experience. Every existing historical religion once did exactly this, and there is no reason why it cannot be done today by women concerned with a spirituality of women's liberation."[37]

Interestingly enough, Ruether still considers this "new" canon, "which makes women as subjects the center rather than the margin,"[38] to be Christian. She declares her allegiance to a transformed Christianity, rather than to an alternative tradition. Again, interestingly enough, she refers to this transformed tradition as a "God/ess" religion, so designated, perhaps, to indicate its theological distinction from both the "God/Goddess" or type-one gender complementarity, and the "Mother Goddess" of the post-biblical separatists.

Ruether's "quest for the goddess" includes a critique of the dualistic, hierarchical thinking which she argues has informed the western theological tradition, including its God-language and imagery. Transcending the binary model, Ruether maintains, involves the appropriation of "God/ess" language which neither perpetuates male/female dominance (the problem she has with androgynous imagery) nor constitutes a reversal of dominance (such as she reads in the radical feminists, e.g., Dianic Wicca, as described by Z. Budapest[39]). For example, Ruether suggests that "God/ess" language draw its imagery, not from models of kingship and hierarchical power, but form female roles and experience, and "from the activities of peasants and working people, people at the bottom of society."[40]

Discussion

The outline I have given pertains to contemporary feminist scholarship in the context of western religious traditions, for the most part, Jewish and Christian. Cross-cultural research in this area of feminist scholarship has only just begun. While I think it is too early to draw any conclusions as to how cross-cultural research will be utilized by western religious feminists, I will refer to one preliminary study, if only by way of raising questions.

A recent article by Rita Gross, "Hindu Female Deities as a Resource for the Contemporary Rediscovery of the Goddess" suggests that Hindu theistic imagery offers five resources for the "reimaging of the Goddess" in western traditions.[41] Gross first cites the goddesses' obvious strength and capability, their transcendence and dynamic creativity. This quality is most obvious, she thinks, in the stories and icons of Durga, the slayer of the buffalo demon. Second, Hindu goddess symbolism, Kali for example, involves the coincidence of opposites-of death and life, destruction and creativity. Third, Hindu goddesses provide an image of God as Mother, but without limiting female power to biological destiny. Fourth, Hindu goddess symbolism associates women with a wide variety of culturally valued goals and activities. Finally, Gross suggests, Hindu goddess symbolism reintroduces sexuality as a significant religious metaphor in a symbol system where divinity is imaged as both male and female.

Gross's study raises questions for me concerning the appropriation of such resources by western religious feminists. "[I]t is one thing to know that the goddess must return," she writes, "and another to know where to find her." Gross's paper advocates an "intelligent selection and borrowing" from Hinduism by western religions to effect what she calls "the second coming of the goddess," her "contemporary rediscovery" or "return."[42] I cited Gross's early writing above as an illustration of type-one reform feminism, as I think it is. I do not know whether her more recent writing can be accommodated within the same biblical reform position. The more important point is, however, that contemporary feminist writing on "the goddess" raises complex questions with respect to the concept of "tradition," the understanding of language and texts within traditions, the methodology for feminist cross-cultural study, as well as a variety of questions as to what constitutes a "goddess" and what constitutes a "goddess religion."[43]

On the topic of cross-cultural research yet to be done, Diana Paul's study *Women In Buddhism: Images Of The Feminine In The Mahayana Tradition*, argues that two themes or prototypes of woman are found cross-culturally in world religions. According to the first prototype, woman is destructive, close to nature, elusive, temptress, evil, dangerous to the male, therefore needing to be controlled or suppressed by the male. According to the second, woman is gentle, maternal, creative, compassionate, her sexuality rightly ordered in marriage or transcended in celibate life.[44] Paul suggests that the different reiterations and resolutions of these themes within and across traditions should be of interest to students of goddess mythology. I concur with Paul on this point, and suggest further that the study of what she refers to as "sexual typification" may prove especially important in regard to future attempts to relate goddess thematics to the wider feminist theorizing of sexuality, of subjectivity, and of language.

I raise the issue of sexual typification with particular reference to the point made at the beginning of this paper, that North American feminist criticism has come to focus on the exploration of womens' texts and the search for "lost" women's voices. it seems to me that the "quest for the goddess" represents this focus, and that it belongs, therefore, to what might be called a "woman-centered" feminism: centered in the experience, identity, and imaging of woman, and endeavoring, in Ruether's words, "to make women as subjects the center rather than the margin." Across the methodological spectrum overviewed in this paper, writers seem to be working primarily to provide women with the origins, narratives, history, identity, and language which they have been lacking, exemplifying what Toril Moi refers to as a "sexual" rather than a "textual" politics.[45] As Moi points out, however, proponents of a "textual" politics refuse the biologism and essentialism which they see lurking behind "woman-centered" feminism, arguing that "it is not the biological sex of a person, but the subject position she or he takes up, that determines their revolutionary potential."[46] I will not launch into these theory debates here, but I do suggest that future research in goddess thematics might benefit from those "textual" approaches which connect the feminist critique of binary logic to a wider exploration of subjectivity and to the politics of language as a material and social structure.[47]

Notes

1. Barbara Godard, ed., *Gynocritics/La Gynocritique: Feminist approaches to Writing By Canadian and Québécoise Women* (Toronto: ECW Press, 1985), 6.

2. Prominent among the earlier type of work were the following: Mary Daly, *Beyond God the Father* (Boston: Beacon Press, 1973); *id.*, *Gyn/Ecology* (Boston: Beacon Press, 1978); Rosemary Reuther, ed., *Religion and Sexism: Images of Woman in the Jewish and Christian Traditions* (New York: Simon & Schuster, 1974).

3. See the critique of some appropriations of this work by J. Townsend elsewhere in this volume.

4. Rita Gross, "Hindu Female Deities as a Resource for the Contemporary Rediscovery of the Goddess" in *The Book of the Goddess: Past and Present*, Carl Olson, ed. New York: (Crossroad 1983), 217.

5. Carol Christ, "Symbols of Goddess and God in Feminist Theology," in *The Book of the Goddess: Past and Present* Carol Olson, ed. 231-51; reprinted in Carol Christ, *Laughter of Aphrodite: Reflections On A Journey to the Goddess* (Harper & Row, 1987).

6. Phyllis Trible, *God and the Rhetoric of Sexuality* (Philadelphia: Fortress Press, 1978).

7. Ibid., 60-62.

8. Letty Russell, *Human Liberation in a Feminist Perspective* (Philadelphia: The Westminster Press, 1974).

9. Ibid., 80.

10. Ibid., 88 Recovery also involves rewriting the past, not just as "history" but as "herstory", by including women; and recognition that Jesus was "for us all," that while "Jesus lived as part of postexilic Jewish culture which had adopted a restricted view of the role and status of women...he persisted in treating women as full persons."

11. Ibid., 98-99.

12. Rita Gross, "Female God Language in a Jewish Context" in *Womanspirit Rising: A Feminist Reader in Religion* Carol Christ and Judith Plaskow, eds. (San Francisco: Harper & Row, 1979), 168.

13. Ibid., 173.

14. Gross, "Androcentrism and Androgyny in the Methodology and History of Religions" in *Beyond Adnrocentrism: New Essays on Women and Religion* Rita Gross, ed. (Missoula, Montana: Scholars Press, 1977.

15. Naomi Goldenberg, *Changing of the Gods: Feminism and the End of Traditional Religion* (Boston: Beacon Press, 1979), 18, 22.

16. Starhawk, *The Spiral Dance: A Rebirth of the Ancient Religion of the Great Goddess* (New York: Harper & Row, 1979).

17. Ibid., Chapter One.

18. Ibid.

19. See for example, Goldenberg, *Changing Of The Gods*, Chapter 7; Carol Christ, *Laughter Of Aphrodite*, Chapter 10; Pamela Berger, *The Goddess Obscured: Transformation of the Grain Protectress from Goddess to Saint* (Boston: Beacon Press, 1985), chapter One. Cf. Townsend's essay in the present volume, which offers a critique of such constructs of pre-historic religion.

20. Starhawk, 7-8.

21. Ibid., 9. Starhawk's use of the feminine pronoun "She" related in part to her assumption of an essential feminine principle, "the feminine within", immanent in nature, and common to males and females. On p. 10 she writes, "The symbol of the Goddess allows men to experience and integrate the feminine side of their nature, which is often felt to be the deepest and most sensitive aspect of the self." Later, however, (21-22) she explains that the "Divine within" corresponds to a deep "third Self", the Goddess/God within, which is conceived as both male and female.

22. Ibid., 10. *The Spiral Dance* gives also an account of witchcraft worldview, ritual, coven structure, and myth.

23. Ibid., 77.

24. Goldenberg, "The Return of the goddess: Psychoanalytic Reflections on the Shift from Theology to Thealogy." *SR* 16/1 (1987) 38.

25. For Goldenberg's critique and appropriation of Jung, see her essay, "Dreams and Fantasies as Sources of Revelation: Feminist Appropriation of Jung" in Christ and Plaskow, *Womanspirit Rising*, 219-227.

26. "The Return of the Goddess," 41.

27. Joan Chamberlain Engelsman, *The Feminine Dimension of the Divine* (Philadelphia: The Westminster Press, 1979).

28. Edward Whitmont, *Return of the Goddess* (New York: Crossroad, 1982).

29. Jean Shinoda Bolen, *Goddesses in Everywoman* (San Francisco: harper & Row, 1984). Bolen writes "The 'goddesses' are powerful, invisible forces that shape behavior and influence emotions...When she knows which 'goddesses' are dominant forces within her, a woman acquires self-knowledge about the strength of certain instincts, about priorities and abilities, about the possibilities of finding personal meaning through choices others might not encourage" (5).

30. Christ, *Laughter of Aphrodite*, x.

31. Goldenberg, *Changing of the Gods*, 120; see also Christ, *Laughter of Aphrodite*, x.

32. Carol Christ, "Why Women Need the Goddess: Phenomenological, Psychological, and Political Reflections," in Christ and Plaskow, *Womanspirit Rising*, 277.

33. Rosemary Ruether, *Sexism and God-Talk: Toward a Feminist Theology* (Boston: Beacon Press, 1983), 60-1.

34. Ruether, *Womanguides: Readings Toward A Feminist Theology* (Boston: Beacon Press, 1985), ix-x.

35. See for example, Ruether, "A Religion for Women: Sources and Strategies," *Christianity and Crisis* (December 10, 1979), 307-311; "Goddesses and Witches: Liberation and Countercultural Feminism" *The Christian Century* (September 10-17, 1980), 842-847. For the debate which has arisen over christian anti-Semitism and "who killed the goddess", see Ruether, "Female Symbols, Values and Context" *Christianity and Crisis* (January 12, 1987), 460-464; Carol Christ, "Dialogue, Accuracy and Ambiguity," *Christianity and Crisis* (February 16, 1987), 55-56; Judith Plaskow, "Christian Feminism and Anti-Semitism" *Cross Currents* (Fall 1978), 306-309.

36. See Ruether, *Womanguides*, Introduction.

37. Ruether, "Goddesses and Witches," 844.

38. Ruether, *Womanguides*, xi.

39. See for example, Ruether "A Religion for Women," 310-11.

40. Ruether, *Sexism and God-Talk*, 69.

41. Rita Gross, "Hindu Female Deities as a Resource for the Contemporary Rediscovery of the Goddess," in Olson, *The Book of the Goddess*, 217-230.

42. Ibid., 217-18.

43. In asking whether we can meaningfully speak of a Hebrew or Jewish goddess, an essay by Steve Davies, "The Canaanite-Hebrew Goddess" in Olson, *The Book of the Goddess*, 68-79, questions the meaning of the terms "goddess" and "goddess religion." Davies argues that goddesses cannot be read back into traditions simply by finding poetry or metaphor concerning God as male and female; and, that a "goddess tradition" is not simply a way of speaking, but a way of worshipping. He concludes that we cannot speak of a Hebrew goddess, although feminine attributes were accorded to God within that tradition, and although worship of a goddess may have continued for some time after the Israelite invasion of Canaan.

44. Diana Paul, *Women in Buddhism: Images of the Feminine in The Mahayana Tradition* (Berkeley: University of California Press, 1985). See, for example, the Introduction.

45. Toril Moi, *Sexual/Textual Politics* (London and New York: Methuen, 1985).

46. Ibid., 12. For examples of the "textual" approach, see Helene Cixous and Catherine Clement, *The Newly Born Woman* (Minneapolis: University of Minnesota Press, 1975); Julia Kristeva, "women's Time," trans. Alice Jardine and Harry Blake, *Sign* 7/1 (1981), 13-35. For an introduction to Kristeva's theory in relation to North American feminism, see my essay, "Kristeva and the Subject of Ethics," in *Resources For Feminist Research* 17/4 (1988), 17-22.

47. See Alice Jardine, *Gynesis: Configurations of Woman and Modernity* (Ithaca and London: Cornell University Press, 1985), which argues for the need to bring French and North American feminisms together, and which also provides a comprehensive outline of the differences between them. For an introduction to recent developments in theories of subjectivity and language, see Rosalind Coward and John Ellis, *Language and Materialism: Developments in Semiology and Theory of the Subject* (Boston: Routledge & Kegan Paul, 1977).

THE GODDESS: FACT, FALLACY AND REVITALIZATION MOVEMENT[1]

Joan B. Townsend

Introduction

Within the wider feminist movement and, in particular, within a femininist approach to religion, there is a group who propose "the Goddess." The idea of the Goddess has a strong appeal to some Western women, who are often relegated to subordinate positions in sacred as well as secular society. There are two approaches to the Goddess. Erich Neumann, a follower of Jung and an example of the first approach, uses the concept of mother goddess as archetype. He specifically states that, as archetype, it has nothing to do with historical or sociological sequences in the real world.[2] The other approach, a more fundamentalist or literalist view, typified by a number of other writers, alleges the existence of an ancient, unified religion of *the* Goddess as historic fact.[3] My concern is only with this latter position, and it is the focus of this paper. I capitalize "the Goddess" to denote and to emphasize the specific kind of goddess discourse which I address here.

The Goddess paradigm sets forth several basic and related assumptions about the prehistoric and early historic past, from the Upper Paleolithic to the emergence of states, as well as assumptions about the nature of social organization. These assumptions provide the underlying justification for an attempt to "revive" the Goddess religion, in order to enhance women's status within Western society. A fundamental premise within this movement is as follows: Where "the Goddess" religion exists, women have status and power equal to or higher than that of men. The assumptions from which this premise developed have created the historical fiction of "the Goddess" in the minds of advocates.

This model of feminine reality fits within revitalization movement theory with nativistic and millenarian elements.[4] The movement grows from the seeds of justifiable discontent of women with their roles in Western society and their religious, social, economic, and political positions of inferiority to men. The Goddess movement proposes to build a society closer to the desired ideal of full equality (at least) on all levels with men, and a more peaceful world. The perceived conditions in which women find themselves conform closely to classic definitions of deprivation, which has so frequently been argued as a causal factor in the initiation of religious revitalization movements particularly among oppressed peoples.[5] In keeping with nativistic aspects of the revitalization model, a golden age is constructed for the past. Then there was a calamity; the golden age was destroyed, bringing with it tragedy. If, however, certain rituals, beliefs and other activities occur, there will come a millennium in this world, the golden age of the past, or something similar, will be forthcoming, which will be more in keeping with the participants' needs and desires. Evil will disappear and good will triumph.

In what follows, I propose to show how "the Goddess" paradigm I am criticizing fits the revitalization model, and to offer a critique of the use of archaeological evidence by its supporters.

The Goddess Revitalization Movement Model

Not all writers supporting "the Goddess" position I criticize here agree on all the elements I have included in the model. For example, Barstow recognizes that early matriarchy is a myth.[6] Nevertheless, I suggest that the following Revitalization Movement model of "the Goddess" viewpoint, which I have synthesized from a number of authors, is a fair characterization of the position of most advocates.

The past was a Golden Age. Originally, society was matriarchal,[7] matrilineal, matrilocal, egalitarian and peaceful. Women held the positions of power equal to, or greater than, that of men. The religion of this primal stage of culture was concerned with "*the* (Mother) Goddess".[8]

A time of destruction followed. Matriarchal (or at least matrilineal) society under the Mother Goddess was usurped by the invasion of more warlike, male-dominated, pastoral societies whose deity was male. This is often equated with the "invasion" of Indo-European speakers into Europe, which allegedly "overthrew" the peaceful "Old European" egalitarian, matriarchal Goddess, agricultural "civilization".[9] Following that conquest by the pastoral, patriarchal, patrilineal societies, the Goddess religion was suppressed and women were subordinated to the rule of men. The male bias in deity and male secular power is reflected in Christianity, Judaism, and Islam and in the socio-political organizations of the state societies that followed. The Mother Goddess religion was not totally supplanted by the god/male oriented religion, however. It persisted in attenuated form in Medieval Europe as so-called witchcraft and today in modern neo-pagan systems such as Wicca.

As a result of the overthrow of the Goddess, conditions in modern society are terrible. The domination of society by men and a patriarchal god has resulted in the persecution, oppression and subordination of women. Societal collapse is imminent with the escalating problems of crime, drugs, immorality, greed, and wars of destruction. An impending dual global crisis threatens: environmental destruction and the destruction of the world through warfare. A revitalization movement is necessary if society is to be saved and world destruction avoided. It remains for women to reinstate the Goddess and female rites surrounding Goddess worship in order to establish equal religious rights and socio-political positions of equality with men, if not dominance.

The Goddess forms a ritual focus around which women can identify and unify to save all of us from destruction and bring about the millennium--a golden age based on the golden age of the past. The Goddess religion is singularly important because it brings with it the peace and harmony of control by women. Consequently, for the millennium to occur, the Goddess religion must be reinstated, and women must be restored to their rightful place as equal with or superior to men.

This millennium incorporates a new paradigm of reality. The Goddess and feminism create a utopian, apocalyptic vision:

> ...a new naming of ourselves, the universe, and the transcendent. It is a fresh perspective on the most fundamental questions--how we conceive reality, what it means to be human, how humans should relate to one another and to the planet, what is valuable and what grounds our values.[10]

I am deeply sympathetic with the goals to create gender equality and a more peaceful world. Similarly, I support the need to recognize that the Divine is not a male-biased entity. Nevertheless, The Goddess movement premise, which holds, as an historic fact that there existed an original, uniform, peaceful, matriarchal/matrilineal society with The Goddess as deity, is flawed and, therefore, is ultimately antithetical to these goals.

Claims regarding the actual existence of "the Goddess" as a single, ubiquitous, prehistoric and historic paramount deity within a Goddess-centred religious tradition, and the "early" or "original" human social condition (e.g., matriarchy) are based on several academic studies from which other writers have developed their positions. These seminal works include the archetype analysis of the psychological history of humans, especially as discussed by Erich Neumann in *The Great Mother*,[11] and the works of Crawford and James which advocate a kind of "universal" prehistoric religion focused on the Mother Goddess.[12] Data from some archaeological excavations in the Middle East and eastern Europe, particularly by James Mellaart, and archaeological figurine analysis by Marija Gimbutas are used.[13] The work of early "armchair" anthropologists, especially Briffault, Bachofen, Morgan, and Tylor, together with works of Marx and Engels (especially as these last two relate to unilineal evolutionary concepts) provide a theoretical basis.[14] Comparative data are drawn from various small societies throughout the world and from a variety of time periods, and used out of context. Some of these primary works I consider valid *for the purposes for which they were written*, while others are seriously out of date or incorrect.

The pseudo-historic/evolutionary argument of "the Goddess" movement harks back to the nineteenth-century armchair scholars mentioned earlier (e.g., Morgan, Bachofen and others), who hypothesized unilineal socio-cultural evolution with an early matriarchy followed by patriarchy. Making a comprehensive critique of this kind of scholarship is especially difficult because there is such an intricate interweaving of fact and fallacy. A thorough response requires an enormous amount of work to dismantle and disentangle the Gordian knot of resultant fiction. Anthropologists, especially archaeologists, and other scientists faced the same kind of problem with the infamous work of von Daniken, *Chariots of The Gods?*, in which he presented "evidence" from around the world through countless ages for the appearance of visitors form outer space who brought all civilization to the world, including that of the Maya, of Meso-America, Peru, the Near East and Asia.[15] A few attempts at rebuttal were made,[16] but little came of such efforts in contrast to the media extravaganzas afforded *Chariots*. The result is likely to be similar with any scholarly attempts to rebut "the Goddess". In addition, to undertake such an analysis would not be in keeping with the goals of the Goddess movement.

Here I will merely initiate a critique of the assumptions, and focus on those related to the nature of religion and social organization of past societies. My argument is not with the myth and the use of myth in giving women a new sense of self and of the divine, but with the tendency of some to treat the myth as historical fact.

Evaluation and Critique of Major Assumptions

The evaluation of the assumptions underlying the Goddess belief system falls into two broad categories: (1) the clarification of social organization as it relates to kinship and power, and (2) problems of archaeological interpretation and the evidence for the "Goddess" religion as defined by those in the modern Goddess movement.

Social Organization: Matriarchy and Matrilineality

Those who support the Goddess paradigm make a number of assumptions about the nature of early societies and the implications for the position of women within them. These assumptions are based on a hypothesized female-focused society, which is understood to have been matriarchal, matrilineal and matrilocal.

Although some authors do not propose that matriarchy existed, it is still part of the argument of others. In order to evaluate the idea of an early matriarchy, it is necessary first to clarify the differences between matriarchy and matrilineality. In terms of social organization, *power* is defined as the right to coerce, if necessary, in order to enforce the will of a segment of a society. It is the right to make final decisions to which others can be forced to comply. *Authority* is the consensual agreement of those in a society for a specific individual or group to lead; there is no real power, however, to enforce the wishes of the leaders if the members of the society decline to follow. *Matriarchy* relates to power and refers to a form of political organization where women hold absolute decision-making power; it contrasts with patriarchy where men hold that absolute kind of power. In each case, the opposite sex is in a subordinate position regarding power. *Matriarchy* in this sense--rule by women as a class--does not exist in any ethnographic, historic or prehistoric societies we know of. Further, true *power,* the ability to coerce as contrasted to *authority,* is not vested in any individuals or groups until complex, stratified societies such as some chiefdoms and the state appear. In less complex societies (popularly known as "tribal" or village societies), individuals lead through authority, which may be ascribed or achieved in specific cases. Although in many cases authority can be a formidable force, it is not and must not be confused with real power.

Matrilineality has nothing to do with political structure nor, necessarily, with matriarchy. Rather it refers to one of the three major kinship system types which determine lines of descent, allocation of people within a society to kin groups, and assignment of obligations for assistance. Kinship systems set out who may or may not be considered kin, with related responsibilities and privileges, and establish rules of marriage, those whom a person may or may not marry. Kinship systems also create conditions under which alliances between kin-groups may be made for the protection and assistance of a society's members.

A bilateral [bilineal] kinship system, in which an individual is a member of the kin groups of both parents, is most common in small societies of band composition and large complex societies such as states, where flexibility both of movement and group membership is most critical. A *unilineal* kinship system, either matrilineal or patrilineal, allocates membership to only one side of the family: mother's or father's respectively. It is more common among societies larger than mobile bands which are at least in part sedentary and involved in cultivation or in harvesting, especially rich wild resources (for example, Iroquois, and some Northwest Coast societies). Such organization is significant when inheritance of real or symbolic property must be controlled. A unilineal grouping may be extended into a lineage which includes all those who are related through a female (or male in the case of patrilineality) member to a known ancestor. Finally, matrilineal (or patrilineal) lineages may unite into a clan on the basis of a hypothesized shared relationship to an unknown, often mythical, ancestor.

Within *matrilineal* societies, women often do have fairly equal standing with men and usually have more independence than in patrilineal systems; women and men have complementary authority. Iroquois society is frequently held up as an example of a society where women are in *power*. This is not the case, nor has it ever been so.[17] In Tlingit and other matrilineal Northwest Coast societies, both women and men were found in positions of authority, but this was related to inherited wealth, prestige, and rank rather than merely gender.[18] In matrilineal societies, usually the person who stands in the kinship position of mother's brother holds considerable authority for that kin group. Authority also is vested in other areas; it rests in the elder generation, and older women frequently have authority over younger men. In many societies the formal political power or social authority is in the hands of men, but women often wield pivotal informal political and social authority behind the scenes.[19] Finally, in examining the question of authority, we must be careful to distinguish between prestige and real decision-making ability, between formal power and/or authority and informal power and/or authority.

Societies are bilateral, matrilineal, or patrilineal on the basis of a variety of factors including economic concerns, population size, and group movements. Kin systems are not fixed forever, but can and do change over time if circumstances warrant. A bilateral organization may evolve into a matrilineal or patrilineal one. Conversely, I have demonstrated a shift from matrilineal society to bilateral with heavy patrilineal emphasis within about one hundred years for Tanaina Athapaskans of southwestern Alaska.[20] Similar rapid shifts can be documented for Northwest Coast and other societies. "What was the *'original'* form of social organization?" is not a productive or even a meaningful question.

In the evolution of a particular kin system, residence locality patterns precede the establishment of kinship lineality allocation (descent groups). Residence is apparently not a result of which sex's production is the more important, or where presumed power lies. Rather, as Gough suggests, situations which might foster matrilocality are those where women gather, fish, or cultivate in small groups, and where their production sites are stable, or if not stable, their movements determine the movement of the group.[21] If men's activities do not require long training under a dominant male, if their activities could be carried on in any locality, or if they were away from home for extended periods of time, then matrilocality would likely be established. If women's production, especially that which was generated in cooperative groups, was sufficiently scarce or valuable so that inheritance rules were needed, matrilineal descent groups might then develop. If conditions changed so that men began to form work groups or activities which controlled group movement, then residence might shift to patrilocality and perhaps ultimately patrilineality. Avunculocality (a married couple residing with the *man's* matrilineal lineage--the man's mother's brother) might occur if matrilineality was still strong.

In recent times we have seen the destruction of both matrilineal and patrilineal systems in small societies as people moved into the unitary market system of the State in which all things are bought and sold.[22] In such developments, kinship obligations, privileges, and alliances no longer are as important to a person as the ability to participate in the market. In such circumstances, it is often necessary for the individual or the nuclear family to move away from either kin group. As a result, neolocality (the isolation of the nuclear family as a residence unit) and bilateral descent within a limited range of relatives develop. Where the emphasis is on men as the direct participants in the market and the attendant direct access to moveable wealth, women are often relegated to lesser roles.

Social systems are extremely flexible and adaptable; it is this characteristic which has led to survival. Through time they have responded with fission or fusion of populations and reorganization of systems in response to specific conditions. Rigid systems would spell disaster. The simple universal, unilineal, evolutionary scheme hypothesized by armchair scholars of 150 years ago delineated a period of savagery, followed by barbarism and then civilization. Associated with these stages were the primordial horde, followed by matrilineality/matriarchy and then patrilineality/patriarchy. Such simplistic schemes are without empirical basis and have no place in today's thinking.

Social Organization and Archaeology

How do we *know*?--how is the archaeological record interpreted? Knowledge of the prehistoric past comes from archaeological research. Until about the 1920s, "scientifically" controlled archaeological excavation was not highly developed. Since that time, the techniques of rigorously-controlled excavation have slowly evolved. At an earlier period, much excavation was akin to random "pot-hunting" expeditions in search of material objects, and was heavily focused on more ostentatious items. Earlier excavation techniques often allowed materials to be extracted without much concern for documenting the setting in which an item was found, although that is the kind of information that is critical for responsible analysis. Only in the last seventy years or so has real concern been paid to the crude or simple items of everyday life, the way of life of the "common people," or the careful documentation of the stratigraphy, or the location, context, and association of artifacts within a site. Much of the data relating to "the Goddess" was discovered prior to the development of "scientific" archaeological methods.

The interpretation of the artifacts, and, more broadly, an understanding of the culture of a people are based on a variety of things. These include the analysis of all remains, artifactual and structural, as well as data derived from geology, climatology, soil and pollen samples. Comparisons of the remains and their provenance are then compared with other sites of the same time period and different time periods, first in the same region and then in other similar ecological niches. Finally, some ethnographic analogies with contemporary societies or those of the recent past may be attempted. Ethnographic and historic analogy is valuable but considerable care must be used. There are several potential problems to keep in mind.

1. *Form and function are not always coterminous.* Similar forms or structures may occur which are not the result of the same cause. Similar form may also be the result of independent but similar developments in two separate areas. Thus, religious rituals or structures may be similar as a result of similar processes in cultural evolution, rather than as bearers of identical meanings. Similarity in some items, figurines for example, may occur simply because we as humans are interested in ourselves, and we might be expected to make some items in our own image. The meanings given the objects in different settings, and their symbolic referents, however, may be completely different.[23]

The form of an artifact (e.g., an arrowhead, building, or figurine) may be similar or identical through several cultures, regions, and time periods. Nevertheless, the meaning of the artifact to the people and its use by those people may differ completely from one society to another. A projectile point, for example may have been used for a weapon as either a spear point or an arrow point (the distinction is usually one of size, but there is a range of overlap). Similar forms may also be used as knives or scrapers. Artifacts which appear to be projectile points may have had ceremonial meaning and may have been used only in connection with sympathetic magic. To cite an example of the difficulty of guessing the use of artifacts, shotgun shells from Tanaina Athapaskan historic archaeological sites might be taken as evidence that the people retrieved and reloaded them for hunting purposes. Informants, however, said that during that time reloading was rarely done. Spent shells were used instead as blunt arrowhead tips for shooting birds or amulet decorations on little boys' caps.[24] Female figurines holding the breasts are sometimes indicative of fertility concepts. The Pyramid texts of ancient Egypt, however, indicate that holding the breasts was an accepted way to depict mourning in that society.[25]

2. *Problems of interpretations of non-material culture.* If there is danger in inferring the practical use of material objects, determining the function and meaning of objects thought to be related to religious, symbolic, or abstract culture (including social and political organization and religious beliefs) is incredibly difficult. At best, such inferences are speculation, and the margin of error is enormous. Archaeologists are often accused, with some justification, of interpreting anything that has no readily-discernable, practical function as a religious/ritual item. "Baton des commandment", mistakenly thought to be scepters of command, which were later found to be spear shaft straighteners, and the many interpretations of cave art are only two of many such examples. Recently,

for example, Babikov mistakenly suggested that ivory bracelets and painted mammoth bones from Mezin were ritual musical instruments.[26]

3. Interpretation of sites in the distant past. Ethnographic and historical analogys are safest when they are drawn from societies which are roughly contemporary in time, in the same or near-by region, and in the same or similar ecological niches. The further apart in time or space the societies, the more risky the interpretation based on analogy. This is true even of the literate, state societies, and the danger is exacerbated when analogies are drawn for non-state societies without written records.

Unfortunately, many archaeologists, especially those who are not trained in North America, may have little or no experience with ethnographic research or the data and theory which are available from contemporary socio-cultural anthropology. This lowers considerably the credibility of their analogies and inferences regarding socio-political organization or religious beliefs.

4. Interpretation of social organization in the archaeological past. In archaeological analysis of pre-contact societies without clear written records, it is extremely difficult or impossible to determine what form of kin organization was practiced. Recently, attempts have been made in the U.S. Southwest and elsewhere to draw such information from archaeological remains, but the results continue to be fiercely debated.[27]

Similarly, the status of males versus females is almost impossible to determine in past societies. Status may sometimes be inferred through evidence from burials. The status of a particular female, however, may reflect the entire family's (and husband's) status rather than her status vis-a-vis males. Burial goods found with a dead body may have little to do with that person's real authority or decision-making power in life.

Political organization is equally ambiguous in the archaeological record. By analogy we are usually able to suggest that the society in question was egalitarian, or stratified, or state, and we may gain an overall understanding of the structure. We cannot necessarily say, however, which sex held decision-making authority or power.

Problems in Archaeological Interpretations Of The Goddess

Before discussing problems with the archaeological interpretations of "Goddess"-related finds, I should make one point abundantly clear. My argument against the historic "Goddess" position is *not* an implicit case for there having been a dominant male "God" within the belief systems of all societies or even all Mediterranean/European societies, nor do I endorse the accompanying assumptions that the gender and role of the deities reflect the status of the sexes in societies.

What do we mean by "the Goddess" in prehistoric and historical societies? Are we suggesting that there was a belief in a single, all-powerful female deity? Or, do we infer that there were many gods and goddesses which differed from society to society, but that a female deity always held the position of superiority and was preeminent? While virtually all researchers accept the view that deities were represented by both male and female beings as well as by animals in various cultures, and that at times the female deity rather than the male might be considered the more powerful or important, the supporters of the Goddess movement suggest the first alternative: *The* Goddess religion was a relatively unified tradition across various ancient societies.

There have been references to a Mother Goddess associated with the earth in the European cultural tradition since classic times but little is known of the actual belief system or worship. Drawing on this tradition, some nineteenth-century writers, notably Bachofen, developed the ideas of a Mother Goddess, matriarchy, matrilineality and other elements associated with the modern movement.[28] It was within this already existing interpretive tradition that female figurines began to be discovered in archaeological contexts in the late nineteenth century, and it was predictable that they would often be analyzed in terms of that tradition. Although Sir Flinders Petrie in 1896 did not associate his Egyptian figurine finds with the Mother Goddess, Sir Arthur Evans working in Crete about the same time soon reinterpreted his material as prototypes of the later Ishtar, Mother Goddess.[29] Once the broad interpretation of figurines as evidence for *the* Mother Goddess was accepted, later analyses were made in those terms without seriously entertaining alternative interpretations. The universal Mother Goddess religion became a paradigm composed of a number of *a priori* assumptions rather than an hypothesis to be proven.[30]

Often, supporters of the Goddess movement maintain that the belief in, and worship of, "the Goddess" have been traced from Paleolithic times in hunting and gathering societies, through the shift to sedentarization and cultivation, to the evolution of the state and civilization. They argue that the female figurines ("Venuses") of the Upper Paleolithic are evidence of the early existence of "the Goddess" religion. These figurines were, however, rarely excavated in context or with scientific procedures. Consequently, the interpretations are highly subject to guesswork. Further, "Venus" figurines were found over a fairly wide area but are tied to a comparatively limited time-period: between 23,000 and 21,000 B.C.E.[31] They appear to be discontinuous with the much later female figurines of the Neolithic. The evidence, therefore, does not support "the Goddess" contention of a continuing tradition. From another standpoint, if we make comparisons with historic hunters and gatherers and simple horticulturalists, we do not find such universalistic concepts of a preeminent deity or an established theology which persists across a number of societal boundaries. The Goddess model, therefore, fails from this perspective as well.

Later Neolithic sites, such as Çatal Hüyük in Turkey, dated 6250-5400 B.C.E., and some others in the Balkans and Eastern Europe, have been excavated recently. Çatal Hüyük, especially, is used by Goddess supporters as further evidence for "the Goddess" religion. We know that at Çatal Hüyük a large number of figurines were found of non-sexed, male, and female individuals, and of a variety of animals. While these apparently did relate to some aspect of the belief system, it is impossible to discern what that relationship was.

The excavator, James Mellaart, speculates that there were special shrine rooms focusing on "the Goddess" and fertility, with a priesthood oriented toward the veneration of the Goddess. Others suggest that these chambers may have been ceremonial locales for sodalities, age groups, or clans and were related to hunting and other group activities.[32]

Mellaart bases his interpretation of Çatal Hüyük as a "civilization" with a goddess as the paramount deity and an alleged extensive trade network on a number of assumptions based on analogy and guesswork. Even his estimation of a population size of 5,000/6,000 up to 10,000 for the site at one point in its occupation is suspect.[33] Others have estimated the population at less than 3,000.[34] If this latter figure is closer to the truth, there are major implications for the social and political organization. Clearly, population sizes of this magnitude do not denote a "civilization"; a "tribe" or "chiefdom" are the most likely organizational possibilities.[35] Since only 1/30 of the site has been excavated, these kinds of assumptions are risky.[36] It is as likely that the "town" was similar to the Pueblo villages of the Southwestern U.S. which are kin-based small societies.

I consider the assumption of homogeneity of the meaning of female figurines across various cultures, regions and periods not valid, and I agree with Renfrew that it is unwise to invest figurines with specific religious meaning such as that of "the Great Mother Goddess".[37] The locales of discovery differ from, for example, habitations in Crete, to painted rooms and grain bins at Çatal Hüyük, to burials in Egypt. This does not support the hypothesis of similar functions.

Some figurines did apparently relate to fecundity. This would seem reasonable for settlements like Çatal Hüyük. In early times there was a comparatively high infant mortality rate and not very great longevity. Female life expectancy was thirty years, male life expectancy thirty-four years. The infant mortality rate was four in ten. Falciparum malaria was a major debilitator of health, and may have been the cause of anaemia which produced porotic hypertostosis, a thickening of the blood-carrying parts of the skull,[38] but a large number of women died in childbirth or from birth complications according to skeletal evidence.[39] Consequently, some of the figurines which suggest pregnancy or birth could be amulets for aid or for fecundity, or even illustrative images for assistance in birthing (e.g., Peruvian medical figurines provide a comparison). It should be firmly stressed, however, that ritualized fertility does *not* necessarily imply the existence of a Mother Goddess.

Figures in some of the illustrations, particularly at Çatal Hüyük have been described as depicting birth position. To my way of thinking these could just as easily show a position for sexual intercourse. Female figurines and presumed female figurines often show corpulent buttocks, stomach, and hips. This need not, however, indicate fertility in all cases. It is quite possible that such figurines are illustrative of a female condition which may have existed at that time: steatophygia. It is still found in some populations which have been fairly isolated for long periods of time and possibly retain some of the earlier genetic material. Steatophygia is found in San (Hottentot, Bushman), Andaman Islanders, and some Pigmy populations of Africa. A Rubenesque, corpulent female form with large thighs and abdomen may have been a mark of ideal beauty for women and, as in recent times, fat may have been a status symbol indicative of ample resources of high ranked families.

In the paradigm of "the Mother Goddess", figures which are male, not-sexed, or of animals are not satisfactorily accounted for, although they are often in places as significant as the female figurines. For no clearly valid reason, when they are discussed it is often in terms of "the Goddess's" husband or son. But, if all female figurines represent the Great Mother Goddess, might all male figurines represent the Great Father God? A cult of a Father God, similar to that of "the Goddess", has not been put forth, however.

Animal figurines are treated fundamentally different from the human figurines found in identical contexts; they are not usually considered to represent deities, although logic would suggest that as an explanation. Most commonly, they are interpreted in connection with general fertility or as toys.[40] Bull images were found at Çatal Hüyük and a number of other Middle Eastern sites and also appear in the Upper Paleolithic. Nevertheless, I am not familiar with any attempt to single out a cult of *the* "Bull" God originating in the Paleolithic comparable to the speculations about a Mother Goddess cult. Hooker even questions the appropriateness of the hypothesized "bull cult" in Minoan religion since bulls are often depicted trussed on tables being ritually slaughtered; therefore, he argues, they were likely sacrificial victims.[41]

Gimbutas offered an extensive analysis of various symbols, including abstract designs such as spirals and crescents, and animals, such as snakes, toads and pigs, all of which she hypothesized were indicative of "the Great Goddess".[42] Care should be taken not to over-analyze designs or objects in order to extract meaning when in fact there may be none.[43] Hayden and others have criticized her analysis, arguing convincingly that there is no necessary equation between the objects or symbols and "the Goddess."[44]

Figurines could be used as icons representative of a goddess. Nevertheless, many could also illustrate individuals assigned to serve the deity. At Knossos, for example, the figures interpreted as Serpent Goddesses by Gimbutas and others could just as easily represent votive figures such as priestesses serving a deity.

Some figurines might represent toys; small ones might have been charms or amulets, while others might have been instructive. For example, some figures could merely illustrate the proper positions for sexual intercourse or birth. They may also be used in connection with puberty initiation ceremonies in which sexual matters are a significant part.[45] The two-headed Turkish figures may, in fact, depict a Siamese twins pathology.[46] Certainly figurines illustrating pathologies are common from other areas of the world, notably Peru.

Dolls have been used in various magical and shamanic ceremonies in many parts of the world. Among the Tanaina Athapaskans of southwest Alaska, for example, a shaman had a doll which acted as a familiar and travelled to the other world to retrieve lost souls.[47] The Zuni, Pueblo people of the United States southwest, also use human figures in ceremonies. In a number of societies, a doll will be cared for in a kind of sympathetic magic to encourage the birth of a real child. In West Africa, girls carry dolls to ensure healthy children in the future. The Batak of Sumatra similarly use dolls to bring about a birth. Among the Wambunga of Tanzania, healing of a female is accomplished by driving the illness into a figure. In various societies, figures have a victim's hair or other personal items attached in order to work sorcery against that person.[48] It is probable that some of the prehistoric figurines were used for these kinds of purposes rather than as deities. As Ucko has shown, some archaeologists believe that a single interpretation of all the anthropomorphic figurines, even at a single site, is likely to prevent the discovery of other functions which they may have had.[49] To make a sweeping single interpretation through long segments of time over vast areas is even more dangerous.

In some instances, female figures most likely did have various ritual/religious meanings for the people of those societies in which they are found. Mother goddess or fertility goddess worship did occur in Mesopotamia and Anatolia,[50] but we cannot assume from this that the meaning was the same for all ancient cultures or through time. We cannot interpret figurines in Europe, the Near East and the Mediterranean as indicative of "the Goddess" merely because goddess traditions exist in some locales at specific time periods. Further, we cannot even suggest that those figurines that exhibit female characteristics were deities, much less that the figurines derive from a cult of "the Great Mother Goddess."

If the various figurines found in Europe and the Middle East are iconographic, and *if* they relate to religious expression, they are symbols. As such, although the form may be similar through vast areas, the meaning of the symbol remains arbitrary. The meaning attached to a symbol in one area can, and often does, vary quite significantly from the meaning associated with the symbol in another area. Moreover, very similar figurines may have served several different purposes even in the same society: toy doll, amulet, substitution for one of a set of twins if one died, sympathetic magic to stimulate fertility, shaman's familiar and so on.[51] As emphasized already, as one moves from one society to another over long distances and through time, the more likely the meaning is to vary.

In addition to figurine interpretation, there are other aspects of "the Goddess" position that cause concern. It has been maintained that pre-Indo-European Europe, especially during the Neolithic, was relatively peaceful. Archaeological evidence, however, now indicates that peace was a function of isolation, and hostilities began as soon as the fertile northern and central European lands began to fill up. Some Neolithic communities seem to have had defensive walls; other settlements used a labyrinthine plan, presumably to make enemy penetration more difficult.[52] At Çatal

Hüyük, Mellaart noted that the solid Pueblo-style houses with entry only by ladder from the roof were excellent for defense. I concur with Hayden that the evidence of human sacrifice during this time seems inconsistent with the proposal that the alleged Old European, female-dominated societies were peaceful antitheses of the later alleged violent male-dominated society.[53] Çatal Hüyük, also thought to be a peaceful town by some, shows evidence of much violence. Mace heads and other weapons were found with some male burials, and head wounds were common on skulls.[54]

Renfrew doubts that the Indo-European "invasion(s)" from southern Russia "were as decisive or as great as they are sometimes painted".[55] Certainly they were not organized migrations. Rather, he and others suggest that there were sporadic and comparatively uneventful migrations of groups of people over a long period of time. No family would need to have moved more than thirty miles from the birthplace of their parents.[56]

A Mother Goddess Religion Persisting 30,000 Years

The idea that small societies had an all-powerful deity, a goddess, and that this "religion" has persisted for 30,000 years, through an enormous number of small and later large societies is ludicrous. Upper Paleolithic societies were hunters and gatherers. They periodically moved their camps and lived in small settlements of probably not over two hundred maximum, and often not over one hundred. With the beginning of cultivation after about 7,000--7,500 B.C.E., sedentary life became more practical. But still, for a long time, settlements remained small and cultivation was often secondary to hunting and gathering, as Çatal Hüyük demonstrates. Around 6,000 B.C.E., some areas supported independent towns of perhaps 3,000 or so. The earliest State society seems to have developed around 5,000 to 4,000 B.C.E., with the Ubaid "cities" of the Tigris-Euphrates area. We can begin to talk about a shift in the conceptualizing of deities into a hierarchical pantheon or a single paramount deity, something like what we are familiar with, about 5,000 B.C.E. or slightly earlier.

Historical, Ethnographic, and Socio-Cultural Arguments

Women in Societies with Goddesses

Societies which have female deities do not necessarily hold living women in high regard, in contrast to the contention of those in the Goddess movement. "The author of the Devi-bhagavata-purana, for example, a

(Hindu) text that praises the 'Great Goddess' above all other deities, despises women".[57] The importance of goddesses in Hindu India in comparison with women's position in the society further demonstrates this point.[58] There are numerous examples of women's low status but a few will suffice. The plight of new wives in village India, who may face severe subordination to the husband's family and sometimes suffer persecution or murder if the dowry is not large enough, has made headlines in Western newspapers in recent years. There is also the alienated position of widows. Even though the practice of *sati*, the burning of the widow on the funeral pyre of the husband, has been officially outlawed for over a century, cases are still reported.[59]

In Christian Catholic society, the Virgin Mary is placed in a position analogous to a goddess.[60] Nevertheless, women's positions are not generally high. Instead, the "evil, sinful" real woman is often contrasted with the purity of the Virgin--a purity which is impossible for an ordinary woman to attain. The reverence of a goddess, through contrast, may actually lead to more oppression of women.

Witchcraft of the Middle Ages

Witchcraft was persecuted in Europe from the late fourteenth century to the early eighteenthth century in various parts of Europe and North America. Persecutions varied considerably from country to country and through time. It is unwise, therefore, to make sweeping generalizations and hypothesize one religion with a single, paramount Mother Goddess which was practiced underground for almost 400 years. A closer examination of the witchcraft records indicates that at certain times in some countries there were as many men as women who fell victim, although women were clearly in the majority in the overall craze. Victims were usually elderly, widowed, reclusive, poor, and vulnerable, and thus were easy scape-goats for society. Monter notes that in Western Switzerland and adjacent France, persecutions between the sixteenthth and late seventeenth centuries seem to "coincide with the rise and fall in persecutions of two other peculiarly sex-linked crimes: infanticide and sodomy... Infanticide was even more clearly sex-linked than witchcraft."[61] Almost all those persecuted for such crimes were single women, but younger than the average witch. Infanticide charges extended to any woman who concealed her pregnancy and whose child died before it was baptized. Presumably lesbianism was similarly persecuted.[62] In this region during this period, it appears that almost as many women were executed for these kinds of crimes as for witchcraft.

Midwives were sometimes accused of being witches. The death of a newborn or a stillbirth was often blamed on the midwife "witch," constructing a dual crime of infanticide as well as witchcraft.[63]

Women who practiced healing, some of whom possibly represented holdovers of earlier shamanism or other non-Christian religious systems, were thought to be particularly dangerous. These "white" witches could lead a person's soul astray more easily, so they were sought out especially.[64]

Heretics, especially Waldensians, became equated with sorcerers (witches) as early as 1425-1450, at least in the Jura region of Switzerland, one of the earliest areas of witch hunts. Heresy/witchcraft was not consistently sex-linked and, particularly in that region, men were persecuted as well as women.

> In parts of the three eastern dioceses, the earliest vernacular words for "witch" were directly derived from "heretic." In the diocese of Geneva the term was *herege*, "heretic"; in the diocese of Sion and most of the diocese of Lausanne it was *vaudois*, "Waldensian." In all three dioceses, the words remained more popular than the "correct" French word for witch, *sorciere*, throughout the sixteenth century.[65]

Elsewhere, words for witch almost always were derived from "sorcerer" rather than "heretic".[66]

It is important to stress that witchcraft and witch hunts of the Middle Ages were multicausal phenomena, and witchcraft certainly was not homogeneous. These kinds of considerations make untenable the argument that witchcraft in the Middle ages was merely the persistence of the "underground" Mother Goddess religion that was persecuted for being in conflict with the patriarchal Christian god.

Conclusions

The existence of a "universal" or Mediterranean/European-wide Goddess religion, which is claimed to have existed from the Upper Paleolithic through the Neolithic and beyond, cannot be validated. The supposition that there existed a peaceful matrilineal/matrilocal kinship organization and/or a matriarchy as a political organization in these areas during that period is also unfounded. Similarly, the assertion that violent Indo-European patriarchal pastoralists with a male paramount deity swept over the peaceful Goddess-oriented matriarchy is not accepted by most researchers. Rather, the Indo-European *linguistic* encroachment into Europe appears to have been gradual, intermittent, of long duration, and not related to undue violence. The effect of those linguistic and perhaps social migrations on the religious and social organizations in specific areas is problematic.

I do not deny that female as well as male and non-sexed humans and animals have been revered as deities in the past and today in various parts of the world. Unfortunately, the literature dealing with the cult of "the Goddess" and her relationship to female supremacy of the past and to particular types of social systems is *often* founded on extremely poor research.[67] Much is taken from archaeological data, with little understanding of prehistory or archaeology. On the basis of selected material finds, assumptions are drawn; then speculations and conclusions are drawn from those assumptions. Attempts have been made to synthesize religion and belief systems as well as social and political systems by taking data that seem to support the argument from various times and places with little critical use of sources. These are melded into a hodge-podge, apparently without any real comprehension of the role and functions of religion and belief in human society, the relation of belief systems to the rest of culture, or of the mechanisms and dynamics of social and political organization at various levels of socio-cultural complexity. Sadly, it is this kind of pseudo-history that many women listen to, partly because it is so readily available, and because it appeals to them by giving the illusion of an effective means of acquiring social and political power in contemporary society.

I strongly agree with Barstow when she says that we cannot go back to a Goddess religion (although I disagree with her claim that an actual universal Goddess religion even existed); fertility symbols are no longer applicable to modern society. On the other hand, the concept of a "femaleness" or "goddess" within the deity (or deities), manifesting "female values and experiences" can serve as inspiration to today's women in their spirituality and in their daily lives.[68]

The goddess/matriarchal-power revitalization movement as I understand it puts forth as *historical fact* the myth of the golden age of the past to give ego reinforcement, to weld a bond among women in order to create a unified force, and to provide women with historical precedent for their aspirations. Myths do act as unifying elements around which to organize a sense of belonging, oneness, and goal-directedness. Myths are essential to the social health of a society.

> When the legends die, the dreams end.
> When the dreams end, there is no more greatness.[69]

But the "Goddess" myth is not recognized by the fundamentalist segment of the "Goddess" movement as a purposeful construction; it is portrayed as historic fact. Moreover, it perpetuates the male/female dichotomy and merely replaces one sexist hierarchical model (the dominance of males and a male God) with another (the dominance of females and a female Goddess), and so perpetuates the insidious stratified dualism. The objective, I believe, should be equal responsibilities and rewards which are based on ability, not on gender. Women do not need to look to a "golden age in the past" to justify their bids for equal rights. With regard to those rights, the goal has merits on its own without myth-creating to support claims of equality or superiority.

If we build unity on a fabrication of an alleged Goddess of an alleged old religion and matriarchy, it is built on sand. If the sand of basic assumptions is eroded, as it easily can be with careful scholarship, the myth will collapse, and with it may go the unity and the strength of the movement associated with the assumptions. There are many such examples in the history of revitalization movements. For example, the Ghost Dance of the North American Plains Indians of the 1890's collapsed when the buffalo and the dead did not return as promised, and the ghost shirts did not protect the people. They lost faith in the entire movement.

I believe that more effort and time should be spent directly addressing the problems of inequality, potential war, and environmental crises. We should work toward an egalitarianism in male/female roles. We do not need to continue to perpetuate the gender dualism which is fundamental to the current problems. Stratification, hierarchies, power and control will remain in large, complex societies, but hopefully on such bases as ability rather than gender differences.

In the realm of religion I have no quarrel with women's efforts to change the concept of "god" from a male anthropomorphic being. I do not, however, support merely changing "god" to a matriarchal goddess. I hope that some way will be found to overcome the linguistic problems of the generic masculine as a designator. But I do not believe merely a hyphenated god ("god-goddess") is the answer. It is contrived and begs the question. This dualism---male/female, god/goddess, patriarch/matriarchy---should not continue. It perpetuates the problem by dealing with the Divine in gender terms. The whole conception of the deity must change. To me, the concept of the Divine in Western society is more properly a consciousness, a spiritual being; gender is not relevant.

Notes

1. I wish to acknowledge Ms. P. Rowsell for her reading and critique of an earlier draft of this essay. I am ,however, totally responsible for the analysis and opinions put forth. I also express my appreciation to the University of Manitoba Social Science and Humanities Research Council (Canada) for their continued support of my research.

2. Erich Neumann, *The Great Mother: An Analysis of the Archetype*, trans. Ralph Manheim (Princeton: Princeton University Press, 1955), 91-92.

3. See esp. Marija Gimbutas, *The Goddesses and Gods of Old Europe, 6500-3500 B.C.: Myths and Cult Images* (Berkeley/Los Angeles: University of California Press, 1982); Evelyn Reed, *Women's Evolution: From Matriarchal Clan to Patriarchal Family* (New York: Pathfinder Press, 1975); Starhawk (Miriam Semos), *The Spiral Dance: A Rebirth of the Ancient Religion of the Great Goddess* (San Francisco: Harper and Row, 1979); Merlin Stone, *When God was a Woman* (New York: Dial Press, 1976).

4. Joan B. Townsend, "Anthropological Perspectives on New Religious Movements," in *The Return of the Millennium*, ed. Joseph Bettis, S.K. Johannesen (Barrytown: New ERA Books, 1984), 137-151.

5. See, e.g., David Aberle, "A Note on Relative Deprivation Theory as Applied to Millenarian and Other Cult Movements," in *Millennial Dreams in Action*, ed. Sylvia L. Thrupp (New York: Schocken Books, 1970), 209-14; Charles Y. Glock, "The Role of Deprivation in the Origin and Evolution of Religious Groups," in *Religion and Social Conflict*, ed. Robert Lee, Martin E. Marty (New York: Oxford University Press, 1964), 24-36; Anthony F. C. Wallace, *Religion, An Anthropological View* (New York: Random House, 1966).

6. Anne L. Barstow, "The Prehistoric Goddess," in *The Book of the Goddess, Past and Present: An Introduction to Her Religion*, ed. Carl Olson (New York: Crossroad, 1983), 7-15; esp. 9.

7. E.g., Reed, *Women's Evolution*.

8. E.g., Barstow, "The Prehistoric Goddess".

9. Esp. Gimbutas, *The Goddesses and Gods of Old Europe*.

10. Janet Kalven, Mary I. Buckley, eds., *Women's Spirit Bonding* (New York: Pilgrim Press, 1984), xviii-xix, quoting Mary Daly.

11. See n. 2 above.

12. See also Osbert G. S. Crawford, *The Eye Goddess* (London: Phoenix House, 1957); E. O. James, *The Cult of the Mother Goddess* (London: Thames and Hudson, 1959).

13. James Mellaart, "Anatolia before 4,000 B.C.," *The Cambridge Ancient History*, ed. I. E. S. Edwards, C. J. Gadd, N. E. I. Hammond (Cambridge: Cambridge University Press, 1970), 1:309; *id., The Neolithic of the Near East* (New York: Charles Scribner's Sons, 1975); *id., The Archaeology of Ancient Turkey* (Totowa, N.J.: Rowman and Littlefield, 1978); M. Gimbutas, *The Goddesses and Gods of Old Europe* (see n. 3 above).

14. Robert Briffault, *The Mothers: The Matriarchal Theory of Social Origins* (3 vols.; New York: Macmillan, 1931 [1927]); J. J. Bachofen, *Das Mutterrecht* (Basel: Schwabe, 1861); Lewis Henry Morgan, *Ancient Society* (New York: World Publishing, 1877); Sir Edward Burnett Tylor, *Primitive Culture: Research into the Development of Mythology, Philosophy, Religion, Language, Art, and Custom* (London: John Murray, 1871).

15. Erich von Daniken, *Chariots of the Gods?* (London: Corgi Paperbacks, 1971 [1967]).

16. Barry Thiering and Edgar Castle, eds., *Some Trust in Chariots* (Toronto: Popular Library, 1972).

17. Annemarie Shimony, "Women of Influence and Prestige among the North American Iroquois," in *Unspoken Worlds. Women's Religious Lives in Non-Western Cultures*, ed. Nancy Auer Falk, Rita M. Gross (New York: Harper and Row, 1980).

18. Kalvero Oberg, *The Social Economy of the Tlingit Indians* (Seattle: University of Washington Press, 1973); Frederica De Laguna, *Under Mount Saint Elias: The History and Culture of the Yakutat Tlingit* ("Smithsonian Contributions to Anthropology," 7; Washington: Smithsonian Institution Press, 1972).

19. Carolyn J. Matthiasson, ed., *Many Sisters: Women in Cross-Cultural Perspective* (New York: Free Press of Macmillan Publishing Co., 1974), 423.

20. Joan B. Townsend, "Tanaina Ethnohistory: An Example of a Method for the Study of Culture Change," in *Ethnohistory in Southwestern Alaska and the Southern Yukon: Method and Content*, ed. Margaret Lantis ("Studies in Anthropology," 7; Lexington: University Press of Kentucky, 1970), 71-102.

21. Kathleen Gough, "Variation in Residence," in *Matrilineal Kinship*, ed. David M. Schneider, Kathleen Gough (Berkeley: University of California Press, 1961), 545-76, esp. 553.

22. Kathleen Gough, "The Modern Disintegration of Matrilineal Descent Groups," in *Matrilineal Kinship*, ed. David M. Schneider and Kathleen Gough, 631-52, esp. 640.

23. See, e.g., Colin Renfrew, "The Prehistoric Maltese Achievement and Its Interpretation," in *Archaeology and Fertility Cult in the Ancient Mediterranean: Papers Presented at the First International Conference on Archaeology of the Ancient Mediterranean*, ed. Anthony Bonanno (Amsterdam: B.R. Gruner Publishing Co., 1986), 118-130.

24. Joan B. Townsend, "Ethnohistory and Culture Change of the Iliamna Tanaina," (Ph.D. diss.; University of California at Los Angeles, 1965 [Ann Arbor: University Microfilms]).

25. See discussion in Peter J. Ucko, *Anthropomorphic Figurines of Predynastic Egypt and Neolithic Crete with Comparative Material from the Prehistoric Near East and Mainland Greece* ("Royal Anthropological Institute Occasional Papers, 24; London: Andrew Szmidla, 1968), 418.

26. Referred to in Olga Soffer, *The Upper Paleolithic of the Central Russian Plain* (New York: Academic Press, 1985), 468-69.

27. Lewis R. Binford and Sally R. Binford, eds., *New Perspectives in Archaeology* (Chicago: Aldine Publishing Co., 1968), esp. David Aberle, "Comments", 353-59; Stephen Plog, "Social Interaction and Stylistic Similarity: A Reanalysis," in *Advances in Archaeological Method and Theory* (New York: Academic Press, 1978), 1:143-182; Daniel Miller and

Christopher Tilley, eds., *Ideology, Power and Prehistory* (Cambridge: Cambridge University Press, 1984).

28. See n. 14 above.

29. See Ucko, 409-10.

30. See ibid., 415-17; Renfrew, "The Prehistoric Maltese Achievement," 120, 125.

31. C. Gamble, "Culture and Society in the Upper Paleolithic of Europe," in *Hunter-Gatherer Economy in Prehistory: A European Perspective,* ed. G. Bailey (Cambridge: Cambridge University Press, 1983), 210-211

32. See Walter A. Fairservis, Jr., *The Threshold of Civilization: An Experiment in Prehistory* (New York: Charles Scribner's Sons, 1975), 170, 176.

33. Mellaart, "Anatolia before 4,000 B.C."; *id., The Neolithic of the Near East,* 99.

34. Fairservis, *The Threshold of Civilization,* 158.

35. Ibid., 167.

36. Cf. Mellaart, *The Neolithic of the Near East,* 98.

37. Colin Renfrew, *Before Civilization: The Radiocarbon Revolution and Prehistoric Europe* (London: Jonathan Cape, 1973), 180.

38. J.L. Angel cited in Mellaart, *The Neolithic of the Near East,* 99-100.

39. J.L. Angel cited in Fairservis, 159.

40. See Ucko, 417, 418.

41. J. T. Hooker, "Minoan Religion in the Late Palace Period," in *Minoan Society,* ed. O. Krzyszkowska and L. Nixon (Bristol: Bristol Classical Press, 1983), 138.

42. Gimbutas, *The Goddesses and Gods of Old Europe.*

43. Cf. Mary King, "On the Origins and Meaning of 'Art'," *Quarterly Review of Archaeology* 4(1983): 1,6-8.

44. Brian Hayden, "Old Europe: Sacred Matriarchy or Complementary Opposition?" in *Archaeology and Fertility Cult in the Ancient Mediterranean,* ed. Anthony Bonanno, 17-30.

45. See, e.g., Ucko, 425.

46. Mellaart, *The Archaeology of Ancient Turkey,* illustrations on pp. 21, 25.

47. Townsend, "Ethnohistory and Culture Change of the Iliamna Tanaina"; *id.,* "Journals of Nineteenth Century Russian Priests to the Tanaina: Cook Inlet, Alaska," *Artic Anthropology,* 11(1974): 1-30.

48. See, e.g., Ucko, 425.

49. Ibid., 426.

50. Ibid., 413-414.

51. Ibid., 422-23.

52. See Hayden, 25.

53. Ibid., 27; cf. Gimbutas, 74; and see Yannis Sakellarakis and Efi Sapouna-Sakelleraki, "Drama of Death in a Minoan Temple," *National Geographic* 159(1981): 205-22.

54. Mellaart, *The Archaeology of Ancient Turkey*, 16, 18.

55. Renfrew, *Before Civilization*, 244; see also *id.*, *Archaeology and Language: The Puzzle of Indo-European Origins* (New York: Cambridge University Press, 1987), 83, 98, 148, 265.

56. Renfrew, *Archaeology and Language*, 148.

57. David Kinsley, *The Goddesses' Mirror: Visions of the Divine from East and West* (Albany: State University of New York Press, 1989), xvii.

58. See Klostermaier's essay in this volume for further discussion of Hindu goddesses.

59. Doranne Jacobson, "The Women of North and Central India: Goddesses and Wives," in *Many Sisters: Women in Cross-Cultural Perspective*, ed. Carolyn J. Matthiasson, (New York: The Free Press of Macmillan Publishing Co., 1974), 99-175; also G. Morris Carstairs, *The Twice Born: A Study of a Community of High-Caste Hindus* (Bloomington: Indiana University Press, 1967).

60. See Kinsley, *The Goddesses' Mirror*.

61. E. William Monter, *Witchcraft in France and Switzerland: The Borderlands during the Reformation* (Ithaca: Cornell University Press, 1976), 197-198.

62. Ibid., 198.

63. See T. R. Forbes, *The Midwife and the Witch* (New Haven: Yale University Press, 1966); also Thomas S. Szasz, *The Manufacture of Madness: A Comparative Study of the Inquisition and the Medical Health Movement* (New York: Harper and Row, 1970), 84.

64. Szaz; Christina Hole, *Witchcraft in Britain* (London: Granada Publishing, 1979); and Heinrich Kramer and James Sprenger, *The Malleus Maleficarum*, translated with Introduction and Bibliography and Notes by the Reverend Montague Summers. (New York: Dover Publications, Inc., 1928 [1486]).

65. Monter, 22.

66. Ibid., 23.

67. Sam D. Gill (*Mother Earth: An American Story* [Chicago: University of Chicago, 1987]) has recently provided a provocative and persuasive argument that the "Goddess" and/or "Mother Goddess" was not a traditional belief among American Indians, contrary to what Åke Hultkrantz and others have maintained (cf. Hultkrantz, "The Religion of the Goddess in North America," in *The Book of the Goddess Past and Present*, ed. Carl Olson [New York: Crossroad, 1983], 202-16; and *id.*, *Belief and Worship in Native North America* [Syracuse: Syracuse University Press, 1981]). In a detailed study, Gill traces the first record of a Mother Goddess among North American Indians to an alleged speech by Tecumseh which was directed to General William H. Harrison in 1810. This, together with the European/Euro-American romanticism about Indians in the 1800's and the adaptation and use of the metaphor later by Indians, created the idea that a Mother

Goddess belief was ubiquitous among Indians before the coming of Europeans. The belief is being used by Pan-Indianists and activists, often for political purposes, as well as by some modern Euro-Americans, particularly in the New Age movement. Although Hultkrantz has attacked Gill's work, I find Gill's argument convincing, and it lends support to my own argument (cf. Hultkrantz's review of Gill's book in *Ethnohistory* 37/1[1990]: 73-74).

68. Barstow, 14; cf. pp. 8-9 for her view of "the Goddess".

69. Hal Borland, *When the Legends Die*, (New York: Bantam Pathfinder, 1963).

HEALING THE DIVISIONS: GODDESS FIGURES IN TWO WORKS OF TWENTIETH CENTURY LITERATURE

Kathleen Wall

Literature, Goddesses, and Mythmaking

A current debate in literary criticism involves the relationship of the literary text to the "real world." Theorists at one end of the spectrum defend the task of literature to reflect informatively and illuminatingly the world we inhabit. On the other end of the spectrum, the literary text is viewed as a structure, perhaps only a reassemblage of previous texts, certainly never fixed in its meaning, which is never guaranteed by the authority of the author, and which is always influenced and made uncertain (at the very least) by the historical and discursive context of both author and reader.[1]

It is useful to recognize this problematic relationship between literature and reality in the following examination of goddess figures in contemporary literature, in which we hope to avoid two pitfalls. First, by focusing on contemporary mythopoesis in literature, we are not dependent on difficult-to-interpret archeological evidence or skewed historical documents.[2] Second, imaginative literature's problematic connection to reality provides freedom for the author that does not pertain to the writing of the texts designed either to reflect the "true" essence or history of a deity, or to provide "correct" dogma and guidance for followers. Literature, therefore, may not be so likely to be dogmatic or tendentious in its intent; nor is it likely to proclaim any truth beyond the author's own hypothetical and imaginative depiction of the human condition. Such a depiction, given the implicit contract between the writer of literature and the reader, is always open to the reader's critical acceptance or rejection.

Theorizing that any given literary utterance can be placed along a continuum that has pure fantasy at one unreachable pole and pure realism at the (equally unachievable) opposite pole, we realize that, unlike history or theology, literature can combine an attempt to describe things as they are with inferences or insights into what things might be like. Thus, literature can consider issues that historical or archeological evidence cannot. Similarly, literary criticism can explore the mythopoeic impulse that is evident in some works, regardless of whether it appears to be a conscious or unconscious undertaking of the writer. In the process of making or reforming myths, writers can ask a wide variety of questions: How are myths and rituals made; what social and spiritual pressures bring myths of the goddess into being? What is the effect of belief in a female deity on an individual's relation to herself, her society, to those she loves? Can belief in a female deity effect changes in society's structure, its attitudes towards women? What rituals enable women to attain a meaningful spiritual experience? Of course one must be careful with respect to the application of answers to such questions: the open text of literature is meditative and hypothetical, rather than dogmatic.

I chose, as two examples of twentieth-century literary works that demonstrate unmistakable concern with a female deity, Margaret Atwood's *Surfacing* and Doris Lessing's *The Marriages Between Zones Three, Four and Five,* because they embodied two opposite poles of the literary spectrum and two different aspects of the impact that the assertion of a female spiritual force can have on the individual and her culture. Regardless of how likely we might think the *Surfacing* narrator's psycho-spiritual experience, Atwood has placed her characters as firmly as possible within an identifiable social and geographical context. Lessing's *Marriages,* though we recognize the myriad (and not always consistent or parallel) allegorical relation of the Zones and their social structures to the "real world," contains an immediately obvious fantasy world. We can postulate that Atwood's hypotheses are meant to be entertained within the context of the "real" dilemmas she mirrors in her novel. Lessing's hypothesis might be considered visionary, suggesting that this is how the world might transform itself if we explored certain attitudes toward the feminine and the spiritual.

The emphasis in Atwood's novel is upon the individual quest for a renewing ritual that will mitigate the sterility and waste that exist both in the narrator's personal life and in the natural world. Her quest would seem personal and even idiosyncratic, as does the dilemma that has brought her to an emotional impasse. In contrast, Lessing's protagonist, Al Ith, journeys to Zone Four on behalf of her people, and indeed at the outset she rails against the personal dimension of this task assigned to her. While Atwood's narrator (we presume) returns to society with her gods once again mortal, Lessing's narrative suggests not only that Al Ith's quest is indeed an archetypal one, but that her people and especially Lusik, the chronicler, are actively engaged in the mythmaking process; that they extract, exaggerate and retell events of her journey in order to embody it with a guiding spiritual dimension. Atwood's novel records, then, the personal recovery of a renewing ritual whose impact beyond the pages of the novel is at question for the narrator. Lessing's novel not only records an individual's mythic journey, but concerns itself as well with the public dimensions of Al Ith's experience and with the way in which the public, needing myth, actively engages in creating and recording the mythic dimensions so that they can outlast Al Ith's life.

Chosen, then, for their contrasts, these works nevertheless evince similarities which might provide evidence as to the direction of current mythopoesis. Both novels present sterile landscapes for renewal, though neither author simplistically envisions (golden age) cures; and, although woman's relationship to the earth is evoked, neither author views her as simplistically chthonic.[3] Both novels evince a nervousness about language, a nervousness over and beyond that of contemporary, garden-variety linguistic anxiety, in that they focus on the difficulty of communication between men and women. Atwood is open about her narrator's distrust of language and her desire for a domain where her child will not need the confusing, inadequate intercession of words. In Lessing's novel, the most effective communication goes on without the aid of language. When the intuitive link between individuals severs, when men and women must speak to one another, misunderstanding is almost inevitable. In addition, many of the artists who attempt to keep Al Ith's history alive do so with paintings, using visual rather than verbal iconography. Interestingly, and perhaps not entirely coincidentally, this is an anxiety which some theorists trace back to the inception of written language, which coincided with the alleged original decline in goddess worship.[4]

Both novels examine a world which is [dis]organized into binary oppositions, and in which the heroine's experience and actions seek to dissolve the oppositions. Finally, the most powerfully ordered binary of a patriarchal society, that of dominant, powerful superior male vs. submissive, powerless, inferior female, is not only questioned but resolved. The agency of this resolution is a hierogamy, a sacred marriage believed to be originally enacted between a sky god and earth goddess, the purpose of which is the renewal of a wasteland. Performed by a king and queen or priestess who represents the goddess, it is a ritual which reenacts creation; and according to the laws of sympathetic magic it can have cosmic import and effect re-creation.[5] In Ancient Sumer, for example, "kings were ritually united with Inanna in order to engender the fertility of the kingdom."[6] Similarly, "in Egyptian Thebes, the chief priestess is the divine consort of Amun, and on Cyprus, Astarte is the consort of the priest-king."[7] The sacred marriage also has political importance, playing a role in determining kingship.[8] Thus, the narrator believes her child will be a god, or the first human; and Al Ith's son, Arusi, becomes ruler of Zone Four.

The Marriage of Al Ith

At first glance, Al Ith's marriage to Ben Ata appears to be the political marriage of convenience, the ways of Zones Three and Four having become over time so different that some exchange of ideas becomes necessary. In her construction of the Zones, Lessing has created cultures that are radically different. Al Ith comes from a matrilineal culture; the rule of Zone Three is passed through the "generations of the mothers."[9] In keeping with the "feminine" orientation of Zone Three, its inhabitants are warm, nurturing, instinctive; feelings can frequently be left verbally uncommunicated because they seem to pass between people in a process not unlike osmosis. Men and women are absolutely equal, and emotional intimacy and sympathy between individuals is a matter of course. Children are treated with the loving attention of future adults. Zone Three inhabitants' intimate and respectful relationship to the natural world also resembles that attributed by some at least to matrilineal societies: they talk wordlessly to the animals and send messages by tree.[10] Through their ingenious economic diversity, they have developed the crafts and skills that provide them with a pleasant and pleasure-filled way of life. The only draw-back is that they have become self-satisfied to such a degree that they have ceased to aspire to anything better: they have forgotten that the spiritually superior Zone Two lies on their borders.[11]

Spiritual stagnation is a problem in both zones: Zone Four has similarly become unaspiring, except that, there, to look at the heights of Zone Three is forbidden; heavy punishment helmets are used to keep inhabitants from raising their eyes to the mountains. In other respects, however, Zone Four is the opposite of Zone Three. Patriarchal in its orientation and structure, relations between the sexes are frought with heavy emotional tension. Men bully; women manipulate. Maintaining an army has become the single purpose of life in Zone Four, duty the most vaunted quality. This single purpose has produced an extremely meager economy, and most of the zone dutifully endures the near poverty dictated by that single-mindedness. Because the fathers are away on duty, boys live almost exclusively with their mothers, until the age of eleven, when they leave the one-sided home environment to join the army. Hence, they either live entirely with women or with men, and must purchase their masculinity by rejecting all that might be regarded as soft or tender.[12] Such an arrangement dictates that relations between men and women, mothers and sons, are fraught with a tense struggle for power.

Other Zones play a part in the novel, but the focus of the novel's narrator on these two, and on the marriage of their rulers, emphasizes the conflict of binaries: matriarchy vs. patriarchy, pleasure vs. duty, relations of intimacy and sympathy vs. relations of power. The marriage of Al Ith and Ben Ata is, of course, a political one, designed by the Providers (the quasi-deities of Lessing's Canopus in Argos Series) to temper these binary absolutes that have resulted from political and geographical borders. That the king and queen marry for reasons quite beyond the political, however, is made clear in a number of ways that possess mythic resonance: the geographical compartmentalization of Rohanda into Zones with distinct social values has caused various levels of sterility on the planet. Easy for us to imagine would be the social, intellectual, and perhaps even psychological sterility of countries whose values had become ossified. But on Rohanda, sterility is affecting the life of the animals, who have lost their joyfulness and their will to breed. Al Ith knows that the plant kingdom is next, and finds that her own people are experiencing the same emotional and sexual lethargy.

If their marriage is able to have such a macrocosmic impact, we recognize that it is not merely the political marriage of convenience; rather, it is a marriage with many levels of importance. Her physical descent into Zone Four is coterminous with a psychological journey; she recognizes that, as a result of being in Zone Four, "she was on the verge of a descent into possibilities of herself she had not believed open to her" (76). Her time with Ben Ata introduces her to a psychological repertoire of feelings previously unexperienced and begins her on a metaphorically-evoked, spiritual journey toward the heights of Zone Two. While the social organization of Zone Three is certainly superior to that of Zone Four, she recognizes among her people a self-satisfaction that has led to spiritual stagnation. Her people's defensive self-righteousness dictates that when her journey in Zone Four is accomplished, she can not merely return as queen. Rather, she lives on the fringes of Zone Two until she learns to enter that realm, while all about her quietly gather those who yearn for something more than the emotional comfort and physical prosperity insured by Zone Three citizenship. Such a cosmology, in which the individual's psychological growth is echoed by political developments, by the fertility of plants and animals and by a quest for spiritual transcendence, nourishes the mythopeic cast of mind. Like the goddess, she participates in a sacred marriage that renews the planet; like the goddess she becomes the guide of souls.

Al Ith's "Descent into the Dark" (75) most closely resembles the Sumerian myth of the descent of Inanna. Both Inanna and Al Ith (as well as a number of other goddesses) make a descent to a lower world (in Inanna's case, Ereshkigal's netherworld) in an attempt to renew a wasteland. The descent involves a loss of self: Inanna must remove the clothing and accouterments of state that identify her as "Queen of Heaven," and she hangs dead on a meat peg in Ereshkigal's realm for three days before Ninshubur organizes her rescue. Al Ith similarly undergoes the death of her old self and a stripping away of identity in Zone Four as she finds it necessary to adopt their ways and values, and as she discovers a different, more confining love that she has for Ben Ata. "The return of Inanna from the underworld was at first demonic (even though it restored fruitfulness to the earth, which was barren when the goddess was absent), yet finally...engendered a new model of equal and comradely relationship between woman and man."[13]

Analogously, Al Ith's return to Zone Three is considered dangerous to the peacefulness of her zone, even though fertility has been renewed. Her time in Zone Four, however, had a distinct influence on the relations between men and women, as she supports the women's hopes with her independent mien and changes Ben Ata's attitude toward women. Her questioning of Zone Four's emphasis on war (they have no enemies) further causes Ben Ata to restructure his zone's society. As Al Ith's marriage to Ben Ata questioned, for both Zones, the validity of the borders and boundaries, so does Inanna's descent "involve breaking up the old pattern, the death of a gestalt we were comfortable with one some level."[14]

Finally, Al Ith, her experience, and her myth, effect the breaking down of the boundaries, so that,

> There was a continuous movement now, from Zone Five to Zone Four. And from Zone Four to Zone Three--and from us, up the pass. There was a lightness, a

> freshness, and an enquiry and a remaking and an inspiration where there had been only stagnation. And closed frontiers (298-9).

How resonant this is of Perera's suggestion that Inanna "symbolizes consciousness of transitions and borders, places of intersection and crossing over that imply creativity and change and all the joys and doubts that go with a human consciousness that is flexible, playful, never certain for long."[15]

Lusik views his task as narrator as a synthetic one. As a chronicler of his Zone, it is his responsibility to record the history of his people. He does not try to disguise the extent to which he must piece together his narrative (112), nor is he reticent to admit that there are events which he can only presume to record accurately (142). Instead, he is forthright about his reasons for presenting this narrative:

> One of the motives for this chronicle is an attempt to revive in the hearts and memories of our people another idea of Al Ith, to reinstate her in her proper place in our history. It is not enough that a minority of us seek her out, identify with her, try to live near her, when such a large majority think of her only as we do of those who represent places in ourselves we find it dangerous to approach... (177).

It is difficult, therefore, to ascertain the extent to which Lusik is creating something more than a portrait of a historical personage, given that he views her as a guide to aspects of oneself. We do know, however, that he is well aware of the way in which mythopoesis operates among the storytellers and painters of his realm. As he records his narrative, he frequently stops to muse over scenes that have entered popular memory. He notes that many of these scenes contain inaccuracies. Examining the iconography that has arisen with little regard for truth (and more regard for the mythic power of Al Ith's journey), we notice three things: that the iconography seems to arise spontaneously, that it draws upon images we associate with a variety of goddesses, and that variations on the folk versions of Al Ith's career reflect the needs and perspectives of the culture that gives rise to them. Lessing, I would argue, has given us a portrait of the mythopoeic process.

The first time Lusik introduces us to the tales that have risen up around Al Ith's life, all three aspects of the mythopoeic process are present. First, Lusik does indeed question whether the painters' and storytellers' depiction of Al Ith's confrontation with Zone Four soldiers and the subsequent gathering of animals is at all accurate. He wonders if they have emphasized an event that was originally of little importance to those involved (19). Later, describing depictions of other events in Al Ith's life, he discusses problems of interpretation; Zone Three artists have difficulty understanding, and thus depicting, Al Ith's parade, while pregnant, before the armies of Zone Four. Often the tales speak of events that never occur, such as Al Ith's return to Zone Four on Yori which the tales invent in order to end her exile and bring back her dead horse. By having Lusik discuss the folk variations on Al Ith's life, Lessing suggests a certain inevitable and spontaneous mythologizing of heroic or royal figures, manifested historically in frequent invocations of royal gods. Al Ith is not, strictly speaking, the goddess: rather she is the goddess's representative or royal likeness, the queen who enters into the sacred, renewing marriage. Through her journey in Zone Four, Al Ith is able to effect a change in the natural world, a change in social values and attitudes, and a change in the spiritual orientation of some of her people. This supports their tendency to view her as the royal manifestation of the goddess. In effect, the tendency of the painters and storytellers to embellish her history reveals their desire to give her experience mythic proportions, to elevate her from queen to goddess, to assert and emphasize the shift in her area of influence from the political to the spiritual.

The initial scene depicted by the painters and storytellers also evinces the way in which these embellishments produce an iconography that recalls various goddesses. This particular scene recalls one of the great goddess's most important aspects, that of Lady of the Beasts. There is precedent for this in the already intimate relationship with animals characteristic of Al Ith's zone, but the importance given to the scene (out of proportion with the importance the scene originally had), the title of the paintings, "Al Ith's Animals," and the way in which she functions as a protectress, push the event into the mythic realm. In other paintings that have a similar numinosity, iconography reminiscent of goddesses is continually present. Like Artemis, she is associated with the moon and the night (53). In the paintings that close her tale, she is often seen with Artemis's moon (277), though sometimes it appears so low in the sky that it looks like the Virgin's halo. The descriptions of some of the paintings of her parade before the armies recall medieval paintings of the Virgin: "sometimes the child is born and is held in front of her: a large child, dwarfing her" (183). Or she carries in the palm of her hand one of the most common universal symbols of goddesses: a mountain.[16] At other times, Juno's peacock is present (277). In "the last of the truthful scenes," the iconography is richly mixed and mingled: "This scene is particularly loved by our artists who embellish it with a vast yellow moon positioned so that it is close to, or behind, Al Ith's head. Or there is a delightful crescent set off by a star or two. And they often add a large peacock, whose shimmering tail fills the orchard with reflected lights" (277). This iconographic stew recalls Berger's experience in her search for obscured forms of the goddess in the lives of female saints:

> Goddesses merge into one another with the ease of the three shape-shifting Celtic Morrigan, who transform from eels into heifers into crows while we impatiently insist that they stand still to be described. Sacred figures change their meanings and powers not only with the passage of centuries and with geographical areas but also with different seasons and especially with different recorders. Mythology becomes mercurial when we attempt to force it into patterns or molds.[17]

The final element of mythopoesis, present first in "Al Ith's Animals" but also recurrent throughout the paintings and tales, is the influence of context upon the depiction, the placement of emphasis, or the interpretation of events. Here, because Zone Three views itself as inherently more civilized and more sensitive, more connected to the animals than the soldiers of Zone Four, Al Ith's role as protectress is dramatically contrasted to the brutality of the soldiers who attempt to catch the animals that have gathered. A common element in the tales that depict Al Ith's escort by soldiers into Zone Four is their stupid brutality, their fear of the Zone Three heights, their incomprehension of Zone Three's attitude toward its beneficent, egalitarian ruler. Several other instances point out the ways in which the two zones interpret an event differently: each interpretation (while still possessing mythic numinosity) reflecting the differing social contexts from which they arise. Al Ith ceases to ride Yori, the horse sent to carry her, when he becomes tired. Thus, Yori arrives in Zone Four without a rider. The Zone Four ballads that refer to this event nearly depict Al Ith as the dark queen of the underworld:

> Cold and dark your wedding bed.
> O king, your willing bride is dead
> The realm she rules is cold and dark.(39)

In Zone Three, the ballads that deal with the same event emphasize Al Ith's close friendship to Yori, tangentially indicating that in Zone Three she is not viewed as queen of the underworld but Lady of the Beasts. It would seem that, out of the vast array of mythic motifs, a culture chooses those that reflect its own identity, organization, and world view. Mythopoesis, Lessing implies throughout these materials, is never a neutral, disinterested act; rather she reminds us that it may be one of the most identity- and need-conscious constructs and activities of a civilization. In Lessing's novel, mythopoesis would seem to combine the energies of those who are consciously innocent of their undertaking and who draw upon a vast, perhaps archetypal fund of imagery, iconography, and narrative, with the energy of more purposeful mythmakers like Lusik, who quite consciously manipulates the attributes of a narrative because he envisions the way in which it answers a spiritual need in his fellow humans.

Atwood's Mythic Narrative

Like Al Ith at the outset of *Marriages*, the narrator of *Surfacing* finds herself in a dying and often sterile world. A kind of macrocosmic, natural-world sterility is indicated by the dying birches, the fished-out lake, and the heron killed and strung up by the "American" hunters. A social sterility is suggested in the narrator's lukewarm, unempathetic relationship with best friends whom she has known for two months, with whom she discusses nothing personal, and whose pasts are vague. Her own personal wasteland is indicated by the absence of feeling. After a while, it is not so much her father's death that concerns her but her own, a death indicated by her inability to feel because she is locked inside her head:

> I didn't feel awful; I realized I didn't feel much of anything. I hadn't for a long time. Perhaps I'd been like that all my life, just as some babies are born deaf or without a sense of touch; but if that was true I wouldn't have noticed the absence. At some point my neck must have closed over, pond freezing or a wound, shutting me into my head.[18]

This entrapment in her head, cut off from the feeling body, is but one of the many binaries and borders in *Surfacing* that recall similar oppositions in Lessing's *Marriages*. Just as the Zones on Rohanda represented dichotomies, so is this narrator's world organized in mutually exclusive categories, of which the mind and body, flesh and spirit, are but the first and perhaps most potent. City vs. country is but a version of the mechanized vs. the natural. The narrator's mechanized intercourse with Joe, in which her response is as "crisp as a typewriter" (73), contrasts, for example, with the intercourse meant to lead to her pregnancy, in which "the right season" is the most important consideration. Human relations are similarly organized in terms of conflict and oppositions: e.g., the powerful, knowledgeable male professor vs. the powerless, untalented and naive student. Certainly the relationship between David and Anna is founded on opposition: David's infidelity vs. Anna's need for secure possession; David's criticism of Anna's mind and body vs. Anna's purported effort to castrate David. David, offering to screw the narrator ("tit for tat"), proposes geometrical, vindictive, mechanised sex. The powerless victims, fish, herons, and the narrator, must contend with the powerful, destructive Americans in a possibly false opposition.

Contrasting with her brother's violent, explosive drawings are hers of peaceful fecund rabbits inhabiting Easter eggs: childlike exaggerations of male/female world views. These and other oppositions indicate an intellectual and emotional compartmentalization, not unlike Lessing's Zones, badly in need of healing.[19]

Unfortunately, the absence of a sacred dimension in Surfacing makes such healing unlikely or impossible. Religion was entirely absent from the narrator's upbringing, her father feeling it was an irrational distortion from which he felt he must protect his children. Instead, he offered the eighteenth-century rationalists (who, she later finds, were alcoholics or madmen) as a paradigm for the "balanced life." Consequently, she has spent her childhood and, to some degree, her adult life searching for magic in missing hands, dried scarlet runner beans, barometers that predicted weather, prayers to victim-fish and, more latterly, love. When the last proved unreliable (although she still hopes that David and Anna have some magic formula for a happy marriage), the emotional impact of the failure has caused her to freeze herself off into her head, the logical organ that secretes the rational explanation, and lies to protect her, not only from the failure of love, but also from the abortion that signalled that failure. It is this state of sterile entrapment in her head that renders her emotionally frozen, and cuts her off from psychologically and spiritually potent aspects of human life. In addition to being unable to feel, she is isolated from an experience of a sacred dimension that might heal, redeem, transform the mute, fragmented psyche of which she finds herself in possession. Hence, she laments, "But we refuse to worship; the body worships with blood and muscle but the thing in the knob head will not, wills not to, the head is greedy, it consumes but does not give thanks" (150).

Attempting to solve the mystery of her father's death (which is really her own), involves her in a series of numinous experiences and visions, all of which are aimed toward her own rebirth.[20] The first is the shamanic dive she makes in search of the pictographs she believes her father to have found.[21] She discovers an image (ostensibly the corpse of her father) of something once alive and now dead, that recalls her brother's supposed drowning, the frogs kept and killed in jars, and finally her aborted fetus. She comes to recognize a truth her logical mind has passed over: her part in these deaths--her passive witnessing, complicity and responsibility. Her dive offers "true vision; at the end, after the failure of logic" (156); and feeling, with recognition and acceptance, begins to return. This discovery is inadequate, however; she needs more than this assertion of her own deathliness. She is restored to belief in the sacred, in places of possible sacred vision. No longer does her godly father ("If you tell your children God doesn't exist they will be forced to believe you are the god..." [112]) stand logically between the narrator and the illogicality of some religious belief. But the god's gift of vision, in helping her to acknowledge her complicity in death, her deathliness as a victim, is incomplete, and she recognizes she needs a gift from both parents, father and mother: "More than ever I needed to find it, the thing she had hidden; the power from my father's intercession wasn't enough to protect me, it was only knowledge and there were more gods than his, his were gods of the head, antlers rooted in the brain. Not only how to see but how to act" (163). She needs not only a world view that contains the sacred, a belief in religion or magic, but a ritual that enacts her part in that world.

Her mother's gift is actually of her own making, a misplaced childhood drawing of "a woman with a round stomach: the baby was sitting up inside her gazing out. Opposite her was a man with horns on his head like cow horns and a barbed tail....The man was God, I'd drawn him when my brother learned in the winter about the Devil and God: if the Devil was allowed a tail and horns, God needed them also, they were advantages" (169). Hinz and Teunissen argue that this is a child's depiction of the Great Mother, with her "moon stomach", and the consort god (here pre-Christian in its conflation of good and evil in the same figure);[22] while I have concluded that the pictograph depicts the sacred marriage between god and goddess.[23] The drawing provides the narrator with a guide: "How to act." And, indeed, her act, in taking Buffalo Joe outside to make love that night, replicates the sacred marriage. The effect of the pictograph creates a state of mind that contrasts vividly with that we would expect from her: her father's body having been found, she should be "filled with death." Instead, the inspiration to ritual given her by the picture allows her to assert "But nothing has died, everything is alive, everything is waiting to become alive" (170).

The mythic nature of Atwood's narrative has frequently been commented upon, and various paradigms have been used to interpret the narrator's experience. Josie Campbell views it as a quest not unlike that in Joseph Campbell's *Hero of a Thousand Faces*;[24] she and Grace view the narrator as a Persephone figure, while Cederstrom sees similarities between the narrator and Inanna.[25] James notes similarities between the narrator's experience and Amerindian, shamanic rituals.[26] I have argued elsewhere that the narrator in effect re-creates an initiatory ritual in which young women are introduced to their sexuality and thereby achieve what M. Esther Harding identifies as psychological virginity. The myth which forms the script for this ritual is that of the pre-patriarchal Callisto in which Artemis-Calliste joins in the sacred marriage with Zeus to renew the damaged forests of Arcadia.[27]

Rather than repeat that argument, I would like to emphasize here the narrator's active formulation of her own renewing or initiatory ritual. Searching for the pictographs on the rocks makes a kind of logical sense, because she believes they hold some clues as to her father's fate. Once she has viewed the "dark oval, trailing limbs," however, the impetus to her other activities comes from an entirely different source. The search for her mother's gift, as many have pointed out, is designed to balance her earlier vision: the masculine, rational recognition of death needs the feminine spiritual recognition of a creative force. She knows, as she asserts, how to see. The problem is how to act.

Again, the mythic echoes of both the pictograph and her intercourse with Joe have been well documented. Pratt views their encounter as part of a rebirth journey.[28] William C. James writes that "in an act reminiscent of some ancient rite which recalls connections among the moon, women, fertility and initiation...she compels Joe to follow her out of the cabin that night and impregnate her."[29] As they lay on the ground, moon on the left, sun on the right, male and female lovers, as the two halves clasp, the dichotomies achieve a union, a balance. One can argue that head and body are no longer divided, that she has both seen and acted, that death (her father's and her unborn infant's) is redeemed or balanced by conception. The psychological efficacy of this ritual, from the narrator's point of view at least (and from critics' points of view, it would appear, given the amount of discussion this aspect of the work has engendered), seems assured.

In the context of a study of goddesses, however, and of the mythopoeic motivation of literature, one wants to examine more closely the impulse that led to the narrator's enactment of the ritual. She admits, as she describes her finding of the picture, that its apparent meaning is no longer useful or informative, and that she must involve herself in another language. Recalling that the pictures described herself before she was born, she concludes,

> That was what the pictures had meant then but their first meaning was lost now like the meanings of the rock paintings. They were my guides, she had saved them for me, pictographs. I had to read their new meaning with the help of the power....First I had to immerse myself in the other language (169-70).

Like Lusik, she is actively involved in the interpretation of the iconography which might function as her guide.

What the narrator must do is translate a fragment of childish autobiography into a meaningful ritual that will heal her fragmented psyche and will counter the death she believes she has carried with her. It would have been possible, had she been so inclined, to glean a Christian interpretation of her drawing: to see herself as the child of God who before her birth was magically sentient and who therefore can, through grace, return to that state.[30] Instead, in viewing herself as mother and not as child, her translation is predicated upon the perception, certainly prevalent in goddess religions, of cyclical renewal through ritual. As her mother once assumed the role of creatrix, goddess and consort with the god, who carries the magical child with x-ray vision, so will she now, in her turn, find her way to play the same role by re-enacting the sacred marriage she interprets her drawing as depicting. And in that re-enaction she enters the sacred space in which she is both goddess and initiate. Indeed, as she views herself later, "ice-clear, transparent, my bones and the child inside me showing through green webs of my flesh" (195), it would seem that she believes she has precisely re-enacted the archetype. Like an original creatrix, she has created "a god" (173), "the first human" (206). Like the goddess's initiate, she envisions the moon as midwife.

It can be argued, however, that her "reading" of the pictograph's language is dictated as much by her own psychological need to redeem her lost child and undo the emotional anesthesia resulting from her life in her head as it is by the iconography of the drawing. We can see that her acknowledgement of the abortion's impact upon her might move her to re-read the child in the moon stomach, not as self-portrait, but as a portrait of possibilities. Moreover, some symbolic aspects of the drawing must attract her fractured psyche; for one way of "reading" the drawing emphasizes the union of a myriad of opposites: adult and child, man and woman, god and devil, god and goddess, male and female, left and right, sun and moon, the rational logos and the emotional eros. Thus, the drawing, the union to which it refers, and the act of conception provide, on their various levels, a paradigm for unifying the fragments of her personality. The ritualized mating itself invokes a fusion of the binary oppositions. Not only do male and female join, but the presence of the rational sun on her right and the cyclical, irrational feminine moon on her left symbolize a dissolution of distinctions between rational, masculine, logos-oriented world view that has kept her trapped in her head, and the emotional, feminine, eros-oriented world view that has been denied to her. Even the image of the lost child--"two halves clasp, interlocking like fingers, it buds, it sends out fronds"--suggests the fecund union of opposites.[31]

As with Jung's concept of the archetype *an sich,* whose existence we can neither prove nor disprove because we can only view the conscious manifestations, so can we not here ascertain all the forces that give rise to the narrator's particular "translation" of a childhood drawing. She does tell us very clearly, however, that understanding the drawing involves quite a different language (170). In her act of translating, she moves from vision to act, bypassing the unreliability and indeterminacy of words, which seem on the whole to create false categories. Joe believes her to be either in love or not in love, for example; but she has learned to distrust the word altogether and does not believe that there is any agreed-upon meaning for it. Words have also become the agent of the rational, but she recognizes "there are no longer any rational points of view" (181). Abandonment of language and of the rational is an integral part of her rejection of borders and boundaries, categories and catalogs, and its abandonment figures largely in her chosen exile. She burns the "alien words" (176,190) of the tales she has been illustrating, listens to multilingual water (192), but cannot understand the language of those who have come to bring her back to civilization. Rather, their voices are "language ululating, electronic signals thrown back and forth between them, hooo, hooo, they talk in numbers, the voice of reason" (199).

Language is both "everything you do" (139) and that "which divides us into fragments: I wanted to be whole" (157). By exploring the new language which "the power" (170) has allowed her to understand, she avoids the fragmentation which she believes language makes inevitable, and instead works toward a state in which her unity with the natural world is manifested both by a transcendent and unifying experience and by the manipulation and transformation of language to express that state. Through respecting a series of taboos against those things which fragment us (language, paths, buildings, cultivated food), she creates a state of mind which allows her to achieve a unity with the natural world. Through a series of recognitions, she becomes less human and melts into the natural world in an almost pre-cosmogonic state.

> The animals have no need for speech, why talk when you are a word
> I lean against a tree, I am a tree leaning
> I break out again into the bright sun and crumple, head against the ground
> I am not an animal or a tree, I am the thing in which the trees and animals move and grow, I am a place (195)

Her unity with the natural world, her becoming the earth, is highly suggestive of a spiritual experience through which she transcends her mortality and momentarily becomes the earth goddess. After her experience, she has a vision of her mother, a woman many other critics associate with the goddess or Lady of the Beasts, given her ability to control bears, her involvement in nature, her cyclicality, her records of the seasons, her patient feeding of the jays.[32] The narrator has a similar experience of her father. But he is here transformed into someone who has recognized that many of his habits and attitudes were destructive and need reparation: "He has realized he was an intruder; the cabin, the fences, the fires and paths were violations; now his own fence excludes him, as logic excludes love. He wants it ended, the borders abolished, he wants the forest to flow back into the places his mind cleared: reparation" (201). Her vision of the "thing he has become" similarly defies definition and boundaries, as it assumes a myriad of protean shapes. After the vision is over, she finds her feet fit the prints of the spirit she believed she was watching. As she has become the earth, the goddess, so is she translated into the logos, the god.

Concluding Reflections

Atwood and Lessing's evocations of the goddess are, in some ways, radically different. Al Ith recalls the divine queen who occupies a no-woman's zone between political mortal and representative (or even manifestation) of a female divinity. Hers is, as we have seen, a very public role, made all the more public by her position and the mythopoeic impulse of her people, who have elevated her experience that it might provide them with a guide. The *Surfacing* narrator drifts between initiate and representative of the goddess in a much more private sphere; rather than occupying a mythic narrative, she is concerned with re-creating and re-enacting a ritual that may provide some context, insight, mode of action, or world view for healing a fragmented psyche that occupies a sterile world. Unlike Al Ith, who has indeed effected macrocosmic and social change, the narrator can only hope to return to the discouraging everyday world with some of her perspective intact. While Al Ith is exiled from her Zone, her experience, as kept alive by Lusik, his fellow chroniclers and artists, becomes a guide to a spiritual orientation, and her female influence has had a lasting impact upon life in Zone Four. The narrator in *Surfacing,* her exile ended, returns to a world where the spiritual dimension is almost entirely absent, and most critical responses to the novel do not envision her ability to change the world for the better.

Indeed, if *The Handmaid's Tale* is any measure of Atwood's vision of the future for women, her *Surfacing* narrator will enter a world that worsens rather than improves.[33]

Yet the exegesis of these two novels reveals some surprising similarities in works so otherwise apparently different. Not surprising, perhaps, is both authors' preoccupation with the fragmentation endemic in modern life, unavoidable, perhaps, given the speed and frequency with which we must adopt different roles. This problem of fragmentation stands squarely behind their use of goddess symbolism; her evocation is tacitly intended to heal splits, deny boundaries, and effect unity, whether in the political and spiritual realms described in *The Marriages Between Zones Three, Four, and Five* or in the psychological and social territory explored in *Surfacing*. Indeed, these authors, in evoking the goddess's role in healing the borders between Zones Three and Four, or in fusing once again the narrator's head and body, may present a deified reflection of the more fluid ego boundaries of women as hypothesized by Chodorow and Gilligan.[34] At the risk of being essentialist, one can observe that, along with women's socialization, their experience of their sexuality and their role as mother (carrying the child within, nursing the child without) might indeed create in women this more fluid sense of self that has been hypothesized. Such fluid ego boundaries might be engendered in a positive way in images of a goddess who recognizes the sterility brought about by the deep clefts of our society, and whose spiritual and psychological influence is directed towards healing and ameliorating those disturbing incongruities and inconsistencies we all--male and female--experience. Thus, Al Ith, whose connectedness to the world is evoked by her ability to communicate with people and animals without words, is able to evoke change in the natural world and also to clear the rift between prosperity and poverty, duty and pleasure, mountain and valley, matriarchy and patriarchy, man and woman that has been fossilized in the separation of the zones. In *Surfacing*, the narrator's ritualized conception and exile lead to a potentially life-giving mediation between nature and culture, city and country, land and water, man and woman. While she returns to a society riddled with compartments, a society she will in all likelihood be unable to change, while she must (unlike Al Ith) use language to mediate imperfectly between herself and others, her experience of these moments of an unparcelled life could be seen to give her a vision toward which she works with a hopeful but knowingly futile ardor.

Both works make use of an iconographic stew that recalls a number of female divinities, ranging from Inanna to Diana to Persephone. Their authors suggest, if their work is at all representative, that the literary project exploring the feminine divine is perhaps less dogmatic than the more traditionally religious one, and is involved less in recovery of "the goddess" than in what Lauter identifies as metamorphosis,[35] and a decreased dependence upon traditional myths that may be hopelessly colored by the patriarchal record.[36] As such, these authors actively take up the mythmaking process, much as it is evinced in Lessing's novel. Both make use of the numinous images of a female divinity (of which one cannot be sure the authors are fully conscious) while constructing self-consciously mythic narratives that attempt to confront many of the dilemmas raised by the social context in which they live and write. It is no mere coincidence, for example, that both authors raise the issue of a conflict between men and women and offer a "sacred marriage" as a paradigm on many levels for subduing that conflict.

Yet both authors, in viewing the sacred marriage as one of the goddess's most significant and renewing, creative acts, shift the emphasis away from exclusively female divinities. This is perhaps a result of their shared view of our world: that the battle between the sexes is at this point only one of many aspects of our world's compartmentalization and fragmented sterility. In their work, the sacred marriage not only reduces the conflict between men and women, but renews a multi-valenced fertility, not only in the natural world, but in the parallel worlds of thought, of social roles, of spiritual values. Healing the narrator's divided psyche, questioning Zone Four's warlike purpose, learning to aspire to something more than physical and psychological comfort, accepting one's part in a world that victimizes all life forms--these require a consortium of spiritual forces and insights. They require that we both see and act, that we think and feel; they require the logos insights of the god and the eros insights of the goddess, the antlers rooted in the brain as well as the impulse that comes from the instinctive, emotional body.

Many of these common elements--the hazy status of the goddess figures, the iconographic stew, the focus on the hierogamy as a healing force for psychological, spiritual, and social ills--demonstrate that these two authors at least are less concerned with an effort to re-capture and re-validate the "true" goddess, than they are with the creation and proposal of some feminine spiritual principle. Lauter, in *Women as Mythmakers,* attempts to capture the essence of the mythopoeic impulse for twentieth-century women artists and poets. Her explanation evokes this productive tension between the fluid boundaries and multiplicity of the female experience and the ordering proclivities of the stereotypically masculine viewpoint. In addition, the imagery of her explanation evokes both the landscape and the concern about language evident in both novels. She states,

> Tentatively I would describe [the central issue of myth for women] as a tension between the multiplicity of being (experienced often as an overflow of images, feelings or thoughts) and the man-made structures that are supposed to order being and give it meaning. Instead of a wasteland, we have here a landscape teeming with interwoven forms of life, whose affinity with our own form we need only recognize to enjoy. Perhaps there is no metaphysical gap between event and meaning once we give up the desire to possess the event in language. The job of myth under such circumstances would not be to fill the void of nothingness but to overcome the restrictions on being we have built into our symbolic code.[37]

Hence we take up, once again, the question of the status of both language and literature as a medium for visions or representations of a goddess. While working within the masculine privileged medium, Atwood and Lessing have (like many women writers) made it their own, and laid claim to their ability, using the many facets of language and narrative, to name their own experience. Nervous about the ability of language to effect communication in a literal level, they have nevertheless evoked a symbolic arena of image, iconography and narrative to convey their vision of a world that contains the concept of a feminine spiritual principle. Because, as authors (rather than theologians or historians) they are not tied to a concept of a literally communicated truth, they can attempt to represent instead a symbolic hypothesis. These are not dogmatic novels; they contain no proposals for direct actions that any of us could undertake tomorrow morning. Nor do they codify a concept of "the goddess." They convey, instead, a need for a philosophy, a psychology, a world view that contains the feminine spirit--in all the senses of that word.

Notes

1. Literary scholars will need to forgive this simplification of the debate intended for more general readers. For a fuller discussion of these issues, see Chris Weedon, *Feminist Practice and Poststructuralist Theory* (New York: Basil Blackwell, 1987).

2. Anderson and Zinsser point out that archeological evidence consists only of the durable remains of a culture, and is inclined to be incomplete. Moreover, a number of specialists agree that the use or significance of archeological evidence can be quite difficult to determine. Historical evidence, in the form of texts, might alleviate the difficulties of "reading" archeological evidence. But Lerner theorizes that the decline in worship of a goddess perceived as a primary deity or as equal in power to the god with whom she shared her power occurred in cultures that were preoccupied with war; further, that the first decipherable writing we have comes from warrior cultures in which the assumption of male superiority had already been established. See Bonnie S. Anderson and Judith P. Zinsser, *A History of Their Own* (New York: Harper and Row, 1988), 3-23; and Gerda Lerner, *The Creation of Patriarchy* (New York: Oxford, 1986), 151-152.

3. Although it is true that many manifestations of goddesses are chthonic, and that women are generally agreed to be "close to nature," woman's relationship to nature is a complex one, as MacCormack and Strathern point out in *Nature, Culture, and Gende*r (Cambridge: Cambridge University Press, 1980). For my views on this subject see Kathleen Wall, *The Callisto Myth from Ovid to Atwood: Initiation and Rape in Literature* (Montreal: McGill-Queen's University Press, 1988), 22-3. The topic is too complex to be discussed thoroughly here.

4. Lerner, 150. Again, this is a simplification of a complex debate about the relationship between women and language. See, for a variety of representative viewpoints, Julia Kristeva, "Women's Time," trans. Alice Jardine and Harry Blake, *Signs* 7 (1981), 13-35; Sandra M. Gilbert and Susan Gubar, *No Man's Land: The Place of the Woman Writer in the Twentieth Century* (New Haven: Yale University Press, 1987), 227-71; and Weeden, 74-106.

5. For various views of the hierogamy, see Mary Esther Harding, *Woman's Mysteries, Ancient and Modern* (New York: G.P. Putnam's Sons, 1971), 143-154; J.G. Frazer, *The Golden Bough* (London: Macmillan, 1951), 186-7, 194, 200; Barbara G. Walker, *The Woman's Encyclopedia of Myths and Secrets* (San Francisco: Harper and Row, 1983), 403, 501-508; and Walter Burkert, *Greek Religion: Archaic and Classical*, trans. John Raffin (Oxford: Basil Blackwell, 1985), 108-109.

6. David Kinsley, *The Goddesses' Mirror: Visions of the Divine from East and West* (Albany: State University of New York Press, 1989), 113.

7. Burkert, 109.

8. Walker, 501-503.

9. Doris Lessing, *The Marriages Between Zones Three, Four, and Five* (London: Granada, 1981), 58. All subsequent quotations will refer to this edition, and will be cited parenthetically in the text.

10. Lessing's Zones Three and Four accurately reflect the qualities of matrilineal and patriarchal societies, respectively, as described by some anthropologists. Describing a matrilineal society, Peggy Reeves Sanday writes: "To conclude, the ascribed basis for female power and authority in the secular domain is found in a ritual orientation to plants, the earth, maternity, fertility. This orientation is probably part of a historical tradition that began when the detailed knowledge of wild plants led to simple farming" (*Female Power and Male Dominance* [Cambridge: Cambridge University Press, 1981], 120). Such people have what Sanday describes as an "inner orientation," and are apt to have an egalitarian society, although rule is passed down through women. [Ed. note: Cf. the discussion of matrilinearity and other cultural patterns in Townsend's essay in this volume.]

11. Betsy Draine, in *Substance under Pressure* (Madison: University of Wisconsin Press, 1983), argues convincingly that the Sufic Way is the paradigm Lessing intends to offer in her novel. I would like to suggest, however, that the "Way" is not the only paradigm that influences Lessing's novel.

12. Sanday's description of the effect upon social structure of sex-role identities in patriarchal societies also pertains to Lessing's Zone Four: "A boy who grows up in a household in which his mother and other adult women control the resources will envy the female status, covertly practice the female role, and develop what they call a 'feminine operative identity.' If, upon reaching adulthood, the boy discovers that his childhood view of the relative power of males and females was distorted, that the balance of power between the sexes favors men beyond the domestic sphere, the boy will develop 'a strong need to reject his underlying female identity.' This need will lead to an 'overdetermined attempt to prove his masculinity, manifested by a preoccupation with physical strength, athletic prowess, or attempts to demonstrate daring and valor, or behavior that is violent and aggressive'" (182).

13. Sylvia Brinton Perera, *Descent to the Goddess* (Toronto: Inner City Books, 1981), 15.

14. Ibid., 55.

15. Ibid., 16.

16. Walker, 695-700.

17. Pamela Berger, *The Goddess Obscured: Transformation of the Grain Protectress from Goddess to Saint* (Boston: Beacon Press, 1985), 1.

18. Margaret Atwood, *Surfacing* (Markham Ontario: Paperjacks, 1983 [orig. ed., 1972]), 114. All subsequent quotations will refer to this edition, and will be cited parenthetically in the text. These endnotes do not in any way pretend to represent a complete bibliography of Atwood criticism. For a more complete bibliography, see my *The Callisto Myth from Ovid to Atwood.*

19. James Harrison, "The 20,000,000 Solitudes of *Surfacing*," *Dalhousie Review*, 59(1979), 75. Harrison writes particularly well about the oppositions in *Surfacing*; and the concept has been noted by a number of other critics, though never developed in quite this way.

20. For criticism that views *Surfacing*as a rebirth journey, see Carol P. Christ, *Diving Deep and Surfacing* (Boston: Beacon Press, 1980); *id.*, "Margaret Atwood: The Surfacing of Women's Spiritual Quest and Vision," *Signs* 2/2(1976), 316-30; Annis Pratt, *Archetypal Patterns in Women's Fiction* (Bloomington: Indiana University Press, 1981); and *id.*, "Surfacing and the Rebirth Journey," in *The Art of Margaret Atwood*, ed. Arnold E. Davidson and Cathy N. Davidson (Toronto: House of Anansi Press, 1981), 139-57.

21. For the shamanic echoes in *Surfacing*, see Catherine Sheldrick Ross, "Nancy Drew as Shaman: Atwood's *Surfacing*," *Canadian Literature* 84(1980), 7-17.

22. Evelyn J. Hinz and John J. Teunissen, "*Surfacing*: Margaret Atwood's 'Nymph Complaining,'" *Contemporary Literature* 20 (1979), 221-36.

23. Wall, 166-7.

24. Josie Campbell, "The Woman as Hero in Margaret Atwood's *Surfacing*," *Mosaic* 11(1978), 17-28.

25. Campbell, 19; Sherrill Grace, *Violent Duality: A Study of Margaret Atwood* (Montreal: Vehicule Press), 98; Lorelei Cederstrom, "The Regeneration of Time in Atwood's *Surfacing*," *Atlantis* 6/2 (1982), 33.

26. William C. James, "Atwood's *Surfacing*," *Canadian Literature* 91(1981), 179.

27. Wall, 10-25.

28. Pratt, "*Surfacing* and the Rebirth Journey"; *id.*, *Archetypal Patterns*, 159; James, 180.

29. James, 178.

30. It seem surprising that the narrator actually identifies her drawing as having Christian origins, and that few critics have taken up this thread.

31. Harrison, 75.

32. E.g., Pratt, 159; Wall, 166.

33. Written in 1972, *Surfacing* may have been more hopeful than *The Handmaid's Tale* might indicate, since the latter takes up many of the issues of backlash and indifference to feminist goals.

34. Carole Gilligan, *In a Different Voice* (Cambridge: Harvard University Press, 1982); and Nancy Chodorow, *The Reproduction of Mothering* (Berkeley: University of California Press, 1978).

35. Estella Lauter, *Woman as Mythmakers: Poetry and Visual Art by Twentieth Century Women* (Bloomington: Indiana University Press, 1984), 207.

36. See, for example, my discussion of the patriarchalization of the Callisto myth, *The Callisto Myth*, 12-15.

37. Lauter, 212.

List of Contributors

Alan K. L. Chan holds a Canada Research Fellowship from the Social Sciences and Humanities Research Council of Canada in the Department of Religion, University of Manitoba.

Terence P. Day is Professor of Religion in the University of Manitoba.

Rory B. Egan is Associate Professor of Classics in the University of Manitoba.

Klaus Klostermaier is Professor of Religion in the University of Manitoba.

Dawne McCance is Associate Professor of Religion in the University of Manitoba.

Joan B. Townsend is Professor of Anthropology in the University of Manitoba.

Kathleen Wall is Assistant Professor of English in the University of Regina.

Larry W. Hurtado, Editor, is Professor of Religion and Director of the Institute for the Humanities in the University of Manitoba.